OXFORD
CRIME, DEATH
& DEBAUCHERY

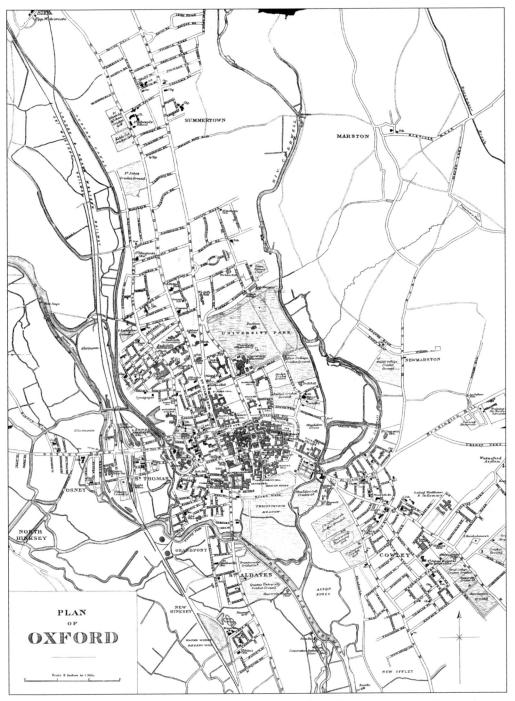

Oxford and the surrounding area, 1913. (Oxfordshire County Council Photographic Archive)

OXFORD
CRIME, DEATH & DEBAUCHERY

GILES BRINDLEY

SUTTON PUBLISHING

 Oxfordshire Books

First published in the United Kingdom in 2006 by
Sutton Publishing Limited
Phoenix Mill • Thrupp • Stroud
Gloucestershire • GL5 2BU

 Oxfordshire Books

British Library Cataloguing in Publication Data
A catalogue for this book is available from the British Library.

ISBN 0-7509-3820-X

> *This book is dedicated to all those who have
> the courage to follow their heart and the
> strength to keep their head
> while others pooh-pooh.*

Typeset in 10.5/12.5pt Galliard
Typesetting and origination by
Sutton Publishing Limited.
Printed and bound in England by
J.H. Haynes & Co. Ltd, Sparkford.

CONTENTS

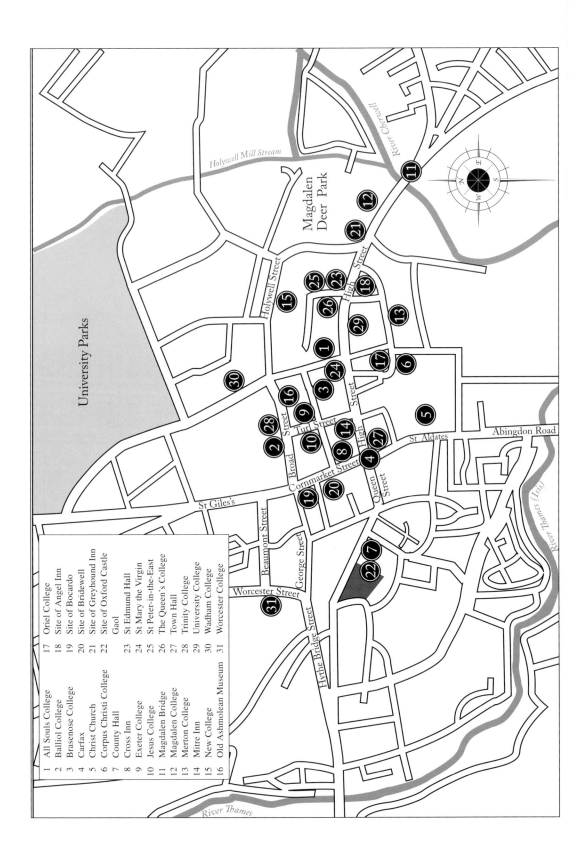

University Parks

Magdalen Deer Park

Holywell Mill Stream

River Cherwell

River Thames (Isis)

Holywell Street

High Street

Broad Street

Turl Street

St Giles's

Cornmarket Street

Queen Street

High Street

St Aldates

Abingdon Road

Beaumont Street

George Sreet

Worcester Street

Hythe Bridge Street

River Thames

1	All Souls College
2	Balliol College
3	Brasenose College
4	Carfax
5	Christ Church
6	Corpus Christi College
7	County Hall
8	Cross Inn
9	Exeter College
10	Jesus College
11	Magdalen Bridge
12	Magdalen College
13	Merton College
14	Mitre Inn
15	New College
16	Old Ashmolean Museum
17	Oriel College
18	Site of Angel Inn
19	Site of Bocardo
20	Site of Bridewell
21	Site of Greyhound Inn
22	Site of Oxford Castle Gaol
23	St Edmund Hall
24	St Mary the Virgin
25	St Peter-in-the-East
26	The Queen's College
27	Town Hall
28	Trinity College
29	University College
30	Wadham College
31	Worcester College

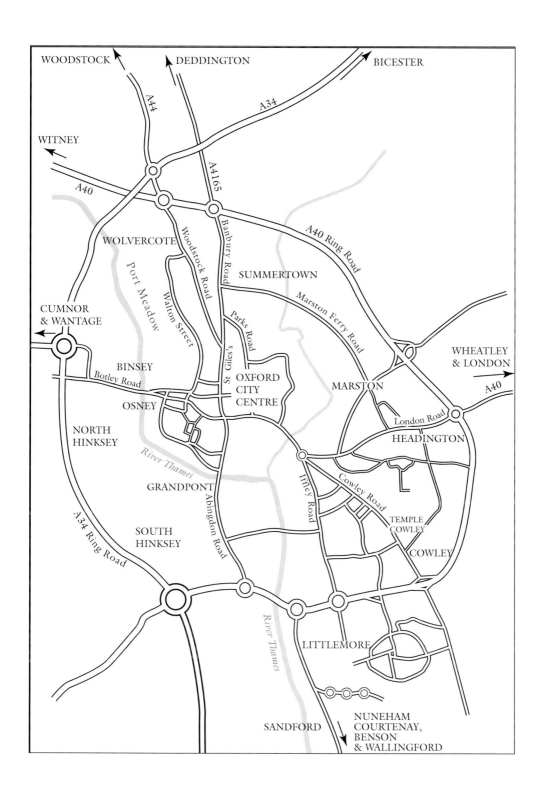

ACKNOWLEDGEMENTS

There are many people without whose support and belief in this project it may never have come into being. They include Sarah Bryce, Michelle Tilling, Jane Hutchings, Helen Bradbury and Simon Fletcher at Sutton Publishing for help, advice and editorial expertise. I owe a lot to Liz Soar for support, encouragement and advice over more years than I care to mention. Thanks are also due to Christina Lindeholm for constant support and as a reader of most of the text; Darren Ravenscroft and Caroline Dalton for useful discussions at a very early stage; Steven Fisher and Mark Murray for housing me during many weeks spent researching at The National Archives in London; Henry Ashton for the use of a new and expensive laptop, for those applications which my own could not handle. Thanks go to several people for the loan of digital cameras.

I am eternally grateful to the many friends and loved ones who have believed in this work from the start and helped in one way or another. Particular thanks must go to Monika Umbrath for her unwavering and constant support even in the final frustrating months of this project; Simon Bailey, Keeper of the Archives at Oxford University, for his help, patience and kindness in granting permission to refer to those documents held in the Bodleian Library from which several stories are taken.

Thanks also go to Carl Boardman and Mark Priddey at the Oxfordshire Record Office for all their help, especially relating to the use of images from the records they hold and their generous permission in allowing them to be reproduced.

Several people provided a great deal of help in relation to photographing the court rooms in County Hall, the Town Hall and Convocation House, and in kindly granting permission for those images to be published herein. The people concerned include Nick Evans and the hallkeepers at County Hall; Sue Scarrott, Owain Pearce and the hallkeepers at the Town Hall; Reg Carr, Ronald Milne and, in particular, Steve Rose from the Bodleian Library.

Thank you to Rosey Wheeler, formerly of Oxford Archaeology, for discussions about the Castle gaol site; Nancy Edwards from MN Associates for setting up a visit to the Oxford Castle site; and Mike Davy from GDG Management for showing me round and likewise for his subsequent support. Special thanks go to Malcolm Graham and Stephen Rench at Oxfordshire Studies for their generous help and guidance concerning the illustrations published in this book.

Overall, thanks go to the helpful, supportive and kind staff at The National Archives, the Oxfordshire Record Office (part of Oxfordshire County Council) and Oxfordshire Studies.

INTRODUCTION

Where there are people there is crime. Similarly, the increase in sophistication in society is mirrored by the increase in diversity of criminal activity. The history of Oxford as a city and a seat of learning is documented in hundreds of books, but little has been written concerning Oxford's criminal past. This book covers a wide slice of Oxford history from its earliest days to the twentieth century; in the main, it spans the years 1632–1849. It charts the diversity of criminal activity in Oxford while it grew into the university city we know it as today. It also covers the areas that were once outlying villages, but are now very much part of the city as a whole, such as Cowley, Iffley and Littlemore. The stories drawn on come from the Assizes, the Quarter Sessions and the University Court, and rely heavily on additional information gleaned from *Jackson's Oxford Journal*.

Many years have been spent elbow-deep in paper while sitting in the Public Record Office (now The National Archives) in London, as well as the Oxfordshire Record Office, Oxfordshire Studies and the Bodleian Library. The purpose of this introduction is to give an idea of the background to the aspects of life and, in particular, crime which run through this book, without getting bogged down in detail.

COURTS

The courts of Oxford are numerous. Those to which this book mostly relate are the Assize Court, the Quarter Sessions and the Chancellor's Court. The Assizes were usually held twice a year and tried the more serious crimes committed locally, such as

County Hall, New Road, built in 1841 on the Castle Gaol site. (Giles Brindley)

County Hall Court Room, which is still used for the coroner's court. (Giles Brindley)

The Town Hall Court Room was used by the Magistrates of the Assize from 1897 to 1969 and the Quarter Sessions until 1985 when all court activities moved to the Court House in St Aldate's. (Giles Brindley)

The Town Hall, St Aldate's, opened in 1897. It was built on the site of the old Town Hall, 1752–1896. (Giles Brindley)

The 'Domus Conversorum', purchased by the council in 1550 and used in conjunction with the neighbouring Guild Hall (built 1292–3), was replaced by the old Town Hall in 1752. (Oxfordshire County Council Photographic Archive – OCCPA)

murder, though from their introduction in the twelfth century until the arrival of the Quarter Sessions in the fourteenth century, they dealt with most cases. The Oxford Assize circuit encompassed several counties which lay close to Oxford, such as Berkshire, Gloucestershire and Herefordshire, and was presided over by a judge of the High Court who travelled through the counties in turn. The Quarter Sessions were originally meetings of the Justices of the Peace. The Oxford Sessions were presided over by a recorder as judge. During the thirteenth century the jurisdiction of the town centre courts rose and they were usually held in the Shire Hall on the Castle site. In 1577 they were moved to the Guild Hall and from 1752 to the old Town Hall, on the site of the current Town Hall. In 1841 they were moved again, to the newly built County Hall on the edge of the Castle site. The Quarter Sessions finally moved to the present Town Hall when it was opened in 1897.

The University Court held jurisdiction over those who were matriculated by the institution. This covered not only students, but a large number of tradesmen as well. In essence it operated under canon law, but later followed common law to bring it into line with the changing times.

Front gate of the Castle gaol on New Road at the end of the nineteenth century. (OCCPA)

Oxford Castle mill and stream from the south. The Norman tower of St George in the Castle gaol can be seen in the background. (OCCPA)

The court was usually presided over by the Vice-Chancellor, with Proctors acting for the defence and prosecution. If a defendant was very unlucky when being sentenced, he or she might have their matriculated rights withdrawn or possibly be banished from Oxford, but there was none of this hanging malarkey.

PUNISHMENT

It is not intended to go deep into sentencing and punishments, but to explain and highlight some of the common themes. At one time court proceedings were used as a last resort when a dispute could not be settled, usually financially, away from the court house. Certainly many cases throughout history were assessed in terms of monetary value as reflected in the levying of fines as punishment. At one point a crime valued at $12d$ or more was considered a capital one and therefore punishable by death.

In fact, most offences, including treason, murder, robbery, larceny, rape and arson, initially were considered to be capital offences. Taking out an eye, disabling a tongue, or slitting someone's nose were added later, to be joined by burglary, witchcraft, damaging forests, sacrilege, letter-stealing and the theft of animals. At one point the list of capital offences topped 200, though in more recent times it was rationalised to just a handful of offences.

In Britain a death sentence generally meant hanging and that was the execution of choice from about the fifth century. Other methods, such as burning at the stake, beheading, firing squad, drowning, boiling alive and hurling from cliffs, have

Executions were usually a public affair attended by great crowds. The gallows were built up to provide a clear view and prisoners often gave a final speech before the sentence was carried out. (ORO)

been used at one time or another. Over the centuries hanging was conducted from trees, the back of carts and later from purpose-built gallows. Hanging was initially a public spectacle, but after centuries of tried and tested use it finally moved behind closed doors, allowing the condemned at least some dignity.

Reprieve from a death sentence became a distinct possibility once people were needed to colonise the new territories of America and the West Indies from 1615 and Australia from 1787. When transportation to America ceased in 1776, overcrowding in prisons led to the introduction of floating prisons (hulks). It was not until 1867 that transportation was abolished altogether. From 1718 non-capital offences resulted in seven years' transportation; capital offences resulted in fourteen years' transportation; and those who, for example, managed to break out of gaol while awaiting transportation often received a life transportation sentence.

The most curious of all crimes was perhaps self-murder (suicide), for which the deceased was convicted and the usual burial rights withheld. Initially suicides, as well as other criminal burials, were performed at crossroads. This seems to derive from the belief that this would confuse the ghost of the deceased and prevent him or her returning to haunt their home. The practice was abolished in 1823, though normal burial rights were still not observed. This often meant burial after 9 p.m. (curfew) without the burial service being read.

Having been executed you still were not safe. Once anatomy became a student pastime, the bodies of murderers, among others, were taken to the schools to be sliced and diced under the guise of the advancement of science and learning. One of these schools was beneath the Ashmolean in Broad Street. The students were only allowed one body from time to time and demand far outstripped supply. Grave-robbing and swiping bodies as they were cut down from the gallows were commonplace. Even the students were not too aloof to do the dirty work themselves, though it was easier to pay a townie to do it.

PRISONS AND SUCHLIKE

Criminals, suspect or otherwise, as well as the poor, were lodged in one institution or another. These included the Bocardo prison, the Bridewell, St George's Tower, the debtors' prison, the houses of correction, the workhouse or house of industry and the city and county prisons.

The Bocardo flanked the original North Gate by St Michael's, at the end of the Cornmarket. The county gaol was on the Oxford Castle site. Prisoners were also confined in St George's Tower, which was Norman in origin, and the round-house on the same site, which was used as a debtors' prison. The houses of correction contained a treadwheel and were located towards the back of the Castle site, close to the Norman tower. Oxford also had a city prison, since gone, located at Gloucester Green. The main workhouse for those who could not support themselves was located in Jericho, not far from Worcester College and close to the Radcliffe Infirmary, and later one was opened in Cowley. There was a workhouse in Headington and mention of others, such as the one in Holywell Parish.

POLICING

This was undertaken at various times by, among others, watchmen, parish constables and policeman. All three were there, in essence, to prevent crime, but there were subtle differences in the formal nature of their position. Watchmen were there to watch and guard, to preserve the peace. In effect, they prevented crime by their presence rather than in active policing. They were often badly paid and relied on those with more to lose to throw some extra cash their way. Constables were intended to preserve the peace and prevent the committal of crime with the power of arrest. It was not until the middle of the nineteenth century that policemen as we know them really come into effect, with more of a formalised structure to their work and organisation.

TRADE AND PRIVILEGE

Usually only freemen had the right to trade within the boundaries of a city and there were three ways to become one: by paying for it after, in theory, being recommended by the craft guild you were joining; by being born the eldest son of a freeman (younger sons could join by paying a reduced fee); or the hard way, by serving a seven-year apprenticeship, which was how the majority were admitted as freemen.

The fourth way to trade was for the *privilegiati*, who could operate without even serving an apprenticeship. They normally came from trades that were useful to the University, such as bookbinders, hairdressers and tailors. Since they were matriculated by the University and subject to its court, they were often known as matriculated tradesmen. By about 1520 a fifth of the tradesmen had matriculated via this route.

When it came to shopping, it should be remembered that walking into a shop and parting with cash is a relatively new concept. For a large part of history goods were ordered and the bills were paid at a much later date. This often meant settling up at the end of the year for all one's expenses. For this reason the system was open to abuse and was the downfall of many. Students ended up having to settle bills termly and the visit of one's father could spell disaster when accounts were scrutinised.

MEDICINE

Medicine has not always involved dancing round trees at midnight with feathers in one's hair. As early as 1800 quackery and fluke chance were on their way out. The 1850s marked a turning point, when public funds were ploughed into the investigation of communicable diseases. For most of history medicine was a scary

The Anatomy School at Christ Church, 1821, where dissection was performed in the basement. Anatomy lectures were originally conducted in the Bodleian and later at the Ashmolean on Broad Street. (OCCPA)

subject. At best, if patients were not being poisoned with medicines containing mercury, arsenic or phosphorous, the medical profession was bleeding them, applying leeches, administering laxatives or even purging them with emetics. If they were lucky, they might have been left alone to rely on prayer or a 'change of air'. If the disease did not kill them there was a chance that the doctors would. The rule of thumb seemed to be not to get ill or if you did, die quickly before you received unwanted 'attention'.

TOWN OR GOWN: WHICH CAME FIRST?

Is the town a by-product of the University or is the University only there because of the town? What is certain is that Oxford would not be Oxford without both, or a few riots between them. Not to generalise, but there are those who would say that the students consider the town to be a playground and that everyone else be regarded as 'local people with their local ways'. On the other hand there are those who would consider that the town's inhabitants think the students are a bunch of over-privileged, under-worked layabouts, who should wash, get a job and stop rowing up and down the river at 5 a.m. In effect, both survive because of and in spite of each other.

It should be noted that heads of houses have been referred to as 'Warden', whether provost, principal, rector or otherwise. No disrespect is meant by this simplification.

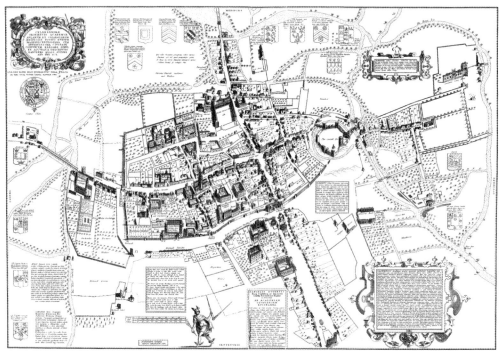

Skelton's reduced engraving of the original Plan of Oxford taken by Ralph Agar in 1578. (OCCPA)

1

FIGHTING, RIOTING AND DUELLING

SOCIAL STANDING

In 1235 Henry Le Ferur was dragged by Adam Feteplace, trader and several times Mayor of Oxford, into the latter's house and beaten. Henry charged Adam with assault and the robbery of a gold ring. Unfortunately the judge stated that the charge Henry made in court was not exactly the same as the one he had made at the time of the assault; Adam was acquitted of all charges. However, the jury concluded that Adam had beaten Henry and thrown beer in his face . . . hardly what you would expect from a former Mayor.

TIT-FOR-TAT

Considering the tender age of some of Oxford's undergraduates, especially during the early history of the University, it is hardly surprising that it was often handbags at five paces. Ferriman Moore, a Balliol scholar, was charged in June 1624 with assaulting John Crabtree of the same college. Moore pleaded not guilty, but was convicted of homicide and manslaughter, having stabbed his fellow college member in the stomach. Moore pleaded the benefit of his status as clergy and applied to the King for a pardon.

It appears that during a snacktime in college the two had squabbled. Then, as now, there was often some fierce marking of territory between graduates and undergraduates. Crabtree, 20, a graduate, chastised Moore, 16, for presuming to drink with him, threatening him, kicking and then pulling Moore around by his hair and ears. Moore had left the buttery and headed for his rooms, but Crabtree followed. A brawl ensued and in the confusion Moore stabbed the other man.

The magistrates took pity on Moore, and his punishment was reduced to burning in the hand – quite common at the time – because Moore had pleaded his status as clergy. Since the magistrates expected a full pardon to follow, and because they feared the student may leave his studies, the sentence was reduced to nothing.

It did not work out as quite expected, as Moore presently disappeared. A year later he mysteriously reappeared and recommenced his studies at Exeter College.

RETURNING THE FAVOUR

During the Civil War Oxford was a royalist stronghold, but not before the parliamentarians were driven out soon after the royalist victory at Edgehill in October 1642. As the soldiers left, one of the London troopers, marching down the High Street, let rip at St Mary's (the University church) and in particular at the statue of Mary above the porch, blowing off her head and that of baby Jesus.

But favours came from both sides when, later, some Christ Church aristocrats stopped the coach of the elderly Lady Lovelace (a Whig) outside the Crown and pulled her from it, calling her an 'old bitch'. Even the Dean of Christ Church was forced to express displeasure with the students.

INCIVILITY IN CIVIL WAR

During the early years of the Civil War, when Oxford was held by the royalists, one Captain Hurst was executed by firing squad in December 1643, by order of the King, for having stabbed a superior officer during an argument. The sentence was carried out in Mr Napper's ancient Great Barn, which stood across the road from his house, Holywell Manor.

DEAD MAN'S WALK

In 1645, towards the end of the Civil War, Cromwell routed a party of the King's troops near Islip Bridge; 200 soldiers and 400 swordsmen were taken at this crushing defeat and the rest fled to Bletchington Park. Cromwell followed and besieged them there. The governor of the Bletchington Park garrison was Colonel Francis Windebank. Against his better judgement, but at the request of his wife and other women, Windebank made a deal and surrendered. Bletchington Park was one of several outposts that were intended to keep Oxford supplied and protected from sudden attack. The colonel was allowed to return to Oxford with his colours to report the surrender to Prince Rupert who, having just been humiliated at Islip, was rather less than pleased with the news. Windebank was brought before a court martial and taken to the meadow wall of Merton College and shot. To this day the path is known as Dead Man's Walk.

NORTH-WEST DIVIDE

Battle commenced between Exeter and Queen's colleges in mid-February 1665, between those from the north and those from west, which was unusual as battles were fought normally between north and south, but each to their own.

MONMOUTH V S YORK

Charles II died in 1685 and two men stood to gain by being crowned king: his illegitimate son, the Protestant Duke of Monmouth, and his brother, the Catholic Duke of York. Less than two years before, in 1683, tension was running high in Oxford, as elsewhere. In April 1683 it was only two months before the Rye House Plot (the plan to assassinate Charles and the Duke of York) would be uncovered.

One night in that April a flashpoint was reached in Oxford. In a pub in Magpie Lane both students and locals sat drinking, in separate rooms of course. The locals toasted Monmouth so the students toasted York. It was all too much for one student who yelled from the other room asking why the townsmen were so rude. This inflamed one of the students, Mr Taylor, who stood up and ripped off his coat and said he would fight any of them. Taylor was cooled down, but the locals continued to toast Monmouth. Eventually the students thought it would be a better idea if they left.

The bill was paid and the students walked out at 8.45 p.m., but the townies did not leave it there. The students were followed at close distance down the High Street with the locals yelling 'up Monmouth'. Unfortunately one student innocently going in the opposite direction was clubbed by the townsmen, who cried out 'kill him, kill him!'. With the mob hot on his heels, the poor student, having been freed, ran for cover in a cutler's shop. Several attempts were made by the city authorities to remove the ringleaders, but without success. Mr Chartlett, a Deputy Proctor, was a no-nonsense type of man. He spied the mob at Carfax at 10 p.m. and went for the ringleader Will Atkyns. Despite Atkyns's protest that Chartlett had no warrant, the Deputy Proctor clapped hands on him and hauled him off.

The 300-strong mob supposed that Atkyns would be taken to the Bocardo prison and they besieged the building. But Atkyns had been taken to the Castle gaol instead. While Chartlett tried to make it through the outermost wicket gate of the Castle, the mob were at the Bocardo screaming that they would rescue Atkyns and they would have the Proctor's blood.

The Bocardo prison, demolished in 1771, abutted the North Gate at the end of Cornmarket Street. The tower of St Michael's Church rises above the gate. (OCCPA)

Chartlett had made it through the first and was now at the second wicket gate with Atkyns. By now the mob had realised their mistake and were heading for the Castle. Faced with a locked gate, Chartlett worked frantically to open it, while at the first gate a gentleman from London, a passer-by, kept the mob at bay with his sword. The gentleman may have fought a valiant rearguard action, but over his head projectiles were flying. While working on the lock, Chartlett was being pelted with stones. Possibly it was some consolation that Atkyns was also receiving his fair share of the battering. The mob broke free at the first gate, but Chartlett had managed to unlock the second and succeeded in closing the door on the rampaging masses, having dragged his prisoner inside with him.

The riot continued outside. Some tried to climb in over the walls, others just screamed that they would liberate Atkyns and have the Proctor's and Vice-Chancellor's blood to boot. Chartlett was now well and truly stuck inside, but managed to smuggle out a note to the Vice-Chancellor asking for help. Meanwhile, Atkyns was merrily telling his guards that he would see all the University members hanged. So keen was Atkyns that he said he would even see to it personally. For his services he offered to charge the very reasonable rate of 2*d* for each hanging.

At 1 a.m., in the dead of night, the Vice-Chancellor with men from Jesus College turned up at the Castle and rescued the Proctor, arresting numerous members of the mob as they went. Several men besides Atkyns stood charged with riot at the next Assizes on 4 September 1683, but the jury threw out the charge against them and all the men went free.

ARROGANCE BEFORE A FALL

Dalton, a junior Fellow of All Souls, was returning from a hunting trip in October 1705 when he met a policeman. Such was his pride that he would not lower himself to move for the policeman and tried to force the man aside as they came into contact, but lost out. As the policeman walked away, Dalton, pride dented, turned around and shot the constable in the back. But the policeman was a big, powerful man and ignoring the wound went up to Dalton, took the gun, arrested him and sent Dalton to gaol to await his trial.

PISTOLS AT DAWN

Sir Cholmly Dearing, formerly of New College, and Mr Thornhill were very close friends. Well, they were close until they had a falling out over a 'matter of honour'. On 17 May 1711, only two weeks after the bust-up, it came to a head. The gentlemen met to duel with dagger and pistol. In this theatrical rendition the first act was also the last. Mr Thornhill was the first to shoot and blew a hole clean through Sir Cholmly. The runner-up in this competition only survived until 3 p.m. that afternoon. Death must have come as a shock for Sir Cholmly and also for his two young sons who survived him. But most of all it would have been a great shock for the woman who had been destined to be his second wife only days later. And this was probably not the final blow-out with friends that Dearing was looking for in the run up to his own wedding day.

DRUMMING UP SUPPORT

Accompanied by a drummer, an officer from the Dragoons was beating up support for volunteers on the Oxford streets one night in August 1715. They were booed and hissed as they went about their business, but carried on until finally they were surrounded. The pair were cornered by a pumped-up mob, which consisted mostly of students. The mob jeered and jostled the soldiers, yelling out 'down with the Roundheads'. The two men were heavily outnumbered, but forced their way out and pushed on towards the Angel Inn with cries of 'God save the Duke of Ormond' echoing in their ears. The good duke at the time was the University's Chancellor. As the troops neared the doors of the inn, out came a gentleman, sword drawn and ready for combat. He put the fear of God into the officer who, under threat, was made to sheepishly call out 'down with the Roundheads'. But this token did not buy the soldiers' freedom, it only served to draw an even larger crowd, who continued the chant. With such large numbers, those who would otherwise not have dared get involved soon joined in. Out stepped a tailor, a well-known Roundhead, to gather evidence against the rioters. He was known locally as 'My Lord Shaftesbury' on account that he, like the Earl, was physically deformed. This was a particularly bad move on his part as he was instantly recognised and jumped on; though it did take a little heat away from the battered soldiers.

The would-be informant was driven down the street, buffeted and pushed towards the East Gate, presumably to shove him outside the city and shut the gate behind him. The tailor saw his 'saviours' as they rode through the gate and into town. He grabbed the bridle of the first horse, which only served to give the mob a stationary target to flog. The stranger was indignant and asked what the hell was going on. The crowd replied the man was a Roundhead and the rider coolly said, 'Please, carry on.' The crowd took great pleasure in this, but presumably the tailor did not.

The East Gate, now demolished, lay at one end of the High Street. Outside the city walls Longwall Street leads off to the right behind the trees. (OCCPA)

Despite the fact that attention had been drawn away from them, the Dragoons were still overwhelmed by force and were being pelted with eggs and rocks. The authorities were forced to step in. The crowd was told that if they did not stop they would be reported to the King himself. Ignoring this the mob stoned on – seemingly mobs do rule and strangers are not always kind.

Two weeks later a group of Dragoons came upon 'four students of note and distinction'. Not much distinction was made and the only note that would have been heard would have been 'ow, ow', as the soldiers gave them a sound beating. It was only when the Vice-Chancellor and others stepped in to rescue them that the students were saved from some rough justice and from being torn to pieces by the miffed Dragoons. It would appear that the score line was one apiece, but the Vice-Chancellor used his power to take the soldiers to task and had all the Dragoons sent away from the city.

Seemingly this was the end of the episode, but it was the Dragoons who would have the last laugh. The final blow was dealt to the University in September 1715 when the Chancellor, the Duke of Ormond, was impeached for high treason and crimes against Parliament. The great man fled for his life to France and Parliament issued a declaration that if he did not surrender himself by the 10th he would be considered guilty and a traitor. It was a bit of a toss-up: he did not return, which left the University perplexed; and they had no Chancellor, although Ormond had not resigned. It was a sticky matter, but it was resolved when a letter was received from Ormond's brother. The communiqué signified that Ormond finally had resigned, which happily allowed the University to elect his replacement, presumably too happy to notice that its former Chancellor had just been condemned as a traitor.

BAYONET PRACTICE

In June 1716 a scuffle between students and twenty or more soldiers led to the soldiers being beaten and students running away with the soldiers' swords to Exeter College. The army officers gave orders that soldiers should carry their bayonets fixed and if anybody, townsman or student alike, offered them the least affront, they should stab them.

BIRTHDAY PARTY

On the Prince of Wales's birthday at the end of October 1716 the lights, as was custom, were displayed in house windows to celebrate the day. Soldiers quartered in the town were told by their major to smash windows where there were no lights. This they happily did, kicking off in the parish of All Saints, smashing windows as they went and throwing burning brands of fire through windows, as well as letting rip with their guns. They abused the Vice-Chancellor and the Mayor, and blew a hole clean through the mace bearer's hat. The carnage was only stopped when their colonel, lodging at the Angel Inn on the High Street, ordered the soldiers back to their quarters. It was a miracle they had not managed to kill anyone by shot or by fire, least of all that they did not burn the whole city to the ground.

BOG HOUSE RULES

Antiquity Hall, so-called because antiquaries including Thomas Hearne used to meet here, was owned sometime before 1718 by Geoffrey Ammon. He was an ingenious man, well respected for his knowledge of history, geography and heraldry, and was often consulted there by antiquaries as well as students. He was a merry chap, but one

Antiquity Hall in Hythe Bridge Street, 1817. The building was the meeting place for many of the city's antiquaries, and the site of a fatal dispute in the early eighteenth century. (OCCPA)

night a dispute arose over the bill and Ammon threw a bottle at the offending Exeter student. The bottle cracked the student across his temple. The student staggered out to the bog house where, rather ignominiously, he died. Ammon was charged with murder, but found guilty of manslaughter instead lived to tell the tale for several years to come.

WORLD CAVES IN

Cuthberth Ellison of Corpus Christi College, who was described as a sad, dull and heavy preacher, was preaching in February 1719 at St Mary's. One of the University Proctors, also present, happened to see some students out in the street. The Proctor left the church and drove the errant students back inside, but he put the fear of God into them so much that they fled into one of the galleries. This caused uproar, as their status did not allow them to be there. Such was the noise and disturbance that people all over the church started yelling that the church was falling down. Panic reigned and the congregation fled in all directions, some jumping out of the galleries, others stomping on anybody who got in their way during the confusion. But not Mr Ellison; as the last of the walking wounded left, he continued to drone on until his sermon was finished.

In a more bizarre incident, sixteen years previously, during Lent an afternoon service was being preached by Mr Stradling, of Christ Church, in the church of St Peter-in-the-East. Several young boys got up into the church tower and proceeded to throw stones down onto the church roof. This so much alarmed the congregation that they stampeded, screaming that the church was collapsing. They had fair trashed the small church in their panic to escape injury. Ironically Mr Stradling was in the middle of his sermon preaching on the end of the world.

HALL OF INFAMY

Battle commenced on the front quad of St Edmund Hall in June 1723. The protagonists were Mr Walter, a gentleman student, and Sam, the college's assistant butler. They were fiercely locked in combat when Mrs Felton, the Warden's wife, arrived on the scene. Coincidently Mrs Felton was related to Mr Walter, but it was only with great difficulty that she parted the two combatants. The fight was by no means over and Dr Felton and Mr Cread, the Deputy Warden, were forced to add their weight in order to quell hostilities. Walter did not appreciate this intrusion, especially not from Cread, and Walter, who had armed himself, began throwing plates at Cread. Walter narrowly missed the Fellow's head, yelling out that it was only yesterday that Cread was a poor servitor at Queen's. Nothing like a bit of upper-class snobbery. The feud was eventually quashed, but it left ill-feeling on both sides of the divide.

Discipline at the time was a little free and easy or at least the students' morals were. It turned out that Mr Rice, described as a 'Welshman of ill character', had 'entertained' a young lady in his rooms the previous evening. The girl stayed until morning, but Sam had discovered this and gone straight to Dr Felton to drop Rice in it. Sam informed Dr and Mrs Felton of the young lady's presence and it was this betrayal that seems to have been the starting point for the outbreak of hostilities. This was a big issue at the time, because women were a no-no in college, except for a few bedmakers and the Warden's wife. New College went so far as to have a statute that basically implied the bedmakers should be so repulsive that no student would want to sleep with them. Sam's betrayal of Rice so much offended Walter that the student had resolved to take the assistant butler to task – after all Sam was a mere servant. On the morning in question, Sam had left college to find a Proctor to search and drag out the girl. But before one could be found Rice and others, who perhaps included Walter, had helped the young lady to escape by smuggling her out of the college.

HAPPY FAMILIES

In his will Thomas Myn, a joiner, had left all his possessions to his wife, Ann, that upon her death they should be distributed among his wider family, much to the annoyance of his siblings, John, Susan and Hesther Myn. It was April 1726 and the siblings were intent upon taking possession of the items before the widow's death. John entered and commandeered the house his brother had built next to Magdalen Parish Church.

The matter was decided in court in favour of the widow Myn and with five bodyguards she went to claim the house on 1 April. John was not at home, but his wife was and she was armed with two pistols with four bullets each. As the party entered the house she let rip at them, but neither pistol went off and she was bundled out of the building. Ann Myn left the five men in charge of the house that evening as she went away.

Returning later that night at 1 a.m. John Myn, in the company of another man, climbed over the garden wall and broke into the house. After blowing out the candle that was lit in one of the rooms, John stabbed Edward Hastings, one of the guards, through the heart. The poor man, a former soldier with a wife and children, died instantly. Myn then moved through the house and came upon another guard, Richard Taylor. Myn made a frenzied attack, repeatedly stabbing Taylor, inflicting several wounds to the stomach. Taylor was a widower and must have thought of his four children as he lay there, bleeding profusely.

The next morning John Myn's wife was arrested as an accessory and committed to gaol. Richard Taylor died a few days later from the multiple wounds he had received. Ann Myn promptly issued a reward of £10 for the apprehension of her brother-in-law.

On 20 April John Myn was apprehended at Coleshill near Faringdon. Word was sent to Oxford and a coach was dispatched to convey him back to the town. He arrived at 3 p.m. on the 21st and was committed to the Castle gaol to await trial at the next Assizes – if he survived that long. Myn had been shot several times before he could be taken. He died of his wounds that very night at 9 p.m. while he sat alone in his cell in the Castle gaol. His body was taken out and buried the next night in Magdalen Parish churchyard.

FUN OR FIGHT?

Copley, Pennington and Bowles, gentlemen commoners of Queen's College, were regulars at Mr Bugge's coffee shop in St Clement's. Bugge's wife and unmarried sister were considered to be very loose, which is maybe why the students all went there. The men drank all day on New Year's Eve 1727. They left – perhaps the gentlemen did not get the action they were looking for, but they must have been high on caffeine. They proceeded to try and grab the maid of Mr Allen, a barber, who was walking down the street in St Clement's. Mr Allen was beaten to a pulp when he stepped in to stop them running off with her. Failing once again to obtain a woman, they attacked an apprentice to Mr Hyeron, the barber in St Peter-in-the-East, beating him about, perhaps because he was the first moving target they came across. The matter was referred to the University authorities by the town as 'a cause for concern'. Maybe they thought the students should have been working rather than chasing women.

A WARM CONTEST

As entertainment goes, St Martin's Parish was in for a treat on 23 April 1766. Two 'brisk' widows of the parish, one a haberdasher and one a midwife, had fixed their affections on the same man, whom they both intended to make their future husband.

One having been favoured with a visit from her lover, her rival was livid. Having found her foe, the women set to with their tongues, lashing each other with words, which rapidly became fists. Both received a battering and were left to display the marks of the other's resentment. No report was made about which side was victorious, but one of the combatants was forced to retreat, leaving the object of her affections in the possession of her antagonist, who readily claimed her prize.

FROM THE RICH TO THE POOR

In September 1766, when inflation was high, the cost of basic provisions had gone through the roof and food was being exported, the huddled masses heard that a wagon was to leave Oxford secretly in the dead of night. On the 23rd a group stopped a wagoner at St Giles's on his way from the Holywell Mill. The group slashed some of the flour bags he was transporting and finally let him go.

The next night a huge mob assembled at Carfax. Having stolen the miller's cart, they removed flour from Holywell Mill. And, with 120 sacks of flour, they distributed it among the populace at large.

The mob then went to the Castle Mill, but found little there and left it alone. At Osney Mill the miller cleverly struck a deal. Rather than have them swipe his goods, he agreed to sell his wheat at a low price. The next night the miller kept his promise. Similarly other businesses were compelled to sell bacon, cheese, butter, fish, ducks, chicken, candles and even soap at reduced prices that were fixed by the mob. Friday 26th saw Mr Butler, a London wagoner, relieved of his load of butter. This was sold for him at 4d a pound, though it is not stated whether he actually received the proceeds.

The tree-lined street of St Giles's, 1833, which led to Oxford's North Gate, with St Mary Magdalen in the distance. (OCCPA)

An early nineteenth-century view of Osney Bridge and toll-house on Botley Road leading out of the city. The bridge collapsed in 1885. (OCCPA)

The city and University officials addressed the crowd and said they would redress the balance, but if events were not stopped, legal action would be taken. This being heeded, the city residents awaited the return of the wagoner with cheese from Burford fair. Thereafter they stopped wagons and forced their owners to sell their goods at the price the mob had fixed upon, threatening to stop any and all transport of provisions out of the city. The local paper stated that by an immediate cessation of exportation it was hoped to quell the unwashed masses.

JEALOUSY KILLS

Jane Harris had left her husband James in May 1821 and stayed for three weeks with Henry Hyatt, also of Headington and a married man. After that she had lived for a short while with her sister. It was from here that James had eventually collected his wife and taken her home. During his wife's absence James had never complained to anyone, but was often known to be depressed.

On the evening of 8 September Jane was returning home from work, accompanied by her husband, when Hyatt came up to her and said, 'Well, Jenny, how d'ye do?' She replied she did not know. James was intimidated and challenged Hyatt to fight. Hyatt declined, but said he would fight James any other time. They parted company and the Harrises went home. When they arrived, James stormed upstairs, saying 'I'll go away'. Soon after he ran back downstairs, but Jane managed to make it to the door before him and lock it shut, so James jumped out of the window. James returned a quarter of an hour later and they both went to bed. He refused to speak to Jane all night, but appeared very agitated and upset. At 8 a.m. the next day Jane fetched some milk and, returning to James in bed, told him he should get up and have breakfast. James refused and shortly afterwards said that he had taken poison. Jane forced a cup from his hand; James said he had drunk nearly all the contents.

Despite medical assistance James finally died two weeks later on 24 September. The verdict at the coroner's inquest was: 'Died from poison, taken when in the state of mental insanity.'

OUT OF ORDER

In 1824 Mr Munday was the owner of the *Oxford Herald* newspaper, which had offices on the High Street. In September of that year he made his opinions concerning the Queen's conduct freely known. For this disrespectful act, vengeance was sought by some of Oxford's inhabitants. Shortly after dark on 18 September a large group of locals, fuelled with free drink courtesy of the candidates who had stood for positions of civic responsibility that day, gathered and proceeded to Munday's house. They smashed his windows and hurled projectiles into the house, inflicting untold damage on the furniture and property inside.

When the mob went back for a second bite at the cherry the city magistrates were forewarned; the police were ready for them and quashed the night's activities before they started.

The four ringleaders of the riots were tried on 19 October. All were found guilty and received sentences varying from four to eight months.

A CULT ABOVE THE REST

In 1825 a cult sprang up in Oxford, which was headed by one Mr Muloch. Muloch was a fanatical man who proclaimed that it was contrary to the laws of God for a man to marry. People believed him and many happily married men left their wives and families.

The deserted wives somehow had to fend for themselves, having lost their breadwinner. There were rumblings among the women of St Thomas's where one of the discarded wives lived. It was all too much for these good and pious female citizens. Having taken great exception to Mr Muloch and his followers, the women learned that the men were holding a meeting on 6 October. Muloch was absent from the meeting at Mr Gardner's house in St Thomas's when the mob descended. The enraged women broke down the door, smashed the windows and destroyed the furniture. The men were beaten into the street where the rest of the parish joined in, hooting and pelting them with shit and anything else that came to hand. Beaten and clothes torn, the cult members were practically unrecognisable. One of their number, Mr Hunt the apothecary, was reported as faring worst than most, if that was possible. Hunt was eventually forced to take shelter in the Town Hall until the mob had been dispersed to avoid being ripped to shreds.

BEATEN FOR MODESTY

At 6 p.m. on 4 January 1826 Frederick Julienne, a 60-year-old carpenter, was found dying in Mr Lucas's yard in the Parish of St Thomas. He was dragged to the house of James Allen where medical assistance was called for and duly given. But Julienne never recovered his senses and died later that day at 4 p.m. Not to waste any time, the body was taken to the Lamb and Flag and a coroner's inquest opened. The hearing lasted until 8 p.m. the next day, when a verdict of manslaughter was returned against William Selstone, also a carpenter. Selstone was committed that very evening to gaol to stand trial four days later on 9 January.

It seems that Harriet Eeley, 'a notorious prostitute', who had lived with Selstone, had brought Julienne to her house on the night of Tuesday 3 January. This act upset

Selstone so much that he ordered Julienne to leave, then proceeded to violently knock six shades out of Julienne, flooring him twice. The post-mortem revealed that there were large amounts of extravasated blood on Julienne's brain, which had caused his death. Monday duly came and the grand jury threw out the charge of manslaughter and acquitted Selstone.

BETTER TO KEEP QUIET

Ann Cox, a smart young lady, was brought into court on 11 June 1830 charged with assaulting and violently abusing an old woman by the name of Mrs Baylis. Although the charge was proved, Cox managed to damn herself, for during her own defence she stated that she called Mrs Baylis 'a damned old bitch'. During the incident in question, when Baylis had taken hold of her Ann had proceeded to deal a heavy slap across the face to the old lady. Ann was fined 10*s* plus costs and released.

A MAN OF LETTERS

Arriving at the subscription room at the Town Hall on the evening of 6 January 1832, Francis Stevens, a printer, announced to the assembled gentlemen that he hoped he did not intrude. Sitting down, Stevens rang the bell and called for a glass of brandy and water. Although not a member, Stevens considered that he had every right to be there since he was also 'a man of letters'. Unfortunately the waiter, William Holmes, did not agree and refused to serve him as he was neither a member nor a guest of one. Stevens asked for a pint of beer or a glass of water, but the waiter again refused. Stevens demanded the waiter ask his master, Thomas Cowderoy, if he was not to be served.

Stevens left the room and returned with Cowderoy. Holmes told him to leave, Stevens yelled 'I must, must I!' and ran to the fire and seized the poker. Holmes and Cowderoy jumped on Stevens and threw him out. Stevens, feeling miffed, brought a case against Holmes and Cowderoy, which was heard on 16 January, at which the Mayor concluded that no more force was used in the expelling of Stevens than was necessary and dismissed the case leaving Stevens to pay 9*s* 6*d* in costs.

A PINCH AND A PUNCH

Mr Middleton, a Cutslow farmer, was returning home from market in Oxford in August 1834 and had stopped at the King's Arms in Summertown to wait for his son. When he entered the pub there was only one other man there. Another soon entered, struck up a conversation and produced a curious lock, wagering that Mr Middleton could not open it. Middleton said that he wanted nothing to do with either of them. Both men pushed Middleton to bet. The waiter stepped in saying there would be no bets laid and took Middleton into the next room.

After waiting another quarter of an hour for his son Middleton left, followed by the two men, who had given the waiter a smack in the mouth for interfering. It was now after 7 p.m. A furlong from the pub, Middleton was accosted by one of the men, James Harvey, who was twittering on about being a friend, saying that he was going in the same direction and would walk with him. Middleton thanked him and told him to get lost.

Harvey kept with him and rubbed him up and down to find out whether Middleton had a wallet in his pocket. The farmer said that if Harvey did not leave him alone he was going to punch him. Harvey jumped on Middleton and both men fell to the ground. Middleton struggled free and got up, trading punches with Harvey; but the farmer was too much for the man and the assailant ran off into the fields. Middleton, not only a better fighter, was the faster man on foot and caught up Harvey 30yd across the field. Further blows were exchanged. Harvey, beaten, ran off and Middleton, despite being bruised and cut, turned back to Oxford expecting to meet him on the Water Eaton path. There Middleton waited and sure enough Harvey came, but saw his nemesis in time and ran away. Middleton followed in pursuit. Mr Cripp's shepherd watched the chase. As the men drew closer, Harvey reached Cripp's shepherd and was clobbered by the man. Middleton and the shepherd brought Harvey back to Oxford.

   Under examination Harvey said his name was Jones, brother of 'Sailor Boy', the bare-knuckle boxer, though his pugilistic skills did not really bear this out. Harvey was promptly committed for trial.

BUMP AND GRIND

Harriet Whitlock went to the evening service at St Martin's Church on Sunday 15 November 1835 and sat in a pew belonging to Mr Midwinter. Mr Nash, servant to Sir Joseph Lock, came up and told her to get out. She told Nash there was no room for him. He told her again to come out and then pushed past two or three other people, grabbed hold of Harriet's wrists and hauled her out. She went to the pew-opener and told him what had happened. Returning with Harriet, the pew-opener insisted that she be allowed to sit in the pew, which Harriet did, next to Mr Nash, who stood on her feet and elbowed her throughout the service to the point where Harriet was ready to pass out. At trial on 16 November, in his defence Nash said that he thought it was his master's pew and that Harriet had no right to be there. He was promptly fined 20s and costs.

FEMALE PUNCH-UP

Elizabeth Burleigh, a prostitute, was brought before the Mayor on 23 January 1835 for spitting in the face of another prostitute, Jane Owen. Using Jane's head as a punchbag, Burleigh dealt Jane two black eyes before she walked off and proceeded to smash the windows of Owen's house. At the end of the court case Elizabeth was convicted and fined 20s plus costs; but unable to pay, Elizabeth was sent to gaol for one month's hard labour and bound to keep the peace and to stay away from Miss Owen on her release.

A WOMAN'S SCORN

To prevent his wife inflicting further injuries upon him, Joseph Biggers, of St Michael's Parish, went to court at the beginning of April 1835. Among other things, she had thrown a knife at Joseph during dinner, which hit him in the face, slashing his lip. His wife Elizabeth had hissed that she wished it had cut his throat and killed him instead. On another occasion she had used him for target practice, throwing glasses as well as brass candlesticks at him. It was the last straw and Joseph called in the police to protect him. When Bossom, the policeman, arrived at the house, so violent was Elizabeth that he was forced to handcuff her and for the safety of all remove a cut-throat razor, which she had hidden inside her clothes. After eleven days on remand Elizabeth was found guilty and sent back to gaol until two sureties could be found to cough up £20 each to bind her for her good behaviour for twelve months.

AN OLD GRUDGE PAYS OFF

Edward Cooper, the University policeman, was patrolling St Aldate's at midnight on 21 July 1835 when he heard a commotion coming from Folly Bridge. When he arrived, there were a dozen people in a circle, one of whom had stripped down to fight. Considering the time of night, it would have been more of a drunken punch-up than an 'organised' prize fight. Cooper told the men who he was and told the fighter to dress. The pugilist refused. Cooper looked for support and saw William Higgs, a watchman, some way off down the street and left to have a word with him; they returned together: Cooper went up to Stephen West, who had the fighter's clothes, and told him to return them. West promptly told the policeman to leave or he would floor him. Cooper stepped forward and was immediately punched by West. With his nose bleeding, Cooper grabbed the man's collar. West pulled the policeman's truncheon from his hand and in a frenzied attack Cooper was beaten to the ground by the crowd.

By this time Higgs presumably had fled in fear of his life, for when they had finished the mob also ran and it was left to Cooper to limp back alone to the police station to have his wounds dressed. It was a fortnight before the policeman returned to duty, so severe were his injuries. It was only three weeks before the incident that West had told Cooper he owed him payment of an old grudge and would settle it at the first opportunity – this he had done. Though no more seems to have been reported on the case, one can only hope Cooper got the justice he deserved.

DOG FIGHT

Thomas Barratt was convicted on 5 September 1836 and fined 5s and costs for stabbing a dog. It seems that Barratt's dog came into contact with Mr Dicks's dog. Snarling and barking, the dogs began to fight and Barratt whipped out his knife and repeatedly stabbed the other dog; one deep wound was so severe that it was 3in long. No more was said of the dog.

THOSE IN GLASS HOUSES

In May 1836 Ann Horser of Bear Lane brought a case against Thomas Harris for riot and assault. Miss Horser stated that Harris and two other people broke into her house at 3 a.m., forcing open her windows, and getting into her bedroom. Harris jumped on Horser in bed. When she told him to leave, Harris punched her, for which he was found guilty and fined 10s and costs. It transpired during the trial that Miss Horser kept a 'disorderly house' (a brothel). This was much to the annoyance of the neighbours, owing to the nightly scenes that unfolded there.

Horser was bailed to answer a nuisance charge at the next sessions, which probably was not the outcome she was hoping for.

THE ART OF PROVOCATION

On 12 February 1840 the University charged George Robert Michael Ward, MA, of Trinity College with a violation of the statutes of the University, in particular for sending to Richard Clarke Sewell, MA, of Magdalen College a challenge to fight a duel and provoking Sewell to engage in deadly combat. Neither of these two men was new to the University nor a rash youngster, as both had already obtained their Master of Arts. In court Ward confessed his offence for which he expressed his deepest regret and begged for mercy.

After a lot of toing and froing over the weeks, on 25 February the Vice-Chancellor pronounced his judgment 'that Mr Ward be banished from the University from the close of the present week to the end of the present Lent term', that is to say he was rusticated (suspended) for a matter of weeks and probably grateful for it. Who said the University was a soft touch?

CHRISTMAS CHEER

William Roberts and William Langley were together in the Jericho pub on Christmas Eve 1841, drinking heavily. They both worked at the Lucy Foundry and messed around arguing about work. Langley challenged Roberts to a fight, but when he refused to accept, Langley punched him anyway, and Roberts reciprocated. Langley threw his friend down, collapsing upon him. Roberts, helped by the bystanders, got up and was taken home, where he died two days later of a ruptured bladder.

Langley was found guilty at trial and sentenced to three months inside with hard labour, the first and last months to be spent in solitary confinement.

OLD COMRADES OF TRAFALGAR

Henry Ward, a 64-year-old inmate of the Oxford workhouse, was released for a few hours on 20 March 1847. Within a short time he was up on a charge of assault. A drunken Ward had felled a young boy, William Worth, severely injuring him. William had been asked by a policeman to go to Pumfrey's and borrow a cart to remove Ward, who that afternoon had been found lying unconscious in the road. When Worth arrived with the cart the policeman had already left, but a group of men succeeded in lifting Ward and propped him up against a wall. On seeing Worth, Ward rushed forward, swinging his stick and cracking the boy across the head. As Worth lay unconscious on the ground, Ward battered him further before he could be hauled off. Worth was rushed away half dead to receive medical treatment.

Witnesses proved it, and Ward did not deny it, but he tried to excuse the attack owing to drink – as he had met an old comrade in town whom he had not seen in forty-five years. The men had drunk heavily and reminisced of old times, of when they fought together at the Battle of Trafalgar. The magistrates were none too convinced: Ward was found guilty and punished with a fine of 20s with 9s costs or gaol for a month. Ward had no alternative but to agree to the latter.

FOOLING AND FIGHTING

Mr Horner, a Balliol student of 1906–10, made a name for himself by being involved in too much horseplay. Finally he went too far with some Eton cronies, starting a fight in the quad and even throwing all the furniture in one man's rooms out of the window. The college banished him forever on 22 June 1912. Shortly afterwards he was wounded in France during the First World War. Returning to active service, he was again injured during the First Battle of Cambrai, but this time he died of his wounds. In May 1915 the college resolved 'that in view of his services to the country' his ban was rescinded. The college war book records that 'he was at times exasperating . . . but that he had an infinite capacity for being forgiven'.

2

THEORY IS BETTER THAN PRACTICE

It was the early hours of the morning of 17 January 1808 and a young man stood at the parlour door in Alderman Parsons's house. Having broken into the house, he had moved swiftly through the kitchen and the laundry and was intent on breaking into the parlour where he supposed the bulk of the family's silver was stored. He had already made a good start; he had amassed a haul consisting of a large silver waiter, teaspoons and tablecloths, and he had even had the cheek to steal the servants' clothes. But the lock on the parlour door held fast and despite repeated attempts to open it he gave up and, discretion being the better part of 'valour', legged it with what he had already collected. When the police came to investigate later that day, they reached the conclusion that the burglars knew the house well, and an inside job was suspected. They compiled a list of all those who had an intimate knowledge of the house's layout. Armed with this list of suspects they set out to question them, which led them to the house of John Grover that very evening.

Grover was living at his father's house, having only returned to Oxford ten days before, after an absence of several years. He had last been in town four years previously when he had lived and worked in Mr Parsons's service. On arrival the police found father and son sitting in front of the fire and intimated that they would like to have a little 'chat' with John. He stood up and told them that he would come with them as soon as he had put his coat on, and went upstairs.

The pace changed. Grover bolted and forced a window in the garret; he looked down and realised he was 20ft above the ground, but now was no time to be afraid of heights and he jumped. In doing so he cut and tore his arm and hand a great deal. He hit the stone floor of the yard below at 8 p.m. Inside, the carefree policemen waited for Grover to trot down the stairs with his coat on. But Grover, now bleeding profusely, was making off in a hurry, escaping over the buildings at the end of the yard. By now it was obvious to the police that John was not coming down, and they went up to search for him. In Grover's bedroom they hunted around and opening a chest they found all the articles stolen from Mr Parsons that morning. Not only that, they also found clothes which had been stolen from Mr Joy, the tailor, three days previously, as well as the contents of a parcel stolen from the Mitre Inn a week before. Not a bad start for somebody who had only been in town for ten days.

Half an hour had passed and, as the police feared, Grover was gone. Leaving Oxford by the Abingdon Road, he finally reached London the next day. The police suspected that Grover would head to Portsmouth and board a ship, and that he would have little money owing to his hasty and forced exit from the city. The price on his head was advertised as 20 guineas, to be paid to anybody who lodged Grover in any of His Majesty's gaols. A week later Grover was marched back into Oxford by officers from Bow Street Police Station; the police's hunch had proved correct and they had arrested him at Portsmouth. Grover was interviewed the next day and sent

Reward for apprehending a Felon.

WHEREAS JOHN GROVER the younger, stands charged with having committed three burglaries and robberies in the City of Oxford, between the 8th and the 18th of the present month: the said John Grover is 20 years old, 5 feet 10 inches high, dark eyes, well looking, upright, and of a good size; is the son of John Grover, a working brewer of Oxford, has been always of unsettled habits, has lived in a variety of services, and two or three months ago deserted from a sloop or other vessel called the *Royalist*, Captain Maxwell, on board which he had entered as Captain's servant. The said John Grover the younger, escaped from the officers of justice in Oxford on Sunday the 17th instant, as they were about to apprehend him, by leaping out of a garret window, and cut or tore one hand and arm a good deal in his fall, some marks of which are most likely still remaining. He left Oxford on Sunday evening about half past eight o'clock on foot, and there is good reason to think that he intended to get to Portsmouth, and go on board some ship as fast as he could, and that he took the South road through Abingdon. From the hurry in which he went off, it is believed that he was very poorly supplied with money. He had on a straight-cut mixed coat, a pair of corderoy breeches, and boots, and took with him a small bundle, which contained a remarkably-shaped blue jacket, with yellow mushroom buttons. A Reward of TWENTY GUINEAS will be paid immediately to any person or persons, who shall apprehend and lodge the said John Grover in any of his Majesty's gaols, by Thomas Henry Taunton, of the City of Oxford, Attorney at Law, to whom it is requested that any communication upon this subject may be addressed.

ford, Jan. 20, 1808.

Notice of a reward offered in 1808 by the Oxford authorities for the apprehension of John Grover. (Jackson's Oxford Journal) to gaol to await trial. But Grover had other ideas and three days later, when the guards were making their rounds locking up, Grover made his escape. He had left the area in which he was confined and made his way across the exercise yard, remaining in the yard long enough to carefully place planks of wood against the boundary wall.

Finding his cell empty, the alarm was raised and, rushing out, the prison officers found the planks against the wall and concluded Grover had made his escape. In fact, John had concealed himself in a wood stack where he was frantically working to free himself from his fetters, having procured a file from a cell where another prisoner, by virtue of privilege, had been working. During that night and the whole of the next day he worked away until he was free. The authorities, fully believing Grover was gone, set out to apprehend him and offered a reward for his recapture, this time raising the amount to a handsome 70 guineas. Grover sat and waited in the wood stack until early the next morning, 5 February, when he made for the wall. Having made his escape in theory, all he now needed to do was to achieve it in practice. He started to climb the wall, but it became increasingly difficult and the attempt soon became a desperate one. Scrambling towards the top he slipped and, falling, crashed onto the stone yard below. Screaming out in pain, he was soon recaptured by the prison officers who were alerted by his howls.

At the Quarter Sessions on 29 April John Grover (aged 21) was charged with the burglary at Mr Parsons's house; the trial lasted seven hours and finished at 9 p.m. He was found guilty and the awful sentence of death was passed upon him.

3

COUNTRY SPORTSMEN

At 3 p.m. on 3 July 1829 five men were observed on Port Meadow by a group of Wolvercote locals; two were stripped 'as if to fight', but no fight ensued. Instead all five proceeded to drive cattle, ducks and geese about in a hectic and violent manner, giving the ducks in particular a good boot as they went. The men continued their afternoon's sporting activity by riding horses and a donkey that were grazing on the meadow.

William Robinson worked for Mr Rowland at Wolvercote and on his way back from lunch at 3 p.m. saw the men and called in on William Eeley, 19, in Wolvercote, who worked at Mr Wheeler's shop. They went across the meadow to the men in an attempt to separate them from the ducks. Robinson told them they should know better. One of the men, named Beesley, asked what it had to do with Robinson and another told the pair to go home. Beesley was obviously known to Eeley as he said, 'Tom, you ought to know better than destroy poor people's property.'

'Do you mean to say that I have one in my pocket?' retorted Beesley, and a duck quacked. Beesley was forced to pull out one of Mrs Wren's ducks, not quite dead, from his pocket.

Beesley punched Eeley and the others joined in, punching Robinson as well, and the pair walked away with the men in pursuit, but soon everybody was running. One of them, Medden, caught up and punched Robinson into a ditch before they could reach the village, where a large crowd had by now assembled. The men thought better of it and headed for the local Crown pub, and Robinson was left to scrape himself up and he and Eeley returned to their respective jobs.

At 4 p.m. the group regaled the Crown with their bravado, stating that they had been driving donkeys, horses, ducks and geese around the meadow, and that they would have some ducks or geese before they returned home. They had already had a skinful before they arrived at the pub, and recounted to the assembled company that they had driven off two men who had interrupted them in their pursuit of geese and ducks, saying they would 'sort them out' if they came across them when the five of them left. They departed about forty-five minutes later.

Back on the meadow Medden and Beesley rode horses up and down, Beesley even abusing some poor woman on the towpath, whereupon all five chased geese and Medden caught one, depositing it on Richard Williams' land and cutting a large stick from an elm tree while there. Eeley returned to the meadow, this time with Richard Horn, another local to try for a second time to stop the men. Medden pushed Eeley and he and his companion fled to the village. The five men headed for the Plough at Upper Wolvercote.

Eeley had ended up by Richard Williams's farm, where his father worked. When the farmer came out of his parlour at around 6 p.m. and discovered his labourers had downed tools in the yard, he stepped out into the lane where he found Robinson and Eeley Jr deep in conversation with the three labourers. The farm

MURDER.
FIFTY POUNDS REWARD.

WHEREAS THOMAS BEESLEY and WILLIAM NEWMAN stand charged, (together with THOMAS MEDDEN) upon the Coroner's Inquest, with the *Wilful Murder* of John Barrett, at Wolvercot, near Oxford; and whereas the said Thomas Beesley and William Newman have escaped from the persons in whose custody they were placed to convey them to the Gaol of the county of Oxford, a Reward of FIFTY POUNDS is hereby offered to any person or persons who shall apprehend and lodge the said Thomas Beesley and William Newman in the Gaol of the said county of Oxford; or TWENTY-FIVE POUNDS for either of them.

The following is a description of the said Thomas Beesley and William Newman :—

Thomas Beesley, about 30 years of age, about 5 feet 7 inches in height, middle sized, light complexion, rather freckled face, rather dark hair, whiskers a little sandy, has the appearance of boatman or bargeman, had on a pair of fustian trowsers, red plush waistcoat, with brown fustain sleeves, and a pair of half-boots, a black leather cap, bound round with fur; walks rather stiffly with one leg.

William Newman, about 20 years of age, about 5 feet 10 inches in height, slender made, very much sun-burnt; light brown hair, no beard or whiskers, a prominent nose, rather good looking, had on a black hat, old black cloth trowsers, stockings, and low shoes; had a fresh wound on the back part of his head.

The above Reward or Rewards (with all reasonable expenses for conveying the said Thomas Beesley and William Newman, or either of them, to the Gaol of the said county of Oxford) will be paid on application to Mr. John Portlock, St. Giles's, Oxford.

Oxford, July 9, 1829.

A reward was offered in 1829 by the Oxford authorities for the apprehension of Thomas Beesley and William Newman following their involvement with the riot at Wolvercote. (Jackson's Oxford Journal)

workers offered protection and said they would help take the five men into custody, and off they went to the Plough; Williams accompanied them on horseback while Robinson went to get a policeman. They met John Barrett and a boy named Symonds 30yd from the Plough, but Beesley and friends had already left and were now on the canal bridge, 50yd away.

By this time only four of Beesley's group remained, including Cooper who watched from the bridge as Beesley, Medden and Newman 'rushed upon the Wolvercote people with all the fury men could, and down they went'. Blows rained in on the local inhabitants; the attack was furious and sustained. Eeley Jr was beaten up, as was one Henry Rowland. Beesley ran in and out of the men, swinging his bludgeon at any and all who came within reach. Newman and Robinson were rolling in the dirt, each struggling to get the upper hand. Then Robinson, kneeling, managed to pin Newman securely to the ground unaware of Beesley running up behind him; Beesley's bludgeon landed a tremendous blow to the back of his neck and Robinson went down as if dead. He blurted that Beesley had murdered him, passing out before being dragged away, bleeding profusely.

The noise and commotion were tremendous. Newman, Beesley and Medden were now armed and letting rip into the Wolvercote men for all they were worth. Williams yelled at Beesley that the man had killed one person and was going to kill another, calling repeatedly to all three to stop, screaming that they were going to murder someone. Later Williams testified that he had never seen men appear so bloodthirsty. Standing on the sidelines, John Barrett was not part of the affray and did not see Beesley approach as his back was turned. Beesley went forwards, swinging his bludgeon and hit Barrett across the back of the head, instantly taking him out. Beesley panicked; Barrett was motionless. Beesley turned and tried to flee, but was stopped by two men who told him he had committed murder. Beesley replied that he would beat anyone's brains out if they tried to take the bludgeon from him, and then laughed, but they managed to get the bludgeon and subdue him. By now a policeman named William Saxon had arrived and with several other people endeavoured to take the men into custody. Resistance was strong. Newman cried out, 'We may as well all die together' and he and Medden fought on with sticks, yelling 'come on'. When Newman was seized by one man he screamed he would knock anyone's brains out if they tried to take hold of him. Events having taken a turn for the worse, Cooper fled the canal bridge only to be captured half an hour later. The fight was over; the men were subdued. Barrett and Robinson were taken to the Radcliffe Infirmary in Oxford for treatment.

Both men were examined; Robinson had a large wound to the back of the head, but was not likely to die. Barrett, with a fractured skull, was still unconscious and considered to be critical; when he was seen later that night his head was swollen and the scalp was cut away to reveal the fracture. He was bled, the wound was dressed and he was left until morning, by which time his condition had worsened. He was trepanned and two or three ounces of coagulated blood were taken from around the brain, but he died at 1 a.m. the following morning.

Saxon, the policeman, charged the four men that first night with assaulting Barrett and Robinson and ordered several Wolvercote men to assist in taking Medden, Cooper, Newman and Beesley to Oxford for examination by the magistrates. At first the rioters refused to go, but eventually relented and said they would go quietly. Half a mile from Wolvercote Medden had a tantrum. He threw himself to the ground and refused to go any further. At this time there were a dozen men in addition to the constable accompanying the four prisoners to Oxford. They stood and waited, Saxon hoping Medden would yield and that they could carry on. They waited for ten minutes, but Medden stayed put.

Leaving three men with Medden, Saxon sent the remaining men to Oxford with Cooper, Beesley and Newman, with orders to take them to Mr Walsh the magistrate. Saxon set off to find a cart to carry Medden to Oxford. Having found one at Mr

Giles's, it was sent to transport Medden and his escort to the magistrate, while Saxon set off to Oxford to meet up with the majority of his party.

Things were starting to get a little messy. The larger group of men had made their way back to Oxford, but the group had split up: James Cripps and George Bennett had taken Cooper in one direction; the other seven had taken Beesley and Newman in another, intending to meet at Mr Walsh's house. When Saxon finally caught up with them it was Cripps and Bennett he came across first on St Giles's and they told him that they had taken Cooper the shortest way to Mr Walsh's, and that the others had taken a route towards Hythe Bridge Street. They said Cooper had been secured with Mr Walsh, but the others had not arrived by the time they had left the magistrate's. Saxon headed for Hythe Bridge Street, where he met the other men, now accompanied by George Bossom, an Oxford policeman, but not Newman and Beesley. Saxon expected the men to tell him that Newman and Beesley had been dropped off, but the bad news was that Beesley had escaped. Saxon was fired up and wanted to go after him, but Bossom convinced him that it was futile. Worse was to come; Newman had also escaped. For the moment Saxon had to forget about the two fugitives while he set off to meet the men who were bringing Medden to Oxford.

What had happened to Newman and Beesley? On the way to Oxford they had convinced their custodians, including John Thomas and Francis Norriss of Wolvercote, that they could find bail if they were to go via Hythe Bridge Street. Their guards had consented to the plan and while walking down Fisher Row, Newman

Hythe Bridge and the houses of Fisher Row at the beginning of the twentieth century, with St George's Tower in the distance. (OCCPA)

called to a man at an upstairs window, 'I want a bondsman, I'm going to the Castle.' The man asked what for. 'I have been in a riot at Wolvercote.' Had the person who held him obtained a warrant? 'No,' came the reply. 'Then don't go.' The man was Robert, William Newman's brother, and immediately going into the street he was followed closely by many others. Robert waved his fists and threatened to fight: 'I'll be damned if you shall have him now.'

The assembled multitude were threatening violence. Francis Norriss was frightened to try and take Newman onwards, the small group having been surrounded by dozens of men. Robert took hold of his brother by the collar, but Thomas already had him by an arm and a tug-of-war ensued, Thomas telling them all he was taking William Newman to gaol, as Robert, with the assistance of others, forced William out of his grasp. The brothers ran away together, watched on by George Bossom, who now made for the group.

In the confusion Beesley saw his chance, made his escape, and ran down the road to a man in a punt, who took him across the water before anybody could get to him. They all watched as Beesley disappeared into the distance.

The next day, 4 July, Medden and Cooper were formally charged with stealing ducks and assault on William Eeley, William Robinson and John Barrett (Barrett was still alive at this point), and they were bailed. Oddly, Gardiner, one of the Oxford policeman, had given Eeley 10s to 'make peace' with Cooper and shortly after the hearing closed at the Town Hall, Eeley had left to visit Cooper, but it is not known whether the two 'kissed and made up' or why Gardiner had become involved.

Barrett having died on the 5th, a coroner's inquest was held the next day and a verdict of murder was returned against Beesley, Newman and Medden. A reward of a £25 each was offered for the apprehension of the first two.

View of Oxford Castle in 1835, with the Round House (for debtors) and St George's Tower visible above the walls to the right. (OCCPA)

The Plough as it is today, overlooking the area between the inn and the canal bridge which was the battleground for Beesley, Medden and Newman in 1829. (Giles Brindley)

Beesley and Newman were finally captured and the trials of all the men began on 3 March 1830. William and Robert Newman were tried and found guilty of rescuing William (who had 'rescued' himself) from custody and sentenced to three months' hard labour. Newman, Medden and Cooper were tried for assaults on 'William Robinson and others'; Cooper was acquitted, but Newman and Medden were found guilty and sentenced to eighteen months' and one year's hard labour respectively. Newman and Medden were acquitted of Barrett's murder; Beesley was found guilty of manslaughter, not murder. The judge commented, '. . . it appeared there was nothing like premeditation or malice on the part of the accused [Beesley]', before sentencing him to fourteen years' transportation. Beesley remained in the Castle until 15 March when he was taken to the Portsmouth hulks to await transportation.

4

SEX, POLITICS AND RELIGION

ROSAMUND

Henry II, son of Queen Matilda, had a residence at Oxford known as Beaumont Palace adjoining today's Beaumont Street. In about 1160 Henry used to hunt at Woodstock, visiting the particularly beautiful Rosamund there. Tradition has it that Henry's Queen Eleanor came to hear of her husband's 'little visits' and was enraged by jealousy. Where Rosamund lived could only be reached by a secret route known to the King alone. Eleanor hit on a plan to tie the end of a ball of coloured silk to her husband's coat the next time he went hunting. She followed the thread and burst into the room where Rosamund sat. Eleanor gave the young girl two options for her own suicide. The terrified Rosamund chose poison, but the King was said to have been enraged and saddened by the death of his lover. The well in Blenheim Park where it is said the young girl bathed still bears her name: Fair Rosamund's Well.

MOTHER CLAP

Brothels and prostitutes were so common in 1666 that the clap was rife among the students, especially among those at Exeter and Christ Church colleges it was reported. Since it was not the kind of thing people would pop into their local doctor to discuss, because of the shame of being involved with something as rude as 'carnal knowledge', there were a great number of quacks in Oxford. They made a good living out of the students, whose health was often no better after they had received 'treatment'.

NO LOVE LOST

A bastard child was laid at the door of Mr Paynter, Fellow of Exeter College, on the morning of 18 April 1685, by one of his former pupils whom Paynter had had expelled. The student was John Jago, who was removed from Exeter for reasons of debauchery, though exactly what this had entailed was not stated. Having attempted to defame his tutor, Jago, who had since been enrolled at St Mary Hall (now Oriel), was banished, not only from the Hall, but from the University by a proclamation which was pinned in several public places around the city on 6 May.

HEAVENLY MUSIC

In August 1688 a young boy brought a cat into University College Chapel under his coat. During the service he pinched it and pulled its tail, and the cat made such blood-curdling noises that the boy was forced to flee the church to avoid the wrath of the entire congregation.

A SHEEP IN WOLF'S CLOTHING

Centuries before women were formally allowed to study at Oxford something rather interesting occurred.

In 1697 two students entered themselves at St Edmund Hall, one a commoner, one a gentleman commoner. These two were to share rooms, but it turned out that the gentleman was in fact a woman. Properly attired as a gentleman she went about things as all students.

Everything would have been fine except that in November 1698 it was discovered that this 'gentleman' was pregnant. It turned out that the father was none other than her room-mate. The young lady was forced to leave and moved to live at Carfax; the commoner was given the option of leaving before he was expelled.

LOOK BEFORE YOU LEAP

At the beginning of the eighteenth century Dr Mayow of All Souls hit upon the idea of marrying a rich woman. When at court in London he lodged with an Irish lady and her daughter. The ladies told Mayow that they had great fortunes.

The cash signs flashed and one day, when the mother went into the city, Mayow ran out and married her daughter. He did not enjoy his triumph long as he soon found out that the family was, in fact, poor and had had the same idea as Mayow himself.

WORKING REPUTATION

A meeting of the Magdalen College Fellows was held on 17 February 1706. The learned gentlemen met to discuss firing all the female bedmakers. They had concluded that the women were scandalously lewd and debauched individuals and that it was not fitting for them to be in college.

At the meeting Dr Frayrer objected to the plan. He was a 'great patron' of these loose women and the fellows frowned upon him for these 'activities'. It is unclear what the outcome was, but certainly the college, in its moral stance, would have kept an eye open for any 'goings-on' in future.

WHOOPS-A-DAISY

Miss Hester Luffe lived with her father in St Peter-in-the-East in 1709, and was considered to be very beautiful. So beautiful indeed that wherever Hester went men followed. One day in winter she went to the parish church, which was thronged with her admirers. On leaving, Hester slipped in the street and when her dress flew up she discovered, much to her embarrassment, what pleased the young gentlemen. Later Hester fell in love with a nobleman of Christ Church and he with her. But as Hester was not of noble origins, the young man's friends objected and he was immediately sent 'travelling', leaving her behind, presumably he had been sent away in the hope that he would come to his senses. Hester was so distraught that she soon wasted away and died of a broken heart.

IMMOVABLE?

Dr Edwards, the Warden of Jesus College, died in July 1712. His death left the position of Warden vacant and an election was held in the chapel the following month; in the red corner, Dr Wynne, and in the blue corner, Mr Harcourt. At the end of the contest it was tied seven votes apiece. The most senior Fellow, Mr Tremellier, pronounced he had the casting vote and declared Harcourt the victor. However, somebody else had declared Dr Wynne the winner. Unfortunately by this time Harcourt had staked his claim by occupying the Warden's chair in the chapel. He must have been very surprised to see Dr Wynne's supporters heading for him. The scene was farcical; while one of the opposition attempted to remove Harcourt, the man clung to the chair believing that they would take him away only over his dead body.

Confusion and arguments reigned, with bickering over whose votes did or did not count. Only after both sides had spent large sums of money in legal costs was the visitor (the college's official arbiter) brought in to make a final decision. This time Dr Wynne was declared the man for the job. But really the only winners were the lawyers who had mopped up the cash on both sides. Although the matter was officially resolved, Dr Wynne's opponents continued to hiss that the only reason the visitor favoured Wynne was that they were both Whigs.

WEDDING COSTS

Sarah Smith, servant to Goody Brazier, a bedmaker at Queen's College, was suspected by her master of being pregnant. In October 1720, in order to find out who the father was, Goody, with assistance, locked her in the college kitchens, refusing to allow her out until she confessed. Sobbing, she revealed the father to be Mr Potter, a student of the college. This caused uproar in the college and she was brought before Mr Hill, one of the Fellows, to whom she related the same story. The considerate college sought a husband for her, generously offering 20 guineas to any man who would have her. They found one in a pub landlord at Stanton St John. Three days later they were married in St Clement's Church; she was a beautiful 16-year-old, he about 60. Potter did not fare any better in the end, as he died of smallpox three years later.

AN EXPENSIVE WIFE

Mrs Stubbs sold beer in Oxford. Mr Stent, previously at Wadham, had promised her £600 if he did not marry her daughter. One hopes that Stent had at least seen the daughter before undertaking such a commitment. Time went by, but there was no marriage, even though the daughter gave birth to Stent's son. Instead of marrying her, Stent chose to look after his son himself. It was not until Stubbs's daughter became Mrs Neal in 1720, when she married an Oxford barber, that Stent paid over the previously agreed £600. It seems that Stent preferred this to marrying the daughter, perhaps because it was the cheaper option.

UNFAIR DISMISSAL

Dr Gardiner, the Warden of All Souls in 1724, was not the most well-respected person and he was considered to be a drunken and debauched old sot, reportedly saying of the poor servants, 'Starve them, and they will be humble.' He dismissed one of the bedmakers, Mr Holman, possibly because Holman complained that the Warden had cheated him out of 10s on Mrs Holman's death. Mrs Holman, like her husband, had been a bedmaker and the Warden had given the widower only 30s on his wife's death rather than the usual 40s. It was even more cheeky considering the Warden was well known to have regularly slept with Holman's wife and had even been reported as being the father of her only child. The son looked so like Gardiner that there was little doubt among the general populace as to the identity of the father.

ON THE RUN

On George Street lived the Wigans family, whose pretty 17-year-old daughter left home on 17 December 1725. After she had been missing for five days the University

Proctors were notified of her disappearance. On 23 December they tracked her down to Jesus College and found her with one of the students. During the same raid they found another girl in another student's room. The girls were committed to the Bridewell as common prostitutes and Wigans was given forty lashes, but would confess nothing and eventually was released. Her companion was not so stout: after five lashes she started to confess and after another five confessed all, saying that Wigans had slept with five or six of the students, and that she had spent all the five days she was missing in the college.

HANDSOME PROPOSITION

Dr John Irish, Fellow of All Souls College, died on 3 August 1728 aged 85. He was a scholar and considered to be charitable, but otherwise led an ordinary life with one exception. When he was a tall, handsome young man and a student at St Edmund Hall, a fine lady came to stay at the Angel Inn. She was childless and did not expect to have any by her husband. She was so enamoured with John that she spoilt him. She explained her situation to him; she wanted him to take her to bed for at least one night. A gratuity was offered for his services if things succeeded, which, looking at him, she had no doubt they would. John readily agreed and so fully satisfied her that in thanking him, as he rose from her bed, she gave him a purse of gold. She left Oxford soon afterwards and later gave birth to a healthy baby boy, who was her pride and joy. Each year she sent Irish a purse of gold until the day he discovered that he had a son. When Irish found out her name the money stopped and John heard no more from her.

GROPING FOR ATTENTION

Love of one's fellow man is a wonderful thing and Warden Thistlethwaite of Wadham thought likewise. In 1739, at a time when men were men and women were centuries away from being members of a college, the Warden had plumped for the butler, asking him to dinner and endeavouring to kiss and tongue him and to put his hand down the man's trousers. The Warden declared that he would not give a farthing for the finest woman in the world, but loved a man as he did his own life.

The butler was not the only person to suddenly find the Warden fumbling around in his trousers; the college barber came in for some attention. The Warden asked, 'How does thy cock do, my dear barber?' giving it a good grope and attempting to kiss him. The barber, none too pleased, called him a son of a bitch and asked him what he was up to, finally punching him backwards into a chair. Abusing the college servants was one thing, but then Thistlethwaite indecently assaulted one of the undergraduates, Mr French, and was forced to flee the country, heading for Boulogne.

While Thistlethwaite was en route, Mr Swinton, one of the Wadham tutors, was charged with buggering a college servant, but conveniently there was not enough evidence to prove the offence. Swinton ended his days as Archdeacon of Swindon.

LOW CLASS – NO CLASS

A 'thoughtless' girl of 19 eloped in October 1770 with a married man, leaving behind him a wife and children. The local paper stated snobbishly, 'It is extremely unhappy when people in narrow circumstances ape the vices of the great.'

ESCAPE FROM THE TOWER

On 23 July 1781 Richard Geden was convicted in court of 'sodomical' practices and sentenced to two years in prison and to be whipped thrice during this time, though it is not known by how many lashes.

Geden made new friends inside, namely Nicholas Hemmings, a thief, and James Eldridge, a deserter. On 10 September of the same year they forced the door of the felons' hall at 7 p.m. and made their way up the tower. When they broke through the wall of the tower staircase they found themselves 10ft above the ground. Although it was still daylight they decided to make a run for it. Coming out of the hole, they were watched by locals as they lowered themselves down their knotted bed sheets. Not surprisingly, the locals raised the alarm and informed the governor of the convicts' activities. Hemmings was recaptured, as was Geden who had broken one of his legs in the escape attempt. Eldridge, being without fetters, had managed to blend into the crowd and get away, and nothing was heard of him again.

TAKEN OUT BEFORE THEY ARE DONE

Reusing graves after an appropriate time has been common practice for centuries, but there were those in St Peter-le-Bailey who were perhaps a little too enthusiastic, or maybe they spied a money-making opportunity.

About 15 September 1790 the rector of St Peter-le-Bailey Church received word that a body had been removed from a stone grave and dumped in the bone house under the church's tower. At the same time ten other coffins were discovered, some of which contained bodies not long dead. The exact details were considered too

St Peter-le-Bailey Church in the 1830s before its demolition in 1874. Queen Street leads towards St Martin's Church and Carfax in the distance. (OCCPA)

The mill at Iffley in the early twentieth century before it was destroyed by fire in 1908. Little now remains of Oxford's mills. (OCCPA)

shocking to relate to the public, but as soon as word got out the church and yard were filled for weeks with husbands, mothers and children lamenting and searching for loved ones. The parish reburied the bones and promised a full investigation.

NIGHT-TIME ACTIVITY

Six girls were brought before the court on 7 September 1818 charged with indecent behaviour on the public streets. The judge told them that he had been informed that 'the streets were nightly infested with persons of their description, annoying the peaceable and quiet inhabitants of that place, by repeated riots and indecent and obscene language'. The magistrates and police were determined to suppress this behaviour and would prosecute the guilty, further saying that they would deprive publicans of their licences if they allowed drunkenness and after-hours drinking, hoping that this would clear the streets of the riff-raff.

KILLED BY CONSCIENCE

Among the congregation at Iffley church on Sunday morning, 30 May 1824, was James Florey, an 80-year-old pauper of that parish who received relief from it. The church clerk announced that a meeting would be held on Tuesday to debate the conduct of someone who received regular relief and allowed a prostitute to conduct her 'meetings' in his house. The person alluded to was Florey. The elderly man knew that it was him they were after and said that he would never be able to face the parishioners again.

Elizabeth Tucker, wife of John of Iffley, had lived with Florey for the last three years and slept in the same room as him. At 1 a.m. on 1 June Elizabeth was woken by noises. She called Florey twice, but as there was no answer Elizabeth said she was getting up. Florey told her he was looking out of the window and thought he saw his daughter. Speaking in his usual tone, he told her to go back to sleep. She woke again half an hour later and, in the shadows, saw Florey's undressed body hanging at the end of a rope held by a nail in the wall. Elizabeth rushed out to find assistance, leaving Florey's body hanging. Help came in the guise of William Robins, but Florey was already dead. That day an inquest was held in Iffley and the jury returned its verdict: 'The deceased hung himself while in a state of temporary derangement.' It can perhaps be considered a cruel act for the church authorities to announce their intentions to the whole parish, rather than show some compassion to a poor and elderly man.

GET YOUR COAT, YOU'VE PULLED

At the beginning of May 1828 a gentleman stepped off a coach in Oxford and made straight into the bar of the inn outside which the coach had stopped. Having a merry time, he drank away until a pretty girl caught his eye and she invited him back to her house in St Thomas's Parish. Off he wobbled.

When he returned to the inn later that night, he realised he was £220 short, which instantly sobered him up. He persuaded a policeman, Pavoir, to help him search the girl's house. But the gentleman, a shade worse for wear, could not remember where the house was nor the name of the girl. The policeman eventually deduced from questioning him that he had gone home with one Mary Barton.

The two men set off accompanied by another policeman and paid Mary a visit. When they entered the house Mary immediately produced the man's money, saying she had found it on the bed and was just about to go and search for the gentleman to return it. No one believed her since Mary had had to rip the pocket off the gentleman to get at the roll of notes. They searched Mary and in doing so another note fell out of her clothes, which put an end to all doubt. By the time they had finished with Mary they had managed to recover all the cash, which was handed to the gentleman. The next morning the policemen were rewarded for their trouble by the gentleman, who rapidly left town having decided not to prosecute the girl. Perhaps he had a wife whom he did not want to find out about the matter.

YOUR WIFE OR MINE

John Corbett, alias Corbutt, alias Corby, of the Parish of St Thomas, was charged with bigamy on 3 January 1831 and duly appeared in court. He had married Anne Smith on 12 January 1829, but his first wife, Elizabeth Barber, was still alive. He had married Barber, a widow, on 1 July 1827 at Magdalen Parish Church. But Barber was not, as she first claimed, a widow. She had married one John Barber in 1793 at Pembrey, who was still alive and well. This proved fatal to the prosecution's case and Corbett was duly acquitted.

SUNDAY BEST

Ann Hurcomb and Hannah Wilkins were two prostitutes from St Thomas's Parish. On 16 April 1832 they were in court charged with assaulting another prostitute, Ann Mercer. Mercer lived in the upmarket end of the parish and was considered more 'high-class' than her colleagues. Parading the streets in her finery, Mercer was approached in Magdalen Parish by Hurcomb and Wilkins. The two women asked her for something to drink and were ignored. Rebutted, they grabbed hold of Mercer's dress and said they 'would have some'. This was starting to look like a turf war. The terrified Mercer made a break for it, but as she headed into a nearby apothecary's shop, the other two ripped the dress right off her back. At the close of play Hurcomb and Wilkins were found guilty and fined the cost of the dress – 1 guinea, plus court costs – but since they could not pay they were sent to gaol for two months each.

St Mary Magdalen Church, 1833, with the Martyr's memorial in the foreground and the Taylor Institute to the right. The church dates from 1194 when it was rebuilt by the Bishop of Lincoln. (OCCPA)

BEAT A RETREAT

Ann McKenzie set out after 1 a.m. on the night of 21 April 1832 and headed across St Thomas's Parish to the house of Ann Day. McKenzie and her servant stood listening outside the door. They heard Mrs Day and then the voice of James McKenzie, Ann's husband, and learned by the conversation that James intended to spend the night there. Mrs McKenzie banged on the front door, demanding Mrs Day send out her husband. A young woman came to the door and informed the women that James was not there. Then Day stepped out from behind the young woman and bashed Mrs McKenzie, forcing her to retreat without her husband. Day was charged with assault and fined £5, which she could not pay and was forced to go to gaol for two months instead.

LETTER BITES AUTHOR BACK

Mr Weller, an Oxford horse dealer, was tried for libel at the Assize Court on 19 July 1832. The libel that Weller stood accused of had imputed that Henry and William Cleeve were guilty of an offence, 'abominable as any which could be perpetrated by human beings', namely that they were buggering each other. This was alluded to in a letter written by Weller to their uncle in Exeter.

William Cleeve had married Weller's daughter, Susan, but the couple had never been happy in their marriage. William's brother Henry had lived with the couple for eighteen months when they were at Blenheim Park, but Henry left when they moved to Winfold in Cambridgeshire. During this time Susan had received some brutal treatment at the hands of her husband. On one occasion William held Susan while his brother beat her, tearing out her hair and throwing her to the ground. She ended up with blood streaming from her nose. Susan accused her husband of sodomy with his brother, having found them in bed together in an 'unnatural situation'. But William threatened to kill her and ordered Susan to leave the house.

Thereafter Susan was very depressed and made regular visits to her father. On each occasion he had great difficulty convincing her to return home. Susan finally left William, though it was considered that it was 'improper' for her to do so.

Susan asked William for an allowance, but he refused and she was forced to go to court to try and obtain it. William retaliated by launching a case accusing her of adultery, but the charge was dropped before it went to court because William could not produce any evidence. Faced with a court case, William sold his property to his brother, Henry, and fled the country for Rochfort in Belgium. Weller was frustrated that he now had to support his daughter when he considered it to be her husband's duty. Weller had no option but to write to the Cleeves' uncle asking for his consideration in the matter, stating that it was high time a settlement was made between Susan and William.

When the case came to court it came down to the matter of whether the letter had been written maliciously. The judge commented that, in law, malicious meant a wilful act, stating that it was difficult to prove that writing a letter was not a wilful act. The jury retired for a short time before finding Weller guilty.

FOR THE LOVE OF A GOOD WOMAN

In St Thomas's Parish on the afternoon of 7 February 1835 Frederick Symonds, surgeon and apothecary, was visiting a patient who lived opposite Mrs Philpot's, when someone came running across the road to find him. The person was screaming that someone had cut their throat and the surgeon must come quickly.

It was after 3 p.m. and Symonds crossed the road to Mrs Philpot's and climbed the stairs to a first-floor bedroom. Here he found the body of James Langston, covered in blood and lying on his back on the bed. Langston was fully clothed except for his coat, neckerchief and shoes; his left hand was resting on his stomach and in his right hand, resting on his thigh, was a blood-stained cut-throat razor. There was blood all over the bed and floor and between Langston's legs was a chamber pot half filled with coagulated blood. His throat had been slashed through the left side of his neck, through the jugular vein, carotid artery and windpipe. Symonds concluded that Langston had died only fifteen minutes before, as the body was not yet cold. He deduced that Langston had been sitting up when the first incision was made while leaning over the chamber pot to collect the blood, but becoming faint he had fallen back on the bed and died.

An inquest was held on the body that evening at the Lamb and Flag where the day's events unfolded. James's wife had come from their home in Woodstock to visit Mrs Philpot's just before 2 p.m. and had asked after her husband when she met Philpot's son at the door. She was told her husband was not there. Persisting, she asked to see Mrs Philpot (the son's wife Maria was present but silent). Ann Philpot came downstairs and Elizabeth told her that Langston had left home on Thursday and had not been seen since. Philpot said that he had visited her that particular day, but had left at noon. Elizabeth implored Philpot to tell her if her husband was there, but the woman said, 'No', James had gone to his mother's and might have 'I upped and left' for all she knew. Elizabeth continued to implore her to say if he was there. Philpot said she wanted to know as much as Elizabeth, and that she would go into town in search of information. Elizabeth left, and Philpot donned her cloak and bonnet and went into town.

Shortly afterwards Langston had arrived at the house and was met by Maria who told him that her mother-in-law was not there. Langston said he would wait upstairs for her. Maria said that his wife had already been to the house, but he made no reply and went upstairs, taking some bread and meat with him. It was when Philpot returned an hour and a half later that she discovered James's blood-soaked body lying on her bed and called for help.

It was telling that during the inquest Maria said she had no knowledge that Langston had a wife and family, but that he always went upstairs when he visited Philpot. Elizabeth stated that her husband was a father to three children, a courier at Woodstock, who had, particularly recently, been ashamed of the manner in which he had been living and had left on Thursday, taking no money with him. Philpot said that Langston had visited her on that Thursday; that he looked very ill and could hardly walk through the door, and had told her that he had been ill for the previous four days. She said she had known Langston since he was a boy and that he came to her house every two or three weeks, but Philpot's meetings were not confined to the house and she regularly saw him two or three times a week at other places.

The case was closed and a verdict of suicide was recorded against Langston, the jury expressing their indignation at Philpot's conduct in encouraging the deceased's visits, as he had a wife and children. Since James was guilty of murder, albeit of himself, the coroner directed that his body be interred in St Thomas's churchyard between 9 p.m. and midnight and within twenty-four hours of the inquest, without the funeral service being read (9 p.m. was the hour of curfew when no decent person would be about). Accordingly, the burial took place the following evening at 9.30 p.m.

The following day, Monday, a large number of people gathered and paraded an effigy of Philpot about the parish before stopping outside the woman's house, where they built a bonfire and burnt the effigy right in front of her. Among the rabble were boys armed with tin kettles, shovels and fire irons, banging them for all they were worth, playing their 'rough music' in a cacophony of sound. Spying a young girl coming out of a house near Philpot's, they ran after her down the passage in which Henry Roberts lived, banging away as they went. Exasperated, Roberts loaded his gun with number four or five shot, took aim, and proceeded to blast away at them, hitting three of the boys repeatedly in the face and head. He was bailed in court on 14 February to answer a charge of malicious wounding at the next sessions.

NYMPHS OF THE PAVE

On 15 April 1836, Diana Pickett was convicted and fined 20s plus 17s costs for assaulting John Wright, one of the University policemen. A large proportion of this particular day was taken up with complaints from the 'ladies of the parish', accusing one another of using indecent language. The complaints were all dismissed, with the assurance from the judge that if any further complaints were made the women would all be sent to gaol as vagrants for a month.

VENTING SOME SPLEEN

Ann Rogers was convicted of trespass on 17 March 1837 on Charles Freeborn's land. Freeborn was a dealer in dogs, foxes, badgers and other animals. Two of his foxes had broken loose and amused themselves with Rogers's washing, which was hung out to dry. As a result, Rogers had gone and remonstrated with Mrs Bull, Charles's housekeeper, using language best understood by 'ladies of a certain caste', i.e. prostitutes, but which led to blows. Rogers was beaten off, but vowed revenge. Having fuelled herself with a due quantity of 'blue ruin' (gin) for courage, she returned with her friend, Ann Batts, and one by one punched out Mr Freeborn's windows, smashing thirty-seven in total before she was stopped, by which time she had cut her hand to ribbons. Many 'ladies' gave evidence for both sides. Rogers was found guilty and fined 20s for the damage plus 24s costs.

5

L O V E ' S   L A B O U R S   L O S T

Biding his time in Oxford gaol, William Humphreys was brought before the magistrates on 19 February 1782. His tongue moved so fast it nearly caught fire, as he sold out Thomas Haddon and William Holmden who had been his partners in many robberies. The can of worms he opened that day started a chain reaction of events, which reached deep into Oxford's underworld and was to take another three years before reaching its final conclusion.

Humphreys told the authorities of a robbery that the three of them had planned. They had decided to go to Deddington Fair on 22 November 1781 and rob anybody they came across. On the day itself Humphreys was ill, so he stayed at home but lent his horse to Holmden. At the end of a full day's work, as Holmden and Haddon passed the King's Arms in Deddington, they saw the postman's horse loaded with mailbags and the postman nowhere to be seen. Haddon and Holmden snatched the mail bags and made off with the booty. As they departed Holmden slung one of the bags into a churchyard, perhaps because it contained nothing of interest.

The same night they made for Joseph Simmonds's house on George Street in Oxford. Simmonds was a blacksmith and in his workshop all three went through the mail looking for cash. Anything that did not take their fancy went in the furnace, until they were down to their final haul: one letter and a bank draft. Night had turned into day and Haddon and Holmden returned to Humphreys to relate the night's events. Then they visited John Bounds, a sergeant in the Oxford Marines. Bounds had supplied them with fire arms in case of trouble. They showed Bounds all that was left of the mail bags before destroying the final two pieces of evidence in his fire, except that is for the huge sack of mail dumped in a churchyard.

As a result of Humphreys selling out his friends, Haddon was apprehended at Warwick, Holmden in Portsmouth, and both were immediately imprisoned. Holmden was not one to sweat it out either; he implicated Simmonds and Simmonds's servant, Paul Ragg, as accessories in helping to open and dispose of the stolen post.

At 9 p.m. on 27 February 1782 Mr Jones from Worcester walked down George Street with an arrest warrant. Simmonds, caught in bed, claimed his servant was not at home. But as Ragg tried to make his escape downstairs Jones turned around and caught hold of him. As he did so, Simmonds pushed past both of them, jumped down a flight of stairs and rushed out of the front door half-naked and shoeless. Making a run for it across Gloucester Green, he eventually climbed up the outside of the chimney breast of a house opposite Worcester College and refused to come down, that is until his pursuers threatened to shoot him down. Simmonds finally relented and was committed with Ragg to the Castle gaol.

With Simmonds and Ragg behind bars, the police, waving a search warrant, went back to Simmonds's house. Tearing the place apart, they found in a concealed underground compartment one hen and one cock; a very amicable arrangement.

They had been stolen only the night before from Mrs Watson of the Catherine Wheel at Sandford and were returned to their rightful owner. The police also discovered a large number of possessions belonging to Mr Phillips of Magdalen Parish, who had passed away and whose house was uninhabited. The police not only found stolen property, but an elaborate backdrop to criminal activity. They discovered pick-locks, a pocket pistol and a dark lantern. They even found counterfeit coins and the means of making them: crucibles for smelting which contained silver, iron or a mixture of both.

The police set off again, this time for the house of Joseph Simmonds's brother Robert at Wallingford. When they searched his home they found a large amount of stolen property. But the police were not satisfied and they returned to Robert's house the next day with a second search warrant. This time they found thirty stolen sheepskins. Robert was arrested and taken to Oxford gaol.

Meanwhile Haddon, who was still in Warwick gaol, pointed the police to the whereabouts of three horses stolen from Hereford. One horse was in the possession of John Simmonds, father of Joseph and Robert. Now anybody and everybody was selling out their accomplices. Bounds and Martin Brown, another accomplice, were both fingered, arrested and bailed in Oxford on 13 May charged with supplying firearms to Haddon and others.

Four days later Bounds was charged again, this time for assault. Bounds must have had a temper, because having been charged with assaulting his captain and several other soldiers, as he was being taken to his prison cell he smashed all the windows within reach. The authorities were obliged to have him fettered and heavily loaded with chains just to keep him in order.

All was quiet for a month; most of the key players were in gaol and there was no hint of trouble. Between 9 a.m. and 10 a.m. on 12 June Bounds was sitting in the box (toilet) in the Castle yard when a message was delivered to him. The message said that Joseph Simmonds wanted a word. Along with Belcher, another inmate, Bounds went to the locked gate that led to the lower yard and separated Simmonds from the other two men. From behind the locked door Simmonds slipped a note through which dropped to the ground. As Bounds bent down to pick it up the other man told him quite flatly that it was not for him but for Belcher, and Bounds handed the note over accordingly.

Back in the box, Belcher read the note to Ragg and Bounds. Belcher stated that he would assist Simmonds with all that was in his power. The note from Simmonds to Belcher told him not to worry, that Simmonds would keep him informed. Perhaps Simmonds had promised Belcher a part in his 'business activities'? Simmonds explained that he wanted a girl to take a note from the gaol to the outside world and for her to await a reply. If she was willing she should then buy cheese and return to the gaol with the reply hidden between her breasts. She should then give Belcher the cheese and slip him the note when no one was looking. Simmonds said that if Belcher did not think this was possible, Belcher should suggest another method, otherwise Simmonds would send word for the little girl who regularly came to the gaol with oranges. Simmonds said she knew where to find them, asking that Brown, who was still on bail, send some wine to them late one evening before the inmates were locked back in their cells. At 11 a.m. the girl came and Belcher gave her a note telling her it was from Bounds, so that if anybody asked it would be less suspicious than coming either from him or Simmonds. In fact, the sign-off to Simmonds note told Belcher not to mess up.

It was just after noon that day when George Chambers, Joseph Turner and Benjamin Danter were hard at work attempting to break through the gaol wall on the staircase leading up to St George's Tower. Simmonds and another prisoner sent their cellmate Thomas Bates up to the men to see how they were getting on. Bates found the trio trying to force their way through the wall. Their reply for Simmonds was that they thought that it was impossible to break through, at that time at least, and asked for Simmonds to send out for more saws if he had not already done so. In fact eleven saws, two turning saws and a specially adapted lever had already been seized from the dungeon and condemned cell two months previously on 26 April. It all goes to show how well organised the prisoners were and the large volume of illicit items they were able to smuggle in. Simmonds told Bates that he could not advise the men any further as he had not had a reply to several previous notes he had sent to accomplices on the outside. Simmonds sent another note to Belcher, which was carried in a tobacco box by Bates himself. Simmonds then sent Bates again to see how the work was going. If there had been no further progress, Bates was to direct the men to the top of the tower to see if they could break out, using blankets to escape.

Simmonds' note had reached his wife that afternoon, by which time Bates had filled in Bounds on what he had missed, namely that there was a big escape attempt in progress. This pleased Bounds. Simmonds had told his wife he needed more saws and he needed them now. Mary Ragg, like her husband, was a servant to the Simmonds family. She had been sent out by Mrs Simmonds to deliver a note to William Rawlins, a silversmith, and to return with him. When she arrived at the silversmith's shop, Mary said that Mrs Simmonds wanted to speak to Rawlins. He asked what Simmonds wanted and Ragg said she had a note for him, so he asked her to tell him what the note or its purpose was, as he did not have time to leave his business to go and see Mrs Simmonds. Ragg only knew what she had been told. Rawlins gave in, saying he would come in five minutes, but would not stay. When Rawlins arrived Mrs Simmonds explained that she wanted to borrow a horse from him for a gentleman. The silversmith had none to lend. Had Mr Whitehead? No, his were elsewhere. Mrs Simmonds asked Rawlins if he knew where she could find a boy who would take a parcel to the Castle, but Rawlins did not know, so Ragg was sent to Gloucester Green to find one.

Mrs Simmonds was beginning to sweat. Ragg returned empty-handed and Simmonds headed for William Best to ask for the use of one of his sons. She drew a blank, but eventually she succeeded in hiring a horse from Mr Latham, the Jesus College Lane baker, and finally one of Best's sons was put on standby to deliver it. Now all she had to do was get the parcel to her husband.

Simmonds told Rawlins that after her husband's trial all his property would be signed over to the silversmith, so Rawlins readily agreed to deliver the parcel to Joseph. On Rawlins' return Mrs Simmonds asked if anybody else had been present when the parcel was handed over. Rawlins said Ragg and Bounds. At this point Simmonds turned white, saying Bounds would betray them and she would not have wanted it delivered in front of Bounds for all the world. Rawlins asked why and Simmonds refused to answer, but she eventually conceded that they were to break out of gaol that night. This was why she was so desperate to find a horse; it was for Joseph to make his final break for freedom.

After Rawlins had left the gaol that afternoon Belcher told Bounds he had now got the equipment. He asked Bounds to throw the parcel over the wall to Simmonds in the lower yard, but Bounds refused.

The nails to the coffin lid were being hit home. Rawlins considered he had been dragged innocently into the whole affair and went to the magistrates. Bounds had set off to blow the whistle and Bates had sent word to Mr Wisdom, the gaol's governor, that he wanted to discuss 'particular matters'. It was only a matter of time before the whole house of cards was to come tumbling down.

Bates had been directed to the cock loft above the gaol gates where he was to meet the governor, but instead he bumped into Belcher. Belcher took Bates into the loft and gave him the parcel and told him to go to Simmonds. Bates must have been sweating. If Wisdom walked in it would be obvious what was going on and there would be reprisals if the other inmates found out what Bates was up to. Belcher left and Bates tore open a corner of the parcel to reveal two saws. Minutes later a panicked Belcher appeared and grabbed the parcel back, saying they had been found out. Belcher said he was going to throw the parcel down the toilet – an open affair in those days – and rushed off. But it was Bounds's subsequent note that led the governor to search the toilets at 10 p.m. that evening after the prisoners had been locked up. Eventually he discovered the parcel among the filth.

County of Oxford.

A CALENDAR of the PRISONERS,

FOR TRIAL

At the SUMMER ASSIZES for the County of Oxford,

TO BE HOLDEN AT THE

TOWN HALL, IN THE CITY OF OXFORD,

ON

SATURDAY the EIGHTEENTH Day of JULY, A. D. 1840,

BEFORE

THE RIGHT HONORABLE SIR JAMES PARKE, KNT.

One of the Barons of Her Majesty's Court of Exchequer,

AND

THE HONORABLE SIR JOHN WILLIAMS, KNT.

One of the Justices of the Court of Queen's Bench.

Front cover of the Calendar of Prisoners, which listed the trials for the Summer Assizes of 1840. (ORO)

Before the escape attempt Mrs Simmonds had sent a tender note to her husband directing him to James Mills near Wood Green, who would look after him, and saying that she had a horse standing by. She signed off, 'God bless you, pray do not think of coming home.'

Court opened and trial commenced on 10 July 1782. Joseph Simmonds and Paul Ragg were found guilty of being accessories in the mail robbery and sentenced to one year inside. Rawlins was acquitted of assisting in Simmonds's escape attempt by conveying saws to him. Humphreys and Holmden, having been witnesses for the prosecution, walked out free men after selling their friends down the river. Haddon, despite assisting the police, was found guilty of robbery and sentenced to be hanged.

On 16 July the door to the condemned cell was opened to reveal Haddon's body. He had tied his sheets to a window bar and hanged himself. An inquest was held that day in the gaol into Haddon's death. The verdict was suicide (self-murder) and a warrant was issued directing that Haddon's body be buried after 9 p.m. in the public highway. That evening the body was carried out of the gaol to the Botley Road. No coffin was allowed despite Haddon having provided one. As his body was thrown into the grave his friends jumped in after it, ripped open his chest and filled it with flaked lime to prevent it from being dug up and used by the students for anatomy lessons.

This was far from the end. William Humphreys popped up again and dropped even more people in it when he gave further evidence to the magistrates on 5 November. Humphreys told of a plan to steal vegetables from a garden near to the Castle Green, which was discussed on Christmas Day 1781. Most of the names were, by now, familiar, but there were a few new ones. Joseph Simmonds and Paul Ragg had pick-locks to open the necessary doors along the way and were joined by James Slatford and Robert Simmonds. Since Robert was involved, he too must have been released from gaol in the meantime. Here the water becomes muddied. The merry band robbed Ann Griffin in Oxford around that time, but if it was vegetables they went for they came back with a whole lot more. On 20 January 1782 they broke into the house of Mrs Fredericks at Bampton, stole £7, but were disturbed by a servant girl before they could make off with more. Ragg had been lent a hat by William Best. When the hat which Ragg wore blew off on the night of the robbery Best had a dilemma. If it was discovered he could end up being blamed for the robbery. Best was forced to go out and search for the hat. He found the hat eventually and removed it at daybreak before anyone noticed. Returning to the nervous men, he told them they were lucky not to be found out. But it was Humphreys and not the hat that gave them away . . . or was it? Whichever way, they were arrested on the back of Humphreys's evidence on 17 November 1782, along with that of Mrs Fredericks's servant who remembered seeing the hat which the robbers had left behind, and with it Best's ideas of having 'gotten away with it' were blown out of the water.

The bungling burglary collective were in court on 5 March 1783. The burglary at Mrs Fredericks's was unproven and instead the robbery at Ann Griffin's was the focus of attention, because they had walked away with 20lb of tobacco, 30gal of beer, 18gal of ale, a loin of pork, 4lb of butter, a firkin of wine, a brass kettle, a saucepan and a trowel. Luck seemed to be on Robert's side, as he was found not guilty. However, Best, Ragg and Slatford were to be transported for seven years to 'one of his Majesty's colonies on the coast of Africa'.

Had Joseph Simmonds escaped a conviction? No, he was sentenced on 5 May for his part in the robbery and, like his friends, he was given seven years' transportation to Africa. On the same day Bounds and Brown were in court for supplying firearms, but were discharged and walked away.

On 17 July Best and Simmonds scaled the walls of the gaol. They were seen by Oxford cordwainer John Smith as they crossed the Castle green at 11 p.m. A reward of 10 guineas each was offered together with a description of the men. Best was soon recaptured near Botley and returned to gaol. The reward on Simmonds's head was increased to 30 guineas for capture within three months, or 20 guineas thereafter.

Bounty-hunters John Smith and Richard Spinlove caught up with Simmonds at 7 p.m. on 23 October 1783 in New Tothill Street, Westminster, London. Spinlove had spotted Simmonds in London the previous day and arranged to have dinner the next evening with him and one of Simmonds's brothers who lived in London. Before the meal, Smith went to Bow Street police station, collected four policemen and they burst in on the Simmonds's at home. Joseph fought ferociously as he was returned to gaol on the 24th. He was taken to the lower dungeon. *Jackson's Oxford Journal* confidently stated that it would be with no small difficulty that Simmonds would attempt another escape.

Charges were laid against Joseph on 7 November 1783 and Best on 3 December for being at large before their sentence for transportation had expired. Undeterred, Simmonds procured a knife from a fellow inmate, carried by mouth, and converted it into a chisel. Joseph filed off the bolt head that held his fetters in place and replaced it with a similarly shaped piece of pewter, which he stuck on with wax. Unfortunately for him, his scheme was discovered on 15 December.

Best was convicted on 3 March 1784 and condemned to death, but his sentence was later commuted to life transportation. On 18 March Best, Ragg and Slatford were taken from Oxford gaol under heavy guard to the hulks for transportation.

In April Mrs Simmonds delivered to Owen, one of Simmonds's cellmates, two files in a clean shirt and the men, having obtained two clasp knives, cut away at the thin bars in front of the cell window. By now desperate and with a breakout planned for the next day, Simmonds made his cellmates swear to secrecy, but when the cell was unlocked the next morning, 15 April, William Furnell, alias Cherry, betrayed them to the keeper. The implements were seized and Simmonds among others was chained and bolted to the floor of the dungeon.

On 23 April Simmonds was sentenced to death. He asked the court to commute his sentence to banishment for life and they recommended leniency. But it was not until 12 May when he received His Majesty's pardon that his sentence was commuted to transportation for life to Africa. Joseph remained in gaol for another eight months until, on 3 January 1785, he was taken to the hulk *Censor* at Woolwich.

6

WATERY GRAVE

Eliza Braine, having previously worked for the Burgesses as their servant for two years, returned to the King's Arms at Sandford on 11 August 1833. She had come to assist them while the Nuneham fair was on, a busy time of year.

Arriving at the King's Arms, Eliza complained of being ill, but the family and servants were suspicious as she looked pregnant, in fact heavily so. Each had challenged her, but she told them she would swear on any Bible in the country that she was not 'in the family way'.

On returning from Nuneham fair on the 15th with another of the Burgesses' servants, Eliza had gone to bed early saying that she was unwell. On her way upstairs Mr Burgess had implored Eliza to confess, but Eliza retorted that it was cruel for him to accuse her of being pregnant. The Burgesses decided to send another servant to sleep with Eliza to 'keep an eye on her'; they did not make the best choice as Caroline Weston slept like a rock.

At 4 a.m. Mrs Burgess was awoken by the sound of a dog barking. In the still of the night she could hear scrubbing noises. She leapt out of bed and headed for the servants' room where she found Eliza on her hands and knees scrubbing the carpet

The King's Arms at Sandford is adjacent to the river lock and is the largest of the village's three public houses. (Giles Brindley)

with a towel. Blood had soaked through the carpet and stained the floor, which was now awash with water. Around Eliza lay bloodied napkins, an apron and chamber pots; one half full of bloody water and the other, having been emptied, bloodstained. Caroline was still asleep in the nearby bed. Mrs Burgess told Eliza that she could not deny her pregnancy now, but she did.

Mrs Burgess shook Caroline awake and demanded that Eliza tell them where the baby was. Eliza denied there was any baby, proving it by saying that there was nothing in the room that had come from her, except that is for the large amounts of blood. The house was searched. A trail of blood ran from the back door, which was found unbolted, through the house and up the stairs to the bedroom, where one of Eliza's bloodied shoes was found. Blood was eventually found on a coping stone on the riverbank just below the lock. Since Eliza had denied giving birth and, despite turning the house upside down, no baby had been found, the doctors were called in one by one through the course of the day. All examined Eliza at length and concluded she had just delivered a child.

The Burgesses were not the first to suspect that Eliza was pregnant. Eliza had returned to them from Mrs Appleby's at the Red Lion in Abingdon. The family there knew it, but Eliza denied it. Only a month before, in July, Eliza had been found by Mrs Faulkner, Mrs Appleby's daughter, being violently sick from the effects of morning sickness. Eliza told Faulkner that she thought there was something alive in her and taking Faulkner's hand put it on her side. Faulkner felt the baby move and told Eliza that she would lend the girl her baby clothes. But Eliza was still confused. She said she wished that was her problem, because she would 'soon be out of trouble'.

However, they were still without a body. That is, until almost a week later, on the 20th, when two boatmen, John Westmacott and John Boyce, saw the body of a male child about 15ft from the lock at Sandford and went after it with a boat hook. On the first attempt they hit it on the back of the head and it sank. On the second attempt they successfully dragged the baby's body out of the water.

An inquest was held the next day in the pub itself. The cause of death was twofold. After the birth the umbilical cord had been ripped in two, which would have led to the baby bleeding to death; the second cause was a violent blow to the back of the head, which had resulted in bruising and a large degree of internal bleeding. Having torn the umbilical cord and battered the back of the head, Eliza must have taken the baby in the chamber pot and, trailing blood, unbolted the back door and gone to the edge of the river where she tipped the body into the fast-flowing water. The inquest found Eliza responsible for the murder of her newborn and she was committed to gaol to await her criminal trial.

On 1 March 1834 at the trial the doctors said they were sure the baby was alive in the womb, but proved it never breathed. This would seem contradictory, but was entirely probable since it had been hit on the back of the head soon after being born and had never had the chance to breathe. Eliza was saved from feeling the noose around her neck, because the doctors could not prove the boy was born alive. She was found guilty only of concealing the birth and sentenced to six months' hard labour.

7

MURDER, DEATH AND SUICIDE

POOR ALICE

In 1241 Alice of Oxford was crushed to death when part of a house collapsed. It happened at a time when fines were levied in cases of accidental death against whoever or whatever had inflicted an injury – the fine often going to the church or the poor. Luckily no one was suspected of causing her death and a verdict of misadventure was recorded by the coroner.

Evidence was then given that the part of the house that killed Alice was worth 5*s*, which was paid out by the court to the owner of the house owing to his poverty.

LOVE AND DEATH

Amy Robsart was the wife of the renowned Robert Dudley, Earl of Leicester, Chancellor of Oxford University and lover of Queen Elizabeth I. Amy was found dead at the foot of her staircase at Cumnor Place in 1560. Following an inquest her body was taken to Gloucester Hall (now Worcester College) and there it lay until, on Leicester's orders, it was moved to St Mary's Church and buried in the choir. Conveniently, her death left Leicester, in theory, open to marry Elizabeth. During the funeral service conducted by Leicester's chaplain, Dr Babington, the chaplain stumbled when extolling the virtues '. . . of that lady, so pitifully murdered'.

It was insinuated that on Leicester's orders Amy had been strangled and thrown down the stairs, but it is more likely that the woman had met with an accident or committed suicide as the result of a broken heart.

LETTING A LITTLE BLOOD

James Powell, a gentleman commoner of Balliol, was attended by Grundy, an apprentice to Will Day, the surgeon, to let blood. Grundy, who had learned a new way of striking the vein, missed and punctured an artery instead. This led to severe internal bleeding and a blood infection. Rather than have his arm amputated, Powell ignored the problem and died a few days later on 2 April 1657.

ONLY SLEEPING

On Saturday 13 May 1699 George Godfrey came to Oxford to do some business, bringing with him his wife, though some called her his whore because they were not sure if the couple were married. On their return home to Headington Godfrey went to a pub to collect £40 while his wife went to the Black Horse in St Clement's to wait for him. Since it was around 10 or 11 p.m. when he finished, Godfrey thought his wife would have left the pub, and carried on without her.

He met an old friend at the bottom of Headington Hill and as they neared the top three men leapt out and demanded money. Godfrey refused and called to his friend to stand by him, which the man said he would. Two men attacked Godfrey, the third jumped on his friend. The friend yelled out that one of the highwaymen had pulled a pistol. But it was too late, the man shot and instantly killed Godfrey. Everybody scattered. In the confusion the money that Godfrey had in his pocket was left behind.

Godfrey's wife, having waited patiently, set out for home. Nearing the top of the hill she saw the body, but thought it was someone sleeping and walked on. When she arrived in Headington later and heard that it was in fact her husband whom she had passed, she was overcome by grief.

It was said that the three robbers came to an untimely end, but in what manner and what their names were nobody ever found out. The woman married Mr Sellard, a joiner of St Peter-in-the-East. She went blind before she died, but one hopes she was no longer referred to as 'a whore'.

BOWING OUT

In June 1719 Revd John Evans of Wadham owed Dr Dunster, the previous Warden of the college, £300. As the authorities stepped in to arrest him for non-payment on 22 June, he excused himself saying he needed to fetch something. While they waited, Mr Evans returned to his rooms and shot himself dead.

LAST SQUEEZE

Tom Juggins, at 17, like his father before him, was head chef at Christ Church. One night in May 1721 Tom climbed into bed with his younger brother and cousin in their house in Magpie Lane. The next morning the two young boys were at play when relations called in. They were on their way to buy fish at the market and asked after Tom. The young boys said that Tom was not awake and they had not been able to raise him. On going upstairs, his relations found Tom face-down and dead on his bed. They supposed he had tied his neckerchief all too tightly around his neck, as he had a habit of doing, and had effectively strangled himself.

BAD BREW

At one time colleges brewed their own very weak beer as a method of killing water-borne bugs. Mr Browne was at his work in the Queen's College brewhouse on 13 September 1721 when he slipped and fell backwards into a great vat of boiling liquor. His screams brought help and he was dragged out sober, but died from burns the next morning at 5 a.m., leaving a wife and five children.

LAY ME DOWN TO SLEEP

Mr Acton spent his last night on earth drinking in his local. The All Souls Fellow was found dead on the floor the next morning, 17 November 1721, by his bedmaker. He had begun to undress, as his trousers were grasped in his hand.

OVERLOAD

In September 1722 a labourer was killed at Worcester College where he was working. He had loaded the scaffold he was standing on with too many stones and the whole lot gave way. He fell to the ground in a bloody mess of limbs and masonry.

SCHOOL JEST

Jakes and Frogley were 9-year-old boys at school near Balliol College in February 1727. Frogley had taken a pistol to school to 'shoot', in jest, a female pupil. To his surprise the gun was loaded, but in firing it at the girl the bullet narrowly missed her head and instead shot Jakes as he sat in the bog house, killing him instantly.

WORK IS BAD FOR THE HEALTH

In 1730 Webb, a stonemason, was fixing the chimney of a house in Catte Street, which had been loose for some time. As he propped his ladder against the house a stone fell and killed him instantly; another piece injured his assistant. Webb left a pregnant wife and two children.

MOTHER DEAR MOTHER

Mrs Wright visited Mr Leaver, the apothecary in St Peter-in-the-East, on 24 July 1732. There she bought a dose of laudanum (opiates), commonly used to quieten noisy infants. Returning to her house in the parish, Mrs Wright gave the entire dose to her 18-month-old daughter. She was discovered in the act, but before anybody could reach her Wright ran off. Heading for Cowley, Mrs Wright attempted to drown herself by throwing herself down a well, but was stopped from doing so. She was apprehended by her Oxford pursuers and confessed all as they walked her back to Oxford. Wright said she deserved and was prepared to die for her crime. Her husband, a tailor, had previously left her because he could stand her no longer. Since then Wright had slept with Mr Train who believed he was the father of the murdered child. However, Wright confessed that the father was in fact a student of University College, from whom she had received only 13s 6d.

Mrs Wright was taken to the Mayor, but he was busy drinking punch with his friends. After a three-hour wait, the Mayor finally directed that Wright should be taken to the Bridewell in St Michael's Parish, saying that he would deal with the matter the next day – and so he did but not in quite the way he imagined. Wright was found dead in her cell the next morning, having strangled herself with her garters. That same morning the coroner held an inquest on the infant, and in the afternoon on the mother; a verdict of murder was returned in the case of the infant and suicide (self-murder) in the case of the mother. Officially, both trials were for murder, and both committed by the same person.

SMOKING KILLS

To prove smoking is bad for the health, a cautionary tale from 1735 shows how such habits can lead to a premature death. At the winter Assizes John Chambers was tried for the murder of one Thomas Middleton, having stabbed him in the right cheek with a tobacco pipe. Verdict: not guilty of murder, but guilty of manslaughter. Chambers was burnt in the hand and discharged.

OVERDUE DEPARTURE

One Monday afternoon in October 1757 Mrs Trendall, a shopkeeper near the post office who had a long history of mental instability, ran upstairs to the second floor, locked the door and threw herself from the window. Landing head-first in the street, she died instantly.

COBBLER'S END

Thomas Jennings, who was convicted of stealing a small amount of leather from a fellow cobbler, was found hanging in the Bocardo in July 1761. His hands were tied on either side to his trouser pockets, and he had hung himself from the chimney breast in his cell. After being sentenced at his earlier trial he had declared that he would either break out of gaol or put an end to his life.

LEAP OF FAITH

A young man had climbed up inside the tower at Christ Church on 14 October 1775 to measure the dimensions of Great Tom, the tower's bell. When he reached the top of the frame he slipped and fell to the floor below. The floor was rotten and, gave way beneath him. He fell to the next floor, 30ft below, where, ten minutes later, he died.

SNUFFED OUT

Richard Mallam, deputy butler at Pembroke, put his sleepy 3-year-old son to bed on the evening of 27 December 1784 and returned to work. Later Mrs Mallam came in and folded up the bed. When Richard returned two hours after her, his son's smothered body was found in the bed.

FULL STOP

On 2 March 1792 Thomas Turner dismounted his horse on the edge of St Clement's (1 mile from the city), tied it to a gate post and blew a hole clean through his own head. In his pockets were found a notebook, gold watch, coins and a second loaded pistol. Turner was a gold and silversmith of Oxford who had been recently declared bankrupt. He had put a full stop to his life, sparing himself the embarrassment of facing his creditors.

BLOWN AWAY

A University student going out shooting at the edge of the Parks in February 1803 put a little gunpowder in the barrel of the rifle to 'air' it. He swung his full ½lb powder flask over his shoulder and fired into the wind. The flash came back at him,

The University Parks, 1868, looking south. The first 20 acres were purchased by the University from Merton College in 1854 and a further 76 acres added in the next five years. (OCCPA)

caught the flask and it blew up. The explosion catapulted the gentleman across the field. He was fine except for singed hair and eyebrows. Unfortunately his dog, by his side, was killed outright when the brass top of the flask hit him.

THE RIPPER

Richard (aged 12) and Benjamin Barnes (aged 9) were on an errand to a man at work in the parks. Richard picked up a scythe lying on the ground and taking a swing sliced straight through the belly of his younger brother. Entrails spilling out, Benjamin collapsed and was taken to the Radcliffe Infirmary where he died that day, 10 September 1810.

ONE SMALL STEP

John Bartlett, printer, obtained permission to take a party of friends onto the Castle Mound to view the city. On Saturday 25 September 1813 he led his friends down the steps to a subterranean apartment. In the mound is the old

The view from the top of the Castle Mound into the city is dominated by the tower and spire of Nuffield College. (Giles Brindley)

A nineteenth-century illustration of the well inside Castle Mound. It was built in the eleventh century to provide water for the Castle, but is now dry. (OCCPA)

Castle well which by 1813 was already dry. Unlocking the door to the chamber, Bartlett and his two friends, driven by curiosity, entered, finding their way by the dim light which came through the doorway. Bartlett remembered hearing of a well in some part of the hill and cautioned his friends to be careful, but pressed on. Finding a stone step, Bartlett stepped up and told his companions he was about to ascend. But this was not the flight of steps he had expected; it was a low wall erected for safety around the edge of the well, and he plummeted 40 or 50ft down to the bottom of the well.

His friends ran for help and Bartlett was soon extracted from the well. Bartlett was rushed to the Radcliffe Infirmary, where it was found that he had fractured bones in his foot and dislocated his right ankle. However, Bartlett shook violently, baffling surgeons and doctors alike, as but there were few physical signs of injury. After lingering for ten days he died of an undiagnosed condition. He was 25 years old.

FATAL KICK

A young man was leading a stallion to the Air Balloon on Queen Street in May 1819. His journey from Gosford nearly at an end, the horse kicked out and hit 16-year-old Edward Adkins as he stood with his father. The boy was flung across the street. He survived only a few days and died in the Radcliffe Infirmary. An inquest recorded a verdict of accidental death.

HIGH JUMP

On 15 June 1827, as workmen were leaving the new buildings at Balliol College, one man named Price jumped from the roof to the first-floor scaffold. He went straight through the wooden planks and hit the ground 30ft below. His head was cut, one of his legs was broken and he was bruised and battered. Price was taken to the Radcliffe Infirmary. The doctors declared the patient was making a recovery, but Price died two weeks later on 23 June. An inquest at the Radcliffe Infirmary returned a verdict of accidental death.

WATCH OUT BELOW

At 1.30 a.m. on 30 May 1829 the body of a man was found on the pavement just along from Tom Gate in St Aldate's. He was wearing only a shirt and was bleeding profusely from the nose and ears. The alarm was raised and the porters were alerted at the lodge of Christ Church when it was presumed that the man in the street was the servant to Mr Leader, gentleman commoner, at Christ Church. Only the name of his master was worthy of mention. The man had fallen the 30ft from his bedroom window and it was supposed that, in shutting the window, he had slipped and plummeted down; rather dangerously the floor was on a level with the window. The man was attended by Mr Hutchings the surgeon, who found him to be very bruised about his hips and shoulders, with a broken arm and fractured skull. But of so little importance was the event that it wasn't mentioned thereafter whether the servant had lived or died.

A FAMILY AFFAIR

Thomas Copus, his wife and four children – two boys and two girls – lodged with Ann and John Hemming in St Clement's in November 1829. On the afternoon of the 24th at 4.30 p.m. all was well, but five minutes later Copus's daughter Jane came rushing to Ann, as the landlady stood in the house's yard, pulling at her, crying and begging Ann to come and sit with them. Jane blurted out that she was afraid that her father would kill her that night. She told Ann that Thomas had thrown a red-hot poker at her, which had narrowly missed.

Ann had never seen the family argue nor Thomas beat or threaten Jane, so she dismissed the 16-year-old teenager and Jane went away, not to be seen again. Thomas noticed that Jane was gone and sent his little boy and girl to look for her. They returned from the yard to tell him that they could not find their sister. Soon after Jane had left, Ann found the girl's purse hidden in a place well away from the house, between a barrel and a wall disconcertingly near to the river; it contained a key and Jane's handkerchief. Ann told Mrs Copus about this when she returned to the house. Jane's mother was shaken, and said she feared that her daughter was drowned. Thomas Copus, already drunk by this time, was unconcerned when the news was related to him.

However, the elder son was dispatched and Ann went with him, but Jane was nowhere to be seen. The girl had not been gone long when Ann told Thomas that she was afraid Jane had drowned herself. Thomas said that she had probably gone out on an errand.

Now John Hemming offered to go and conduct a search, but Thomas refused, saying 'Blast her, let her drown', as he stormed out of the house into the yard with his sword in hand. Thomas was inebriated and the red mist had descended. John had followed, as Thomas screamed, 'Blast her eyes! I wish I could find her!' and tried to kick down the door to Mr Jones's neighbouring dye house. By now it was nearly 6 p.m. and the search was stopped for the night.

The incident had preyed on John's mind all night and the next morning he set out with two friends, Thomas Young and Edward Hichman, in a boat on the River Cherwell. Eventually they found Jane's body floating near Magdalen Bridge. It was removed and taken to the Black Horse Inn in St Clement's where an inquest was convened immediately. John testified that there were no marks on the riverbank to show that somebody had slipped into the water and said that it was impossible for Jane to have fallen in accidentally. In conclusion, the jury returned their verdict:

> Found drowned in the River Cherwell; but although there is no proof how the deceased came into the river, there appears to this Inquest, from the evidence, too much reason to fear that the deceased was induced to destroy herself in consequence of the ill treatment and violent threats of her father, Thomas Copus, a Sergeant in the Oxfordshire Militia.

A DANGEROUS TURN OF SPEED

Travelling at what was considered a dangerous speed of 7 or 8 miles an hour in September 1831, William Bateman was driving his horse and cart through Holywell Parish while standing on the shaft. Two boys were playing in the street and ran out into the horse's path, one bounced off the animal, but unfortunately James Gilder went straight under the cart, and as the wheels went over him they crushed his spine and ruptured his bladder. Bateman was charged with slaying James on 19 September. Witnesses said that the cart was going too fast for anybody to have moved out of the way. On 20 October Bateman was found guilty and was sentenced to twelve months' hard labour.

STONED AT WORK

William Wellstood, who was employed by Mr Plowman the builder, was at work on 5 October 1833 on Turl Street. At 11 a.m. workmen were winding up stones in a sling to the tower above Wellstood. As the sling reached the top of the winch three of the stones slipped and rained down on the pavement. One hit Wellstood; he died at 4 p.m. that day. An inquest was held later that evening at the Radcliffe Infirmary and a verdict of accidental death was returned.

SCARED TO DEATH

Mary Tanner was on her way back from Oxford races on 18 August 1834 accompanied by Mr and Mrs Baldwin and the Baldwin's 6-month-old son Joseph who was being held in his mother's arms. At Heffield's hut Mr Hughes, bookkeeper at the Roebuck, galloped through the crowd, scattering all, including the Baldwins, who screamed out in fear of their lives. Hughes was so drunk that immediately afterwards he fell off his horse. Mrs Baldwin, clutching her baby, was nearly knocked down by Hughes's horse and the infant cringed and appeared frightened. At 6.30 a.m. the next day the baby was seized with convulsions and died. At an inquest on 22 August the jury returned the verdict: died from convulsions occasioned by fright.

NO WAY OUT

The verdict on the body of Mrs Day, landlady of the Greyhound on the High Street, was that she had died from the effects of taking arsenic while in a state of derangement.

It was the final straw following the brutality wreaked on her by her husband. On 14 January 1836 at 4 p.m. an agitated Sarah Day visited Mr Young, apothecary on the High Street, asking for arsenic. She was angry when his son William asked her what she wanted it for. When Mr Young told Sarah not to be angry as William was right to ask, Sarah said that she wanted it to poison rats. An hour later Sarah's daughter rushed to the apothecary to ask Mr Young if her mother had bought anything from him. His reply was, 'Yes, arsenic.' The daughter replied: 'Oh dear, I wish she had not.' She feared her mother had taken the poison. Young told her to run to Mr Tuckwell the doctor, but instead she went to Mr Rusher, their family surgeon. It was Mr Young who went to Mr Tuckwell and together they went to the Greyhound.

Mrs Day was found by Mr Rusher on her bedroom floor. She was twitching and foaming at the mouth and Rusher administered, with difficulty, an emetic. Then with the assistance of Mr Tuckwell, who had arrived at the house at 5.30 p.m., he pumped her stomach, the contents of which contained a large amount of arsenic. Sarah died around 6 p.m. Mr Rusher testified that her husband was not in the room; he was downstairs, drunk.

The only other injury they found on Mrs Day's body was on her right leg, which Mr Tuckwell had seen some weeks previously. It was a large inflamed wound which she had said was caused by some man kicking her, but she would not say who; it had confined her to bed for some days. George Hodges, Sarah's son, said that he had seen his mother beaten on many occasions by her husband when he was drunk, but when sober the man had no recollection what he had done. Hodges did not think his mother had been without bruises for the last fourteen years, these being caused by her husband.

The day before her death, Sarah had gone to her son and told him that she had been beaten black and blue two days previously and that she was not going home. Sarah wanted George to go to her husband and demand maintenance for her and her three young children. George left to consult with his uncle and returned to tell Sarah that his uncle would come over that very evening and see what could be done for her. George said that he had heard that she was in the habit of drinking. Sarah said she was, and George replied that it was no solution to her problems. Sarah knew this to be true, but said it was caused by the ill-treatment she received from her husband.

That day George returned at 5.10 p.m. and met Mr Day at the front door. He told George that Sarah was a dead woman. George found Sarah lying on the floor; she said she had only had a half of beer. William Bacon, Sarah's nephew, was in the house that evening. A very drunk Stephen Day had come to the bottom of the stairs to ask how Sarah was. Bacon said she was a little better and Day replied that it would be a damned good job if she was not. Day then began yelling at Mr Rusher and Mr

Tuckwell for coming to his house and said that today Sarah was all theirs, but that he would give them what for tomorrow.

Everybody agreed that it was during the last two months that Sarah had hit the bottle, and hard – she was often too drunk to do anything and had given up all hope.

Matilda King had come to the Greyhound at noon on the day in question and found Sarah sobbing. Matilda tried to comfort her, but Sarah said it did not matter because she would not be around much longer. Provoked and perturbed by these words, Matilda returned at 6 p.m. and asked Mr Day what was wrong. He replied, 'She has poisoned herself, the damned old bitch.' Sarah died shortly afterwards.

The jury's verdict at the inquest was that Sarah had poisoned herself while in a state of temporary derangement, but felt it their duty to express their detestation and abhorrence at the brutal conduct of her husband, which was about as much as they could do.

RUN BABY RUN

Three nannies met on 26 October 1838. Martha Bailey, nanny to the Fosters, was herding the children when they met Mary Ann Bateman with a fourth Foster youngster. Last to join was Rebecca Page, servant to Mr Faulkner, who brought an infant with her. The nanny collective with a gaggle of children walked down the Abingdon road and then climbed up Hinksey Hill. By now the pram which Bailey had brought was crammed with four children; the youngest of the five was carried in one of the nannies' arms. At the top of the hill Page had taken charge of the crowded buggy and set off at a fair lick back down the hill. The baby carrier was too much for her to control and the other girls screamed for her to stop. But she could not and the buggy flipped up in the air, turned over and threw all four children in different directions. Mary Ann Foster landed head first. By the time Page caught up Mary was out cold and bleeding from her ear.

Mary, aged 3, was the eldest of the Foster children. With the assistance of a passer-by, who went for help, the child received medical attention. Time was of the essence, but it had taken quite a while to get Mary home, and despite the best efforts of a medical gentleman Mary died two days later on the 28th.

While the girls waited for Mary to be seen they had had enough time to concoct a story in order to shift the blame away from themselves. They had removed one of the wheels of the buggy and had made a pact that they would say that the wheel had come off, hoping that it would look like a terrible accident. But the truth came out during the inquest held on 29 October in the Wheatsheaf on the High Street. A verdict of accidental death was recorded. Since the cause of death was directly attributed to the buggy turning over, the fine of 1s was levied against the buggy. But it was not the end of the affair for the nannies. At the demand of the jury all three girls were hauled before the coroner, Mr Stone, who severely reprimanded them for their shameful and dishonest behaviour.

TAKEN TO HEART

Clements, a servant to Mr Rowell in Alfred Street, was mildly reprimanded on 24 January 1839 by her master and mistress for having acted improperly and told she must leave. Clements went to her room and hanged herself from the bedpost. At the inquest the jury returned a verdict of temporary insanity.

WICKED STEPMOTHER

On 20 April 1841 the eldest of the Brooks sisters went to her brother John, who lived at Mr Grove's in the Cornmarket, to complain of the ill-treatment that she had received from her stepmother and to say that she could no longer live with her. Maria Brooks, 44, was the second wife of James Brooks, waiter at Dickenson's coffee-shop. They lived together in a house on New Street, St Clement's, with James's three daughters by his previous marriage. Maria and the daughters were not on good terms and frequently quarrelled.

Having heard the report from his sister, John Brooks immediately went to his father's house at 9.30 p.m. and remonstrated with the elder man concerning the treatment of his sisters. James declined to listen to his son and ordered him to leave the house. John refused and so James went for somebody to help put his son out of the house. In the intervening period John went in search of his stepmother. Finding her in the house, he proceeded to argue with her, grabbing hold of her by both her shoulders and thrusting her out of the house and across the street. Maria fell backwards and hit her head, but she got up and was able to run back into the house and lock the door, by which time she was close to hysterical. There she remained until the following morning when the surgeon, Mr Stone, called to see her. He found her in her senses, but in a dying state; she died later that day.

An inquest was held two days later at the Port Mahon on 23 April. It was adjourned until 7 p.m. the next day to allow Mr Stone time to conduct a post-mortem. Stone found no general signs of disease or any bruising, but noted that her lungs were wasted away and her enlarged heart was nearly empty of blood. His

Cornmarket, 1840. The street leads north from Carfax towards St Michael's Church and St Giles's. (OCCPA)

professional opinion: Maria was asthmatic and death was caused by 'passion, producing a want of circulation at the heart'. John Brooks was not found guilty of her murder as she did not die of injuries received from him. However, the jury recorded a verdict of natural death, criticising John's 'unmanly and unjustifiable conduct' in staying in the house when repeatedly told to leave and in his abusive treatment of Maria, which accelerated the disease that caused her death.

DRUNKEN ESCAPADE

William Eden was brought into court on 27 April 1841 charged with attempting to shoot Hannah Reeves a week earlier. Hannah was a young girl who had recently arrived from London to lodge with Mary Ann Bryant in St Thomas's Parish. She had known Eden for three weeks when he turned up with a friend at her house at 2 p.m. on 20 April. Although Eden was already drunk, more beer was fetched and all 'romped' together until 5 p.m., when Eden became jealous of his friend. Hannah teased him saying, 'Did 'um teaze him, dear?' Eden punched Hannah in the face, knocking her to the floor. Hannah screamed. Bryant came in and told Eden to leave. He would not go and the pair traded blows. When Eden grabbed Mary's arms she bit him in the face and when he recoiled Mary cracked him over the head with a jug which, although it cut his head, seemed to calm him down.

Eden and his friend left and went their separate ways, but Eden returned alone at 8 p.m., apologising, saying it was only a drunken frolic and wanting to kiss and make up. Between visits Eden had been in the bar at the Prince Albert pub at around 6.30 p.m. and had asked the ostler to go out and get him powder and flint. When the items were given to him, Eden sat in the pub, pulled a gun from his pocket and proceeded to load it, mumbling, 'I'm damned if I do not go and blow that woman's brains out.' But on his return to the house he had sobered up and all seemed well. Mrs Wharton, also in the house, had bathed his head wound and he had gone to sit on Hannah's lap.

All of them drank together and three beer runs and a couple of hours later Eden asked Bryant to go with him to his father's house. Eden wanted to get some cash and then come back and sleep with either Mary or Hannah. Was it a brothel or was Eden just a little saucy? Either way Mary refused, but then ended up going with him, only to return alone twenty minutes later. Mary rushed through the door and straight to Hannah, telling her that Eden was on his way back and that under no circumstances should she open the door to him. There was a knock at the door. Hannah went upstairs and opened the bedroom window. As she leaned out to see who was there, Eden looked up and asked where Mary was and would Hannah open the front door. Hannah refused and Eden replied, 'If you do not open the door, I'll shoot you.'

As Hannah reached to close the window, Eden, only 12ft away, raised his right hand. Hannah saw the flash and felt the blast in her face as the bullet flew past her, hit the window shutter and embedded itself in the wooden frame. Time stood still. Wharton was in the same room as Hannah, with a child in her arms. Mary opened the front door, but Hannah was so shaken she could not remember what happened next. Mary screamed at Eden, 'You have shot my sister, and now shoot me!' Mary was hysterical. Hannah was downstairs when they eventually let two neighbours, who had heard all the commotion, in by the back door.

The events had also been witnessed by William James, a passer-by. He went up to Eden who, in a drunken state, was trying to reload the pistol. James offered to assist in replacing the flint; Eden accepted and James took the pistol away from him for safe keeping. The two men made their way around to the back of the house and into the garden. Mary let them in by the back door. James stepped in first. He still had the pistol in his hand when he asked Mary if 'that was it?'. She promptly fainted and Hannah asked Eden if he still wanted to shoot her. 'Yes' came the answer.

By now a lot of people had gathered in the garden, having heard the gunshot. One of the crowd touched Eden who was so drunk that he collapsed and was handed over to Atkins, the University policeman. Atkins thought all the protagonists were drunk, especially Eden, but he had not heard the gunshots and when he came to search Eden, as he found only bullets in his pocket took no further action. The same was true for Ackers, the City policeman, who searched Eden not long after Atkins. It was lucky for Eden that the pistol had been taken away from him by James. Eden then looked more like a drunken bystander with ironmongery in his pocket than someone who was trying to shoot people. But even then Eden would not go away, saying he wanted to spend the night in the house. The girls would not let him and he eventually drifted off into the night.

Several character witnesses were called before the court on the 27th, who said that Eden was a peaceable, well-disposed and well-conducted young man, though seemingly not so when drunk. The jury's verdict: not guilty. Eden was released.

A BAD APPLE

Thomas Lipscomb choked to death on a piece of boiled apple at the Trout Inn in September 1843.

BLACK WIDOW

Awoken on 23 July 1845 by the sound of smashing glass, Robert Ledom jumped out of his bed to see the shattered remains of his bedroom window. He rushed downstairs and out of the Abingdon Arms to find the landlord Matthew Barnes sprawled face-down in the road, dressed only in a shirt and pants. When Ledom went forward to take his hand the man groaned, kicked twice and died. Ledom looked up, but there was nobody around as it was 1.30 a.m., so he ran across the road to Mr Hadley's who, after being dragged out of his house, helped to carry the body back into the pub. Hadley noticed that Barnes had a black eye.

Barnes had married the widow of the late landlord of the Abingdon Arms twelve months previously and was considered to be a civil man, but had recently hit the bottle and was more often than not blind drunk. Barnes and his wife were, at the best of times, not on good terms and the couple slept in separate beds.

Another of the inn's long-term residents, Henry Owen, had often taken Barnes to bed drunk and it was he who had given the landlord his black eye during one of Barnes's particularly violent episodes. Barnes had told Owen that he would never again be happy, refusing to divulge why and saying that he would either commit suicide or a crime so that he could be transported.

The day before Barnes's suicide he was found by Owen hanging on to his bedroom door saying, 'Harper has been throwing water over me . . . feel the curtains.' But Owen found them quite dry. Fifteen minutes later Owen returned to the landlord who was in a frenzy, saying, 'He has been here again – he has been trying the lock.' But who? Owen never found out. Owen told the court at the inquest that the landlord was regularly drinking 15 to 20 pints a day and a bottle of gin to boot, and that he went to bed drunk two or three times a day, but strangely the landlord had been sober for the three or four days before his death.

The jury concluded that Barnes had thrown himself out of the second-floor window while in a state of temporary insanity, smashing Ledom's bedroom window on the first floor as he fell.

DISCHARGED AND DISPATCHED

James Chard, a 20-year-old mason of Jericho in the Parish of St Thomas, was a man fond of shooting. Having been out since early in the morning on Saturday 16 January 1847, he set off for home at 8 p.m., putting the barrel of his gun in one pocket and the stock in his other. On returning home he went into his father's garden, picked up a stone and threw it at a dog. In doing so, his pocket swung round and the barrel hit something. The lot discharged and blew a hole through his head. A verdict of accidental death was recorded at the coroner's inquest.

DEATH WISH

Thomas Price, 57, having been convicted more than once before, was on remand awaiting trial for another crime. On the morning of 14 December 1847 Stephen Judd, a prison officer, went to Price's cell where Price was already awake and dressed. Judd handed Price his breakfast as well as his braces and handkerchief, which had been washed for Price after he had entered the gaol, and told him to put on his braces and get ready to go before the magistrates at 11 a.m. Judd returned to the cell at 10.40 a.m. to find Price hanging from his braces. He rushed in and cut down the body, but the prisoner was already dead. Price had wrapped his waistcoat around the window bars, passed his braces through the armholes and tied them round his neck. The inquest held in the gaol the next day recorded a verdict of self-murder (suicide) and directed the body to be buried between 9 p.m. and midnight.

JOY RIDING

Mrs Coppuck left her house at Headington Quarry on 7 June 1848 to take dinner to her husband, leaving her 6-year-old daughter to look after their youngest, Eliza, who was 18 months old. She told her daughter that if Eliza was restless to wheel her around in the little barrow. Eliza was happily being wheeled around in the barrow when Mr Coppuck's wagon drew up in front of them. The driver moved the elder child aside and drove on. As he did so, the wheels went over the barrow, crushing in the sides and with them Eliza. The coroner's inquest reported that Eliza had died instantly of her multiple injuries and recorded a verdict of accidental death.

8

SPEAKING IN TONGUES

The Town Hall was officially opened on 28 July 1753, and in its court room two weeks later John Billingsgate was sentenced for several offences including scandal, abuse and swearing. His fate was to have his tongue cut out, and a scaffold was duly erected in front of the Town Hall for the purpose of carrying out his sentence.

As Billingsgate went to the scaffold he was attended by a large crowd of women from the fish markets of London, expressing great concern for their friend, though the significance of this is unknown. He was reported to have behaved decently, as he 'did not swear above a dozen times from his house to the foot of the scaffold'.

When on the scaffold Billingsgate announced to the assembled crowd that he would make final use of his tongue to confess his many sins. He told the gathering that he was born of honest parents, and that he would have never met this end had he stayed in school rather than spending his time gambling in the cockpits. He had moved on to bullying debtors in the hope of spiriting up clients in the form of the unfortunate people's creditors. He confessed to having killed a famous antiquarian and from that day forward had continued on a spree of slaughter until he had finally satiated his desire for abuse. He turned to the sheriff and whispered something, but only the ending could be heard as he concluded, 'Theodocia was a good girl, but God damn Sarah Walker.' At which point he began to rant and rave.

The executioner told him that his time had come and immediately carried out his business. It was reported in *Jackson's Oxford Journal* that, 'Upon taking out the tongue it blistered the hand that held it, and at several yards distance toasted cheese like a salamander: great quantities of water were then thrown upon it, but it was so much inflamed that it was impossible to quench it. Some dogs that came within its influence were seized with a sudden fit of barking and snarling; but what was odd was at the same time they lost the power of biting.'

The tongue was purchased by a logician who was said to use it to touch the lips of those pupils who deserved the 'genuine spirit of altercation'.

Within two weeks Billingsgate had become a deplorable spectacle. After his tongue was cut out he did not get any rest because the remaining stump continued to spasm in his mouth 'so that no medicine will stick to it long enough to have any effect'. Puss oozed from the wound, described as being so evil that it even coagulated milk. Some of the puss was said to have fallen on the hand of the nurse attending Billingsgate, and though 'scratched with a pin only skin deep', on healing she was left with such 'untoward symptoms' that she was advised to travel to Southampton 'to bathe in the salt water'.

So frustrated was Billingsgate with his predicament that people feared he might take his own life, whereupon they removed all cordage from his house, and kept a watchful eye on him. He was seen to wring his hands and turn up the whites of his eyes with 'the impious cast of a fretful gamester who has lost his stake', from which observers concluded that he cursed and swore inwardly. When his frenzy was at its height he would gesture for pen, ink and paper, but these had been denied him, as an early experiment with writing was less than successful. The only intelligible sentence written was: 'Without a tongue I have no more chance in life than a cat in hell without claws.'

A later experiment with reading was equally fraught. A friend had several books delivered to Billingsgate, on subjects known to have been of interest to the man, including the life of an eminent antiquarian, a fable and songs. He gladly received them, clutching them tightly, and then threw them all into the fire. Whereupon he snatched up the fire poker and stood before the fire with such a demeanour as to threaten destruction to anybody who tried to rescue the burning volumes.

A clergyman was sent for, in the hope that prayer would help to ease Billingsgate's suffering. The clergyman sat with him and asked if he would write a few details regarding his birth, education and his prior conduct. Billingsgate took this an attempt to solicit information so as to profit by writing his story. He ran off, and returned with his chamber pot 'with a contexture of the muscles of the face so expressive of indignation that the doctor, to prevent the effusion of Jordan, thought it best to provide for his security by a precipitate retreat'.

Day by day Billingsgate grew weaker, much to the confusion of local surgeons who agreed that the body would be cured if the mind could finally be set at ease. They resolved to prescribe opiates, believing that if these were to prove ineffective ''tis a cause lost'. The local cockfighters, of which sport Billingsgate was particularly fond, were greatly concerned about Billingsgate's well-being and laid bets of £10 to a crown against him recovering.

Nothing more was heard or reported of Billingsgate after that. Whatever the final outcome, his subsequent life, whether short or long, would have been hellish indeed.

9

IF AT FIRST YOU DON'T SUCCEED, GIVE UP BEFORE YOU GET CAUGHT

In 1786 William Coxe met William Mariner, when the latter visited Coxe at home. Mariner told him that he knew where to get £100 if he was interested. Coxe asked where this would be and Mariner said the silver in Magdalen College chapel, a haul consisting of four large candlesticks and a large dish, which sat on the communion table. Mariner said he could make keys to unlock the doors, having seen the originals. Coxe said he was not interested and Mariner swore at him, saying £100 would set them both up, Coxe declined, but one Thomas Gearing, a friend of Coxe's who was present, swayed it, and all three agreed to do the job together.

They started to plan and spent most of their time discussing what time to do it. Mariner favoured 7.30 p.m. via the front door. Gearing made objections and proposed 1 a.m. to 2 a.m. since everybody would be in bed. He said that it would be impossible to get into and out of the college at 7.30 p.m. without being noticed. Mariner said they would only be spotted if they went up the gravel walk and then into the chapel via the kitchens. Coxe wanted to go along the passage leading to the new buildings; Gearing agreed, but Mariner objected and was of the opinion that they would be seen as they went round, owing to the illumination of the lamps. They finally decided to do the business at 7.30 p.m. via the front door and Mariner departed. Coxe asked Gearing if Mariner could be trusted and Gearing replied that Mariner was a stout man and could be relied upon, having done many jobs with him and one Miles Ward, and that they often dropped keys off with him to be copied.

Weeks passed and Coxe finally met Miles Ward in the Coach and Horses pub on the High Street. Ward asked Coxe to walk with him to the King's Head. On their way, Ward asked if Mariner had made the keys and if Coxe was to do the job, Coxe said yes to both. Ward told Coxe that he himself was to have nothing to do with it, save to get them a horse, stolen of course, from the country. Coxe, Mariner and Gearing had, in fact, discussed the robbery dozens of times during the intervening weeks, but no more was said on the matter.

Days later, 25 February 1786, the day of the robbery, Ward turned up at Coxe's house at 5 a.m. and woke him. Coxe, climbing out of bed and going to the window, called to ask who it was. 'Ward,' came the reply. 'Is your wife at home?' 'No,' said Coxe and Ward asked Coxe to let him in, as he wanted to sleep there. They slept until 10 a.m. when Coxe went to Gearing's to see about the keys Mariner had made. They returned together and went to Ward, who was still in bed, with the keys. Ward ordered Coxe to go and get Mariner, but Coxe sent his apprentice instead, who soon returned with Mariner. Mariner, meeting Coxe downstairs, went up to see Ward and Gearing. Coxe followed minutes later. The conversation as Coxe entered was of the robbery, Mariner pulling a set of keys out of his pocket and showing them to Ward. Ward doubted they would work, but Mariner insisted he had seen the originals and these copies would open the doors.

The men, having altered the time of the robbery to 1 a.m., changed their minds again when Mariner convinced them to go at 7.30 p.m. and the discussion turned to how they would carry the plate. Gearing said that the candlesticks were long; Mariner argued they were not so long that they would not fit into his little bag, but he had not got it with him so Gearing asked Coxe if he had a bag. 'Yes,' said Coxe, fetching a bag from a backroom and putting it on a chair in the kitchen.

An hour later they dined together and Gearing left, followed, at 3 p.m. by Mariner who said he would be back in an hour. At some point that afternoon Ward had asked Coxe to go to Gearing's and ask for some shoes since his own were so warn that he could not wear them. So Gearing had returned with a new pair of shoes for Ward. Ward could not get them on and Cox took them downstairs to his shop and attempted to stretch them, but they still did not fit, so Ward demanded to have Gearing's own shoes, which he gave him. Time passed and the men waited. Mariner returned at 7.30 p.m., but by this time Ward was unsettled and told him they had changed their minds again and were not going till the middle of the night. Presently Ward went to bed. Half an hour later a nervous Mariner told him he was scared that he would be missed from his lodgings and after telling the others that the best way into Magdalen was from the Grove, Mariner left.

Coxe left with Mariner and went via Gearing's, who was surprised to hear that the job had not been done, since they were only to go to him afterwards. Gearing agreed that the new time was more appropriate and the three sat and drank together until 10 p.m. when Mariner and Coxe left, each for their own house. Walking over Magdalen Bridge, Mariner repeated his instruction that the Grove was the best way in, and departed. Coxe returned to Ward – who was still in bed.

At 1 a.m. Ward – who had changed his mind about his involvement in the scheme – and Coxe finally departed, bag in hand, heading for Magdalen Grove. James Emanuel, watchman of Holywell Parish, was patrolling that night. His dog had run off barking, heading for Longwall; Emanuel stopped, listened and on hearing footsteps shouted, 'Hello, who's there?' There was no reply so he called again. 'Hello,' came the reply. Emanuel went and cried the hour at the church nearby and, his dog reappearing, called after the man again. Again there was no reply so Emanuel went to him. As he drew close he could see by the light of his lantern that it was William Coxe, shoemaker of St Clement's. Emanuel remarked that it was odd that William should not answer when called and asked Coxe where he was going. 'Home,' said Coxe and saying goodnight he left. Ward had seen the watchman coming and done a runner, leaving Coxe to deal with the situation and only returning when the watchman had disappeared. The two men made their way to Magdalen Grove and Ward quickly climbed the wall, but Coxe could not. Ward offered to lift him up, but Coxe would have none of it.

Time was rapidly ticking away. Emanuel had gone to Holywell Street and called the hour and returned to the bottom of the street near Magdalen, where he stood and listened. Ward was worried in case the watchman came across them, and was forced to come down from the wall. They were dealt another blow when again Emanuel's dog ran off barking. This time Emanuel found the two men under the walk by Magdalen Grove and asked them where they were going.

'About my business,' one replied.

'And what business have you at such a time of night?'

The High Street in the foreground with Gravel Walk behind, 1825. The Greyhound Inn is on the far left; Magdalen College is the building on the extreme right. (OCCPA)

They said they were waiting for a man who was to deliver some tea to them. Emanuel told them they looked really dodgy skulking about. Coxe, who had reappeared after having said he was going home, asked Emanuel to go away. Emanuel refused and Coxe and Ward were forced to walk down Longwall towards the Greyhound Inn. In fact, Ward and Coxe were now off to Gearing's to get a ladder.

Coxe had had enough; they had been spotted twice by the watchman and he tried to dissuade Ward from continuing. But Ward said he would have it done as things had gone badly for him in London. And so it was set. Ward and Coxe returned with Gearing's ladder and proceeded to scale the kitchen yard wall. Making across the yard and into the kitchen through a fortuitously unlocked door, they lit a candle and Ward pulled out a key. This unlocked a door which led into the cloisters and on entering they snuffed the candle; then being illuminated by the lamps, they made their way round to the chapel. They broke into a cold sweat when they heard the outside kitchen door squeaking. Ward rushed back to prop the door open with a spade he found in the kitchen. He returned to Coxe, but it was too dark to see the lock on the chapel door and they were forced to relight the candle in order to find the hole. Ward opened the door with one of the keys Mariner had given him and made his way alone to the altar. He put one pair of candlesticks into the bag and carried the others in his hands. But it was not until he returned to Coxe that he realised he had forgotten the altar plate and sent Coxe back for it. They made their way out of the chapel and retraced their steps around the cloisters, through the kitchen and across the yard. Ward disposed of a candle held in one of the candlesticks by throwing it across the yard. Once over the wall they collected the ladder and headed back to Gearing's.

So far so good Emanuel had continued about his business, although he had returned to his box to retrieve his hanger (a short sword worn on a belt). He had walked the parish streets, occasionally stopping to sit and listen, but heard nothing more for the rest of the night. Coxe returned to Gearing and woke him; Ward went to Coxe's directly. Both men found Ward unscrewing the candlesticks when they entered Coxe's house. Gearing remarked, 'This has been a job long talked about, but thank God 'tis done at last and I wish you good luck with it.' The only reason

Gearing had been brought to the house was that Ward needed money to get to London, but now the two men argued as to whether the candlesticks were in fact silver; Gearing thought not. Meanwhile, Gearing realised that the front door was unlocked and gave Coxe a mouthful, telling him to lock it and put up a cloth at the window so no one could peer in. Some time after 4 a.m. they left; Gearing went home and Ward, with 6s he had been given, went with Coxe to catch a coach, stopping on Dawson's Hill where they sat and waited. Eventually Ward went back down to the turnpike to enquire at what time the coach would pass. The turnpike keeper said 'near six'. Returning to Coxe with this information, they decided to wait at Coxe's house, from where Ward finally boarded the coach at 5.30 a.m.

Edward Kench, coachman for the Birmingham post-coach, on his way to High Wycombe, saw Coxe and Ward waiting outside the former's house at 5.30 a.m. They called for him to take Ward he said the fare was 9s and Ward said whatever the fare he must get to London. Coxe passed Ward a charcoal coloured bag and Kench put it in the boot. Later he testified that the contents of the bag 'rattled like would fire shovel and tongs' and weighed three-quarters of a hundredweight. He charged 1d for its carriage. The two shook hands, wishing each other good luck, Coxe anxiously insisting Ward write to him as soon as he could.

The coach reached its destination of High Wycombe and Kench asked Ward for the fare. Ward offered only 10d (despite having been given 6s) and said he would pay when he got to London as he had no more. He set off in the same coach, now being driven by Robin Allen. Ward was last spotted at 1 p.m. at the Swan at Bayswater still clutching the same bag.

Back in Oxford the theft had been discovered. Emanuel, bumping into Mr Barnes and Mr Smith, policemen, informed them about the lurkings of Coxe. Coxe was arrested and questioned, but this was now two days after the robbery. Even before the questioning finished, Smith decided the booty must have been taken to London and off he headed. As he left Oxford he received news that somebody had departed at 5.30 a.m. on the morning of the robbery with a heavy bag; Smith headed for Bow Street Police Station. With the assistance of the London police Smith traced Ward to his father's house at Walham Green, Fulham, that very evening. During questioning Coxe made a full confession, implicating all his friends. Ward was eventually returned to Oxford gaol, by which time Mariner and Gearing were already there, charged and awaiting trial.

Six days after the robbery the four met again, this time before a magistrate. Ward denied the charge, denied knowing any of the other men and even denied ever being in Oxford – a cunning defence. With Coxe as star witness, at the trial at 8 a.m. on 11 March, Ward was charged with burglary and theft, Gearing and Mariner as accessories. All three had pleaded not guilty. The value of the haul was £10 for the four candlesticks and £15 for the Communion dish, only a quarter of the sum that Mariner had originally promised the booty would be worth.

Mariner said the men had two keys belonging to him which he had given to Coxe, but not for any 'bad intent' and denied everything else. Gearing denied advising robbery or anything suchlike, or giving his opinion as to whether the goods were silver, though he did admit to seeing the candlesticks and to taking shoes to Ward at Coxe's house.

Ward was a different matter; he claimed he had not been more than 20 miles from London in the last month. On the evening of the robbery he maintained that he had been at home in Fulham; in fact he had been at home all day, he said, only leaving the day after at 1 p.m. to buy provisions for his family at Hyde Park and, at 3 p.m., to buy tea at a shop he could not remember on Oxford Street and lamb at another shop he could not remember, nor could he recall how much he had paid for it. Ultimately, he had been spotted by one Peavey Saunders at 1 p.m. in Bayswater . . . he denied being there and likewise denied that when he got off the Oxford coach he had gin or gingerbread in the Swan and definitely did not ask the landlord, Robert Colley, to change a shilling.

Now Ward had to explain the presence of a stolen watch in his pocket. He said he had bought it three weeks before at the Green Man in Ewell, Surrey, from a man he believed was a smuggler, the address of whom he did not know. Ward boasted several witnesses to prove his alibi, but his counsel was eventually forced to back down and say that they were not trying to dispute Ward being in St Clement's on the evening of the robbery. The defence argued that the whole trial hinged solely on Coxe's testimony, which was unreliable as he was an accomplice, but the judge said it was up to the jury to decide if the men were guilty and the trial proceeded to its conclusion.

The men were members of a notorious gang. Ward was found in possession of several stolen saddles and horses, Gearing of stolen goods and poaching equipment.

The use of a horse and cart in an execution, as pictured in 1797, was at one time common. The 'drop' would be performed as the cart drew away, leaving the convict to hang until dead. (OCCPA)

In fact, all three had started the trial day on a charge of stealing geese and wheat and Gearing ended it by facing a charge of stealing leather from a shop in Birmingham. The local paper hoped that the trial would dispel the commonly held belief among criminals that an accomplice, not directly involved in a crime, would escape the same punishment as the perpetrators.

Gearing and Mariner languished in gaol, but they were removed early amid security fears as the Castle gaol's structure had been significantly weakened by the demolition of outer walls owing to extensive rebuilding and improvement work. On 25 April 1786 they were conveyed to the hulks at Woolwich to wait until there was a convict ship ready to sail to Africa where they would begin their life transportation sentence.

Ward was not so lucky: at noon on 27 March 1786 he faced execution. He approached the gallows without fear, and resigned to his fate he prayed fervently and shed tears. Standing under the gallows he proclaimed the innocence of Gearing and Mariner and lambasted Coxe, who had got away scot-free, stating that Coxe had proposed robbing the Tan Yard at Little Gate, leather from Mr Pietley's outhouse, Mr Spicer of New Inn Hall Lane, the linen draper's at Long Crendon, and hiring a horse and cart and robbing Coxe's father-in-law, a shoemaker at Brackley. And the cherry on top: robbing Mr Aston's shop near Magdalen Bridge by taking bricks out of the end wall, as Coxe had observed that it was only one brick thick. On the same day Ward was joined by John Grace, and John and Richard Cox, who had been condemned for sheep stealing. When all four were standing on the cart below the gallows Ward, with great composure, asked his companions, 'Are you all ready to die? If you are let us take leave of one another.' They all shook hands, but before the brothers could let go of one another the cart had drawn away and there they long remained, hands tightly clasped. After hanging for the usual time, Ward's body was cut down and placed in a handsome coffin and taken by his mother back to Walham Green.

10

NO PLACE TO HIDE

The gates of the Cross Inn heaved under the weight of bodies. John Costar, wielding a wagon lever, prized the doors open and fifty men rushed in and proceeded indiscriminately to attack anybody and anything that stood in their way. It was the early hours of 10 October 1819 as the angry mob stormed across the coaching yard to the inn. They soon broke open the front doors and, crashing through, armed themselves with anything that came to hand – spits, pokers and the like – and began taking the inn apart, smashing windows and furniture and yelling that they were going to set the building alight. Upstairs the inn's guests and servants listened to the terrifying sounds of destruction coming from below, having been woken from their sleep. The mob were after three men in particular: Mr Seward the landlord, William Griffin the ostler and a waiter at the inn.

The yard and inn were the scene of utter confusion and uproar. Mr Holmes, a coach proprietor, got in the way and was summarily dispatched. William Griffin was tracked down, beaten, punched to the ground and stamped on. He managed to escape, though only as far as the inn's cellar. Here he hid, behind a stack of coal, only to be found and dragged out by several of the mob, before finally escaping their grasp. Time passed, but the violence continued and several residents of Carfax experienced it at first hand when they came to see what the confusion was, receiving several blows for their curiosity.

The inn's residents had long fled their beds and taken refuge in any hiding-place they could find, including the cellar where Griffin had hidden. There was mayhem. The furious assemblage had, by then, removed one of the city's policemen from the equation after he had stepped in to quell the riot. The mob continued to wreak havoc until the Mayor, James Adams, and one of the University Proctors stepped in to find many of the combatants severely wounded while others were venting their fury amid the carnage. It seems that by sheer force of personality, or possibly status, the Mayor was able to cease hostilities – for which he was commended – for surely only extreme force could have otherwise stopped such a mob.

The whole affair had started much earlier. The spark came when shortly after 1 a.m. John Wheeler lay in the street outside the Cross Inn bleeding profusely from his head, the gates shut upon him. He was carried home near dead and a cry of murder went abroad, leading to John Costar and the great body of men rushing back to the inn's gates.

But what had led to Wheeler's slumped body being found in the street? At 1 a.m. Wheeler, along with John Timms and Thomas Kempson, had arrived at the Cross, having spent the whole day drinking heavily. The labourers called for a quart of beer, but were refused by Mrs Seward the landlady as all had gone to bed. The men were not put off, as others were still up and drinking, and demanded the beer, pushing the landlady and 'treating her rudely'. They were turbulent and intent on causing a disturbance. Mrs Seward called for help and her servant attended. Mr Griffin and Mr Holmes stepped in and told the men to leave, whereupon a scuffle ensued.

The men were turned out of the inn with nothing more than a bit of pushing and shoving, but tempers flared when they were put outside the gates. Punches were thrown, Griffin and Holmes were beaten back and fled to the inn, by which time Mr Seward had been forced from his bed by the disturbance. The inn and yard were cleared of the intruders. Mr Seward, none too pleased, followed Griffin into the street in pursuit of the men. Griffin had armed himself with a splinter bar from a coach and cracked Wheeler across the back of his head with a hefty blow, flooring him. A half-dressed Mr Seward, hot on the heels of Griffin, gave Wheeler a good whacking with a large stick while he lay unconscious on the ground. Griffin and Seward finally returned to the confines of the inn and the gates were shut.

On their return, Costar and the group had firmly placed Griffin and Seward at the centre of their resentment and had vowed vengeance. At the end of the night, after the Mayor had put a stop to proceedings, four men were carted off to gaol: John Coster, James Thornton, William Piesley and Samuel Glassington. A further six were apprehended the next morning, when all ten were brought before the Mayor and magistrates for questioning, which lasted nearly all day. All the men were released on bail and just over a week later, on 18 October, eight were formally charged with riot and assault. On that day another charge was laid, but this was against Seward and Griffin for continuing the assault by attacking Wheeler after he had been turned into the street.

The full trial began on 10 January 1820 at the Quarter Sessions and continued over the next day. Before giving sentence the judge lectured the courtroom on the ruinous consequences of drinking and how it had fuelled the assailants during the riot, which could have only comprised such lower orders as would have spilled out of the pubs at that time of night 'inflamed by liquor'. Of the men charged only George Rodwell was acquitted, while the others were sentenced: John Costar to six

Sir James Parke, nineteenth-century Justice of the Assize, from the Berkshire Assize Calendar for summer 1840.
(Oxfordshire Record Office – ORO)

months; Thomas Coppuck to four months; James Thornton, Charles Auckland, John Timms, Thomas Kempson and William Piesley to three months each. The judge commented that had Seward and Griffin's actions been in defence of the family or premises, they would have been unquestionably justified. Since this was not the case, they had used unwarrantable violence towards Wheeler, though allowance was made for the landlord's irritation in being woken, the uproar in his house, the rudeness to his wife and the violence used towards his guests and servants, all of which amounted to provocation, and under these mitigating circumstances Griffin and Seward were fined £5 each.

11

STUDENTS, FELLOWS AND THE UNIVERSITY

TAKE-AWAY BREAKFAST

Warden Cotes was not a universally popular appointment as Warden of Balliol and one of the Fellows, John Smythe, had it in for him to the end. In 1543 Smythe was fined for the offence of making off with the Warden's breakfast. So unruly was Smythe that the Warden had to get an injunction requiring him to do as he was told.

MAGIC, A PINCH OF SALT AND COOKERY

Adam Squire was elected as Warden of Balliol in 1571. Despite being a mathematician, he was a colourful character, described as quarrelsome, lewd, lecherous, hypocritical, fantastical and a spendthrift. He nearly shot himself in the foot and risked his job when he convinced some gamblers to pay for 'magical assistance' that very year. He made himself appear even more ridiculous when he performed the ceremony at his own wedding; perhaps he hoped to save some money. Squire's father in-law, the Bishop of London, made him Archdeacon of London, but while an inspection was made of his district, Squire was caught in bed with somebody else's wife. The errant husband hit on a plan: he gambled and forged a love letter to his wife from a knight and handed it to his father-in-law as an excuse for lapsing in his duty to his wife. The Bishop was very upset, but looked on Squire more favourably because of the letter. When he discovered it was a forgery, the Bishop flew into a rage and, locating a butcher's cudgel, went around and gave Squire a tremendous thrashing.

Bearing in mind Squire was elected to a responsible position as head of a college, he was not setting too good an example. In fact, from 1572–3 he recruited Christopher Bagshaw, a Fellow of Balliol, to his faction. Squire, a Protestant, loathed the senior bursar Robert Persons, a Jesuit. Bagshaw was Catholic and anti-Jesuit and falsely accused Persons of dodgy accounting (thirty years later he was still going on about Persons cooking the books). Finally Persons was forced from the college at the beginning of 1574. He was given the choice of resigning or being dishonoured and thrown out. Squire continued as Warden until 1580.

STRICT MERTON WARDEN

During the time Sir Thomas Clayton was Warden of Merton his treatment of one of the Fellows can only be described as cruel and insensitive.

In 1681 William Cardonnel was a college bursar. Unfortunately he allowed his tongue to get the better of him and it was to prove his undoing. On Clayton's suggestion one of the college gardeners had been sent to Cardonnel to solicit payment for his work on the Warden's garden. The bursar misjudged the likely consequences and was frustrated, saying 'the Warden be hanged'. The Warden was not one for subtlety and exacted a humiliating punishment: he made Cardonnel give a public apology on his knees. The poor fellow was wrought with guilt and hanged himself from an oak beam in his rooms during the night of 23 October 1681. It was sad for all concerned, but the Warden remarked that he now had one less enemy and then directed that Cardonnel's body be buried in unhallowed ground in the old chapel yard.

This final act owes more to the customs of the day relating to suicide, which was considered to be self-murder, than it does to the Warden's lack of compassion.

BAD FRUITS

Mr Gilby, a Fellow of All Souls, died of tuberculosis in August 1705. His death was believed to have been caused by a piece of cherry stone going down his windpipe. This was thought to have led to a corruption of his lungs, though most people considered his death to have been the result of hard drinking.

FLOWER POWER

Dr Hudson, the bursar of University College, had turned the wasteland of a college garden into a thing of beauty in 1706. It had been turfed and trees and flowers had been planted. Days after its completion several college students trashed it during the dead of night. Suspicion fell on one Robinson who, among others, was upset that the college had dictated that students attend college dinner or be fined. Possibly then, as now, the students preferred not to eat the college food. At the time there were numerous accounts of local chefs being fined by the University for taking dinners to students. This was very much against the wishes of the college authorities and they took the local tradesmen to court – their own naturally.

THE BEST THINGS IN LIFE

Dr Thomas Sergeant of All Souls died on 23 October 1708. He was a rich and miserly Fellow, who died without a will that would give in death as he had failed to do during his life. The 'good' doctor was a recluse. He rarely came out of his rooms and would not answer his door, but if the presence of oysters was announced he would be out like a shot, as he was fond of good food and drink. His epitaph read:

> Here lyes doctor Sergeant Wth in these Cloysters,
> Whom if Ye last Trump do not wake then Crye Oysters.

AND THE LIST GOES ON

In December 1710 a book was published in London on the life of Dr Sacheverell, formerly of Magdalen College. He had disowned his uncle, mother and benefactors, who had financed him both through school and University. Among his many crimes listed, his sermons were said to be illogical, grammatically poor and nonsense. To add to this, he had little skill in Latin, divinity and astrology, preferred fiction to fact and gave little for his pastoral responsibilities. He was also accused of being insulting, quarrelsome, rude to the Fellows, insolent, ill-natured, maliceful, foul-mouthed, scurrilous, profane, immodest, lewd and proud.

If that was not enough, he was also considered to be a dodgy dealer who was addicted to drink, gambling and was considered to have been responsible for the death of a young woman. In addition, he had written to both his glovemaker and laundress, informing them that he refused to pay them and swearing at and abusing them . . . but luckily that seems to be all.

FELLOW ROBBER

During the evening, about dinnertime, on 6 June 1713 Thomas Butler's house in Holywell Street was burgled and £20 stolen. Mr Butler was the keeper of the Holywell Parish cockpit and the loss of the money was a great blow at the time, since he was a poor man and had put the money out to pay for his entire year's rent. After the robbery it transpired that Cotton, a Fellow of New College, was to blame; which tallied with reports of his bad reputation.

HAZARDOUS WATER SPORTS

In a time before it was commonplace to learn to swim, anything involving a river was considered a dangerous sport. In the afternoon of 8 May 1722 Mr Hazell, a student of Queen's College, was fishing from a boat near Sandford Lock with two fellow students. They got into rough water, and as the boat was being dragged rapidly towards the weir two of the students jumped out and scrambled back to the bank, but Hazell stayed in the boat. His companions screamed at him to jump, but it was too late. The boat overturned and he was drowned.

BEER ABOVE ALL OTHER

Dr Stonehouse, Fellow of Magdalen College, was so fond of his beer that on returning one wet March evening in 1724 he did not stop to change his rain-soaked clothes, but went directly to the common room and drank four pints of beer in a couple of hours. Later he died of pneumonia.

The Turf Tavern, once known as the Spotted or Split [sic] Cow, is hidden behind Holywell Street and was home to the Holywell cock pit. (Giles Brindley)

EXPENSIVE ACCOUNT

In April 1725 Mr Dike, a student of Wadham College, was visited by his father who was to remonstrate with the young man over his extravagant lifestyle. But on his father's arrival the son was not to be found. He had shot himself.

RUNS IN THE FAMILY

The nephew of Dr Gardiner, the Warden of All Souls, was a Fellow of Merton in 1726. In August that year he slashed his throat on account of an argument he had had with his family. What was possibly even more surprising about this family was that the young man's sisters were so fond of men that they were known to leap out of windows after them.

THE GOOD DOCTOR

It was 6 December 1751 and the University Court was in session. The prosecution was headed by the Worshipful Radcliffe Howard, Doctor of Laws and Fellow of All Souls College, and also by the Revd George Wilmot, MA, Fellow of Balliol College. The judge was the Revd John Brown, DD, Master of University College and Vice-Chancellor; the accused was William Lewis, Doctor of Medicine of Christ Church. Having committed the charge to paper on 15 November 1751, Howard and Wilmot presented it in court, unanimously denouncing William Lewis who 'hath in manifest violation of the wholesome laws and shameful acts, manifestly tending to corrupt, debauch and vitiate the mind and morals of a modest youth of the age of 15 years, namely William Rouse of Magdalen College'. The men stated that all these acts of lewdness and indecency would be later specified and presented to the court, but no further records are to be found. The dons asked that the Vice-Chancellor instantly decree a citation to be served on Lewis that would require him to appear in court to answer for his 'indecency, immorality and lewdness' as the law and justice required. The Vice-Chancellor rejected the petition and informed them that it was within his power to hold proceedings either at that court or in his own lodgings and adjourned until 9 December, when he would hear them between noon and 2 p.m. in his own rooms if they had anything new to add.

On 9 December Wilmot and Howard presented the charge again, and again the Vice-Chancellor rejected it, saying that he had made a judgement relating to Lewis with respect to Rouse, a chorister at Magdalen. He added that he would consider the charge against Lewis, should the alleged new facts be of the same kind, but with the exclusion of anything relating to Rouse. The men insisted, saying that they did indeed have new evidence, but that moreover they had a right to the citation requested without presenting the evidence, protesting that the Vice-Chancellor's ruling was 'null, unjust and iniquitous and that they would appeal there from to the Worshipful House of congregation'. There being no more records to illuminate the proceedings, it is unclear if the matter proceeded further.

However, a prior statement made by Rouse and a bond made by Lewis show the events that led up to the charges laid by Wilmot and Howard. Rouse's statement before the Vice-Chancellor on 3 April 1751 said Lewis had:

. . . given great offence against good manners by indecent and obscene language in a private conversation with the said Wm Rouse and thereby occasioned public scandal and suspicion of libidinous intention towards the person of the said Wm

Rouse which libidinous intention however the said Wm Lewis has it by his solemn oath in the presence of the underwritten witnesses utterly disowned and purged himself of . . .

The Vice-Chancellor had therefore taken security for Lewis's good behaviour for life, binding him in the amount of £500 to be paid within a month should he be convicted of this or any similar offence with a person of the same sex. Similarly two sureties were bound for £250 each for Lewis's good behaviour.

THE BEAN COUNTERS

Releasing information to the local paper at the end of December 1762, New College announced that it had been robbed of £600, a large sum of money. No stone was to be left unturned; search warrants were issued and people sent out to execute them. The college authorities were in a high state of excitement. It was an extraordinary theft, since the money belonging to any college was secured in a locked chest fitted with several different locks, one for each bursar of the college who alone held the key for that particular lock. They suspected a gang of highly organised criminal masterminds. The college even went to the King and obtained a royal pardon for anybody brave enough to rat on his accomplices.

The college boldly advertised a reward of £100 for information. Then finally, on 30 January 1762, it announced with stunning brevity the humiliating fact that it was all an accounting error and that no money had been stolen.

DANGEROUS SLUMBERS

The body of James Butler, bedmaker at Corpus Christi College, was found one May morning in 1781 in Cornmarket. He had been run over by the wheels of a carriage. Butler had left the Cock and Bottle near Worcester College at midnight to make for another pub, but on the way he had found a rather dangerous place to sleep: the middle of the road.

WHILE THE GOING'S GOOD

At 9 p.m. on 23 April 1815, as George Field was walking in Christ Church meadow near the Isis, he was assaulted, knocked over and held down

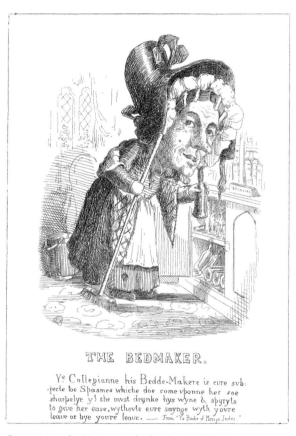

THE BEDMAKER.

Yͤ Collegianne his Bedde-Makere is eure svb:
-jecte toe Spasmes whiche doe come vponne her soe
sharpelye yͭ she must drynke hys wyne & spyryts
to give her ease, wythovte eure saynge wyth yovre
leave or bye youre leave. —— From "Ye Booke of Merrye Jestes."

Caricature of a University bedmaker. (OCCPA)

by three men, while another picked his pocket of a wallet containing a £5 note and two £2 notes. They stamped on him before escaping. His cries brought some

FIFTY POUNDS REWARD.

WHEREAS about Nine o'clock on Sunday evening the 23d of April inst. as GEORGE FIELD, by Trade a Shipwright, of the King's Yard, at Chatham, was walking in Christ Church Meadow, in this University, he was overtaken in the Gravel Foot-path, near the River Isis, by four Ruffians, who suddenly knocked him down, and forcibly took from his watch-pocket a small Purse, containing a Five Pound Bank of England Note, and two of the same Bank of the value of Two Pounds each; after which they violently stamped on his breast, and left him apparently lifeless.

For the apprehending and bringing to Justice of the offenders, the DEAN AND CHAPTER OF CHRIST CHURCH hereby offer a REWARD of FIFTY POUNDS, to be paid on conviction: and the same Reward will be paid to any one of the persons, concerned in the above mentioned offence, who will discover and lead to the conviction of his accomplices, and means will be used to obtain for him a free pardon.

Oxford, April 28, 1815.

N. B. Three of the offenders were dressed in dark coloured coats, and one of them wore a light frock.

A reward for the apprehension of George Field's assailants was advertised in the local newspaper by Christ Church in 1815. (Jackson's Oxford Journal)

watermen to his assistance, who found him covered in blood and battered. Field told his rescuers that he was a shipwright from Chatham. Christ Church took pity on him and advertised a reward of £50 in the local paper for the apprehension of the villains and even offered to do all in its power to obtain a pardon for any of them who would turn in their accomplices. So much was the college's desire for justice that it added a further reward of £100 a week later. Donations for Field poured in from the ladies and gentlemen of the University and city. A large sum of money was collected, but

Field was nowhere to be found. He had done a runner before it could be given to him, after he had heard that people were making enquiries about his story and about his 'relation' Mr Connolly, of the Swan Yard at Newington Butts, who, it turned out, knew nothing of any George Field.

In May the police finally tracked Field down to St Albans. Unfortunately this was his undoing. Having played an identical trick at St Albans, he had almost pulled it off, even to the point where three soldiers had been arrested on suspicion and were languishing in gaol awaiting trial. Field's fatal error was to hang around after he had been given all the donations. The situation was rapidly reversed and the soldiers were released. Field was arrested and tried in St Albans on 13 July 1815. At his trial were a long line of policemen, including Mr Smith from Oxford, as well as men from Cambridge and Fareham. Field, alias Philip Hewitt, alias Philip Gibbons, was a 'most incorrigible villain'. His web of deceit was unravelled before his eyes, it being proved that his tricks dated back at least fifteen years. He was found guilty and sentenced to seven years' transportation.

The secret of Field's deception? He was able to cause his nose to bleed and, after swallowing the blood, skilfully spit it out for several days afterwards, thus giving the appearance of a man who had been severely beaten.

RESPECT FOR AUTHORITY

Three stones came smashing through a first-floor window at the Revd Mr Hewlett's house in St Aldate's at 8 p.m. on 10 December 1818, the first two landing on the bed of a little boy who was asleep, the third missing the child's head when it was deflected by a piece of furniture. Mr Hewlett rushed to the window and saw three students, complete with gowns, legging it down the street.

SPORTING TIMES

Some University students were amusing themselves on 16 June 1840 with a little early evening target practice, while hanging out of the window of their lodgings. About 70yd away, on St Giles's, a young man was walking down the street and heard the whizz of a bullet as it flew past his head and embedded itself in the gates of Mr Tustin's, the butcher. Nobody was arrested for the shooting.

GUARD OF HONOUR

At 6 a.m. on 12 May 1840 one of the Magdalen College servants looked out into the deer park when on his way to wake up some of the students. There he saw something rather curious: the deer had congregated in a circle not far from the college building. The servant went out and found the deer surrounding the body of the Revd Mr Grantham, Senior Fellow and bursar of the college. Medical assistance was called for, but Grantham had died two or three hours previously and was pronounced dead.

The Fellow's room was on the second floor of the new buildings overlooking the deer park. On that Tuesday night he had been tutoring two choristers and on leaving them had returned to his rooms. What followed was later pieced together.

Returning to his room lit by a candle Grantham had reclined on his sofa and fallen asleep. He was awoken by the smell from the snuffed candle and had got up in the dark and endeavoured to open the sash window. The window had been varnished recently and was stuck. Suddenly it came free and Grantham lost his balance. He fell

Magdalen College's deer park, known as the Grove, with the New Buildings in the background.
(Giles Brindley)

two floors to his death below, landing on his head. An inquest held the same day returned a verdict of accidental death. The college took this opportunity to advertise for his replacement in the local paper.

CAMPANOLOGIST – WILL WORK FOR CASH

Arriving back in Merton College, having matriculated that day, Henry Hammond was in his rooms on 14 February 1848 when a man called. This 'gentleman' said he was one of the University bell-ringers and asked Hammond for some money for the bells that had been rung as part of the matriculation ceremony. Since Hammond had only just arrived in college, he was unsure exactly how things worked and questioned the campanologist at length. He was told that it was customary and that everybody gave him something. How much? Hammond asked, and was told 5*s* was the very least; in fact, the student below Hammond had given him 10*s*. Hammond searched his pockets, but could find only 4*s*. The so-called ringer took it, saying he would come back later for the balance. Hammond was still not sure and with doubt in his mind he went and asked one of the college servants about this custom. He found Richard Bishop, who told Hammond he knew nothing about giving ringers money on matriculation.

Hammond discovered that the man was not an eminent campanologist, but a workman named Richard Cater. Since the matriculation of students was conducted by each college on different days, Cater had ample opportunity to move between the colleges and solicit money as he went.

On 10 February Mr Maskel of the University had collared Cater outside Worcester College. Maskel had told Cater he knew what he was up to and had accused Cater of obtaining money from students by claiming it was for bell-ringing. Maskel had been called out by several students who were complaining bitterly about being fleeced by Cater, and by now the Vice-Chancellor had been informed. Maskell had said: 'You know I saw you coming out of Magdalen College. You went to get money off a gentleman there.' Cater had been told by Maskell that if he did it again charges would be pressed. Cater had baulked and said he was going off to London, but that idea did not last very long, as, days later, he had, of course, obtained 4s from Hammond.

Cater's very profitable scam was exposed. He was charged and released on bail to appear in court on 1 March 1848, but never turned up – perhaps he had gone to London after all. He was never heard of again.

ONE FELL FROM THE CUCKOO'S NEST

Despite the University coroner's statement only a month earlier that there were few fatal accidents in the University, John Key, a student of Oriel, was pronounced dead at 7 a.m. on 3 March 1849. Key's body was discovered in the front quadrangle between the chapel door and the hall staircase, just a few feet from the wall. Mr Martin, the doctor, had been called out at 6.45 a.m. and on arriving in the quad found Key lying on his stomach. Key's face was turned to the right, his right arm and wrist were broken and his left arm, which lay under his body, was bruised and the shoulder dislocated; blood was clearly seen to have come from his mouth. Martin concluded

The front quad of Oriel College, 1830s, with the entrances to the Hall (centre) and the Chapel.
(OCCPA)

from the injuries that Key had fallen from the college roof 40ft above. The student had died instantly from a head wound as he landed in the quad below.

An inquest was held that very afternoon in the college's hall. The circumstances of Key's death were even more unexpected than his premature departure. Mr Maughan, a student whose rooms were above Key's, was awoken some time after 3 a.m. by a loud noise coming from the room below, which lasted ten minutes and sounded like several people struggling with someone against his will. Maughan had jumped out of bed and was partially dressed when he heard people going down the stairs and all became quiet. He climbed back into bed, but lay awake straining his hearing. A few minutes later there was a furious banging on his door. Nervously, Maughan half-opened his door, expecting to find an enraged individual, but instead found Key, who seemed quite calm. Key asked to be let into Maughan's sitting room; Maughan refused and told him to go away. This carried on for another five minutes. Maughan was getting bored of the verbal tennis and finally convinced Key that he was not going to let him in, since Key had not given him a good reason to do so. Slurring something about getting out of the window onto the lead roof, Key pronounced that he was a good climber. Still Maughan refused to allow Key into his sitting room and told Key for one final time to go back to his rooms. Undeterred, Key hit on a new plan: he asked for a coal hammer to break down his door. Since Maughan did not have one, he suggested that Key put a chair at the top of the staircase and use it to climb up and through the window above the door. Maughan gave Key a chair and a candle just to get rid of him. Maughan thought Key was possibly emotionally unstable, but not drunk. Maughan shut Key outside and went back to bed. Nothing more was heard by Maughan until 7 a.m. when the alarm was raised.

It still does not explain how Key came to be locked out of his room or how he ended up dead in the front quad the following morning. It was left to Mr Cox, another Oriel student, to explain. Key, along with others, had been drinking from 10 p.m. onwards the previous evening in Cox's room. Just before 3 a.m. Key staggered out. Cox said that Key was so drunk he could not walk or look after himself, so Cox had half-carried Key towards his rooms. On reaching the staircase, Key lay down on the steps and Cox, unable to move him, had given up and gone to bed. A while later, Key was staggering around the quad making so much noise that he woke numerous people. Cox and another friend were forced to go down to collect him. They only got so far before as the red mist descended and Key flew into a furious rage. The flailing student was too much to handle and, calling for two more friends, all four fought to get Key back to his rooms. The quartet finally got the student onto his bed, but in failing to undress him amid the punches Key was dealing, they retreated. When they tried to shut the bedroom door, Key thrust his arms between the door and the post to prevent them. They were left with few options and chose to barricade the door with a sofa, tables and the suchlike. Alone in the dark, Key was quiet and the four men left, locking the outer sitting-room door behind them.

What then appears to have happened is that, the sitting-room door being locked, Key escaped via a window and onto the roof. From there he dropped down onto the staircase by Maughan's room. Confused by Maughan not letting him in, and not realising he had only just escaped from his room, Key decided to return the way he had come. He climbed back out of the window and onto the roof, but there his 'expertise' deserted him and he fell over the parapet to his death in the quad below. The jury concluded the trial by recording a verdict of accidental death.

KNOX'S NO JOKE

During the year 1880 there was a head-on clash between A.E. Knox, the principal of the postmasters (scholars) at Merton College, and five of the college's students. It had started as a practical joke played by the students on a fellow undergraduate. They had removed their friend's bed sheets, but when they were reported to the porter, Knox had summarily expelled the five students. The college's members were stunned and fifty-two of them, including thirteen postmasters, appealed to the college's visitor, Archbishop Tait, but to no effect – and Knox's authority was upheld.

THE ORIEL RAID, AKA THE PICKAXE INCIDENT

For most of its history Oxford was a male-dominated society which only really achieved something approaching equality in the 1970s. When women were formally allowed to study at the University at the beginning of the twentieth century they resided in separate colleges and halls. Men and women alike were subject to curfew at an early hour.

At one time Somerville College (for women) was next to Oriel College (for men). On 19 June 1919 certain members of Oriel decided to enter Somerville College by the shortest route: through the intervening wall. After the liberal use of a pickaxe several undergraduates jumped through the wall into Somerville's quad. They were finally induced to return to Oriel by the college authorities on both sides of the divide.

The commotion had started when the Somerville women dragged bedding into the quad in order to sleep there while the Oriel men, fresh from victory on the river, were celebrating into the night. Upon the inebriated men stumbling into Somerville, the Somerville porter ran for reinforcements, gathering Fellows and the college Warden along the way. The Oriel men ran for cover back through the hole and amid the confusion Viola Garvin seized the pickaxe and darted back to her room with the trophy.

While Somerville's Warden stood on one side of the wall and Oriel's porter on the other, Oriel's Warden's appearance was commanded. The Warden stayed on his own ground, refusing to tackle Somerville's Warden on her home turf and assuring her that all was now quiet, he made a hasty exit back to his lodgings.

The Somerville Warden, being made of sterner stuff, stayed put and organised the college Fellows into an all-night vigil at the hole. She retired to her rooms to swap her second-best hat for her best before returning to sit in front of the hole in an armchair, complete with cushions and coffee, all provided by the students.

What became of the pickaxe? According to one story, after Viola Garvin's assertion that the proof of Oriel's embarrassment, the pickaxe, was in her possession, the Oriel porter came to claim it a few days later. Another story says that Somerville retained the trophy, bringing it out at inter-collegiate debates, presumably to terrify the opposition.

UNRULY CLERGYMEN

Some might say that today's students only drink and sleep, but in the eighteenth century it was very different: they prayed as well. Pastor Moritz, visiting from Germany in 1782, found himself in the Mitre Inn one night and was surprised to see that at midnight, several hours after good Christians should have been in bed, he was surrounded by clergymen of the University. Each one was wearing his gown and bands and was sitting with his pot of beer around a large table. Moritz said that there was often a lot of trouble at the German universities induced by drinking. One of the clergymen said that they were very unruly in Oxford as well, taking a hearty slug of beer and hammering his fist on the table.

Surprisingly, arguments in Oxford were of a religious nature and that evening was no exception. The assembled group even called on a waiter at one point to bring them a Bible in order to settle an argument. The men drank and argued until the sun began to rise. But it was not only day that was about to dawn; swearing, Mr Maud leapt from his chair. He had just remembered that he was due to read the morning prayers at All Souls and rushed off, hopefully arriving before the full complement of the college's members.

THE LUCK OF THE SCOTS

Edward Lhwyd was keeper of the Ashmolean Museum (Broad Street) from 1697 to 1709. During his travels in Scotland he acquired a young boy as his servant from a region north of Knapdale and eventually brought him back to Oxford. It is unclear what the boy's real name was, but he appears as Gilacholuim McMulen on some Ashmolean manuscripts. In the museum account book there appears the heading 'Gilacholuim's sconces or forfeits out of his wages'. These cover the period from 22 October 1703 until the end of 1705, and run to eighty entries, including fines for general absence, neglect of business and drunkenness, with a final entry on 1 January 1707. Perhaps Gilacholuim had learned his lesson by 1706, or more likely his master had given up recording what were almost weekly offences. Lhwyd's patience was not extensive and he was known to explode, but he seemed to have an almost limitless amount when it came to Gilacholuim.

Gilacholuim's list of offences included:

18 December 1704: for playing football during opening hours and leaving the upper study open with one person studying in the gallery and two men working on the lead work. Fined one penny.

19 December 1704: for the same, being absent all morning contrary to being told not to do so. Fined one penny.

For neglecting to make Lhwyd's bed on Easter Monday and Tuesday, or to light a candle on those days; and for staying out on both nights to at least 10 p.m., if not all night; for at least another forty other offences since 28 February 1705, a period of about a month; and, finally, for being absent from work for four months, he was fined £1 10s.

It is not known when Gilacholuim left the museum, though he may have remained until Lhwyd's death. What is certain is that with the last entry in the list of fines his name disappears.

NEW BROOM SWEEPS CLEAN

John London, Warden of New College (1526–42), enforced orthodoxy with an iron fist. His reputation as an odious man stemmed from his own ambitions and his enthusiasm for cleaning out religious 'relics' while he was one of the monastic inspectors appointed by Henry VIII. It was around 1530–32 that one Fellow, Quimbey, with whom he had dealt savagely, was confined in the tower until he died of cold and hunger. Presumably Quimbey had not fitted in with the new ideas on religious thinking. And no matter how extraordinary it may seem today, London actively used astrology to track down other similar offenders.

BY ORDER

In 1674 there was a pub next to Balliol so dingy, horrid and vice-ridden that Dr Good, Warden of the college, thought it fit only for the lowest in the social food chain. Naturally Balliol members went there. Reportedly, Dr Good called them together to lecture them on the evils of beer, telling them that it destroyed body and soul and that they should have nothing more to do with the place. One cheeky Fellow remarked that the Vice-Chancellor's officers drank in another pub, the Split Cow, so why should they not drink? Off Good went, to tell the Vice-Chancellor that his men were setting a bad example and ask that they refrained from drinking beer. But the Vice-Chancellor was a lover of beer and told Good there was no harm in drink and summarily turned the old man out.

Returning to college, Good called his Fellows again. He said he had been to the Vice-Chancellor who had told him there was no harm in beer, that Good truly thought there was, but as he had now been informed to the contrary, and as the Vice-Chancellor allowed his men to drink beer, he gave the Fellows permission to do likewise, so they could now be drunkards by authority.

WASHED AT ROOM TEMPERATURE

Shortly before midnight on 21 January 1661 students of Christ Church entered a room under the hall in college from where they removed all the surplices they could find. They ran to the open toilet block behind Peckwater quad and with sticks rammed the surplices down upon the shit below.

The next day the mischief was discovered and the surplices were pulled out of the toilet and washed. So enraged were the Dean and Canons of Christ Church that they made their protest public, saying that if they found out who had done it, the perpetrators would not only lose their places in college but would also be thrown out of the University. Moreover, they would have their ears cut off. This so pleased the Presbyterian opposition that it was remarked that they would reward the students if they got to them first.

To commemorate this event the 'lamentation of Edward Lowe' was assigned to one Thomas Smith, BA, of Christ Church and read thus:

> Have pitty on us all, good Lairds,
> For surely wee are all uncleane;
> Our surplices are daub'd with tirds,
> And eke we have a shitten Deane.

EDUCATIONAL REFUND

John Bradshaw, originally from Kent, was a student at Christ Church. He was taught by one of the Fellows, John Weeks, whom he paid for his tutoring. On 13 July Bradshaw broke into the loft, crawled across the rafters and climbed down into

Weeks's bedroom from where he removed 25s – perhaps because he felt he was due a refund. It was night and Weeks was in bed. Bradshaw went across the room, hammer in hand, to bludgeon his old tutor to death, but in the process fell over and made such a racket that Weeks woke to find Bradshaw sprawled across the floor.

Bradshaw was taken to the Castle, stood trial and was condemned to be hanged on 27 July, just two weeks after the attempted murder. His sentence was commuted to a year inside shortly before he was due to feel the hangman's noose. Having served his time he went off to be a teacher at a school in Kent.

RING OF FOUR

Smith and Comby were two of four undergraduates of St John's College who were well known for their scandalous behaviour. All four were atheists; they drank heavily and slept with women at every chance. But they were most notorious for their drinking escapades during 1681, when they were often known to go to chapel drunk and vomit into their hats.

TARGET PRACTICE

At the beginning of the twentieth century one father was summoned to remove his son from New College, because he had been caught throwing bottles from the college's new buildings into the windows of the houses on the other side of Holywell Street.

12

A LITTLE KNOWLEDGE IS DANGEROUS

The men's plan was simple: to sell game birds to unsuspecting persons, the sale or purchase of which was illegal without a licence, then to pass on information to the authorities and act as witnesses in the prosecution of the unsuspecting persons. On conviction, the informant would receive a reward from the fines paid.

John Davis of Wheatley gave evidence in court on 22 September 1826 against Edward Boyce for buying six partridges from Davis's associate Richard Munt in St Martin's Parish, contrary to the game laws. When two witnesses proved that Boyce lived in All Saints rather than St Martin's Parish, the charge was deemed incorrect and therefore untrue and was thrown out of court. But the stitching at the seam was starting to come undone. A poulterer, Harris Shayler, returned fire. He laid information against Davis for having game in his possession in the Parish of All Saints; the court was adjourned and all parties were to return on the following Monday to hear the charge. Tempers were frayed – so much so that owing to the ill-feeling being shown towards Munt and Davis they were forced to leave the court under the protection of several police officers – and things were about to get worse.

It was around 11 a.m. and within ten minutes a riot was in progress and the policemen were about as much use as a chocolate fire-guard. Out in the Town Hall yard all hell was breaking loose and the Mayor dispatched several more policemen to investigate the cause. They returned shortly with Davis, clothes dripping wet and face covered in blood. The fact that Munt was unscathed suggests he did not even get as far as the yard before hastily retreating to the safety of the Mayor's office.

Davis began to relate his tale to the Mayor. On leaving the court he had been surrounded by a mob of about 100 people who had eagerly knocked him down and punched him into a pool of water. In gathering him up they had then thrown him through a shop window. To add insult to injury, Davis was forced by the furious shopkeeper to leave his watch to pay for the damage, at which point he was again punched to the ground by the mob and kicked repeatedly in the head. He was then pushed out of the shop and put under the water pump where blows rained down on him while he received a soaking.

For their safety the Mayor directed that the two men be locked in his rooms by the policemen until the angry mob had dispersed. They waited and eventually Munt was the first to try his luck when at 6 p.m. that evening, still under police protection, he walked out of the courthouse and across the yard. There was almost nobody around, but he and his partner had upset one too many people and he was instantly recognised. In a flash he was surrounded by a livid mob who dragged him off in the direction of Magdalen Bridge. This 'diversionary tactic' was a godsend for Davis and he made his exit, slipping away unnoticed and rapidly leaving Oxford.

In contrast, Munt was in the thick of it, still accompanied by his police 'protection', a man named Gardiner. As the rabble passed Carfax, a policeman, James Pavier, saw

them and stepped in to try and sort things out; but the herd carried on. Henry Bell, a
bystander, also attempted to rescue Munt, but he too was drawn into the crowd. By
now the charging populace was screaming 'duck him'. In a last desperate bid for
freedom Munt broke free as they went through St Peter's Parish and dived into a
public house. James Sammons and others followed. Sammons punched Munt in the
face, knocking him to the ground where, in a similar vein to Davis, he was given a
good kicking. The crowd dragged him, bloody and battered, out into the street and
across the stones.

At this point Munt's 'guardian angel', Peter Hope, stepped into view. He took hold
of the victim's arm and supported him as the mob pressed on, jostling and pushing
him forwards. Hope held Munt's coat and offered words of comfort, 'You must be
ducked, and I'll see to it that you are; but if anyone ill-treats you, I'll take your part.'
A second protector stepped in as the rabble passed the Angel Inn: John Noble, a
visitor from Thursby in Leicestershire. Noble struggled against the crowd in vain as
they neared Magdalen Bridge, when they ran down the slope and charged into the
water with Munt. Four men in particular continued to deal out the brutality – Peter
Hope, Adam Chandler, Thomas Cox and James Sammons – while Noble implored
them to stop and was assailed with foul language.

Munt, bleeding profusely and half dead by this point, was being repeatedly
punched by Sammons, which caused him to bleed further. Hope, giving further
'assistance and advice', had convinced Munt to take his coat off. Munt implored
Noble for help and in he rushed, receiving a torrent of abuse. Munt was exhausted
from the struggle and about to collapse. Noble was beaten off and fled across the river
in fear of his own life, followed by Sammons who, at the deepest part, grabbed

*Looking down St Aldate's from Carfax in 1775 to Tom Tower at Christ Church, with the Conduit, left,
and the old Town Hall, right. (OCCPA)*

Oxford's spires from Magdalen Bridge, mid-nineteenth century. The bridge was rebuilt in the 1770s and 80s and widened in 1835 and again in 1882. (OCCPA)

Noble's collar and jumped on him, forcing him under the water. When Noble was finally let up, he made off without looking back, Sammons slinging Noble's hat after him. Munt's motionless body was eventually hauled out of the water and he was left for dead on the riverbank.

At the trial on 26 September Hope, Sammons, Chandler and Cox were charged with inciting a riot, assaulting Richard Munt and attacking him in the River Cherwell near Magdalen Bridge. Sammons was summarily charged with assaulting John Noble. Witnesses proved the involvement of all four men, in particular Sammons who was the most committed and violent of the group. The men made no statements in their defence and were found guilty. Sammons was sentenced to six months, Cox and Chandler to four months. In a slightly bizarre twist Henry Taunton, a policeman, stepped in to speak on behalf of Hope. Several witnesses were brought forward and the jury addressed. Munt stated, as did Taunton and his witnesses, that Hope had assisted Munt and acted in a 'friendly' manner, saying that he had offered Munt more protection than the police. On the same day at the preceding trial Robert Sims stood charged with inciting riots and assaulting John Davis. Sims denied the charge, but called no witnesses. Davis had no clue whether it was Robert Sims who had assaulted him and the jury was forced to acquit Sims of all charges.

13

WATCHMEN 4, DRAPERY MISS 0

The shocking and mysterious murder of 24-year-old Ann Priest, known as Ann Crotchley, was reported in the local paper on 15 December 1827 and a reward of £100 was offered for information leading to the conviction of her murderer.

A few days previously, late on the night of 6 December, Harriet Mitchell had met Ann and the pair had wandered the streets of St Thomas's Parish. Drifting further afield, they arrived at Brasenose College at 11.30 p.m. where they could see a party in progress. The girls called through an open window into the students' room and seven or eight men crowded around the window to catch a glimpse of the two women. Despite being a rowdy affair, reportedly they had no wine when Ann asked for some. Through the window a teapot full of brandy was passed to the girls. Ann gulped down a pint and Harriet polished off the rest of the teapot. Obviously a professional drinker, Ann again demanded wine. Perhaps there was no wine, or perhaps the students were peeved that Ann had cleared them out of brandy, seemingly without effect. Either way the men refused and Ann immediately sprinted off down the street with Harriet in hot pursuit, stopping a night-watchman to ask for directions back to St Thomas's. Just as Harriet caught up, Ann sprinted off again. This time the race led down Blue Boar Street, but Ann never made it to the end; she collapsed and passed out in front of someone's door.

The brandy had now taken effect on Harriet. She staggered to the corner of the street, where she was found at midnight by a passer-by, Richard Llewellyn. As Harriet swayed in the breeze and laughed hysterically at a joke nobody had made, Llewellyn asked her what she was up to. Truthful to the last, Harriet said she had been drinking brandy and was drunk.

Meanwhile, Joseph Hedges was returning home from his job as porter at St Mary's Hall (now Oriel) with his servant James Champ when they found Ann slumped in front of their house. Hedges dragged her into a passageway before leaving to find help. He met Llewellyn and Harriet further down the street and asked if they had seen a watchman. Harriet implored them not to go for a watchman, saying the girl was her friend and would not do any harm.

By now Hedges, Champ and Harriet had been joined by Richard Field, a watchman, and John Williams, a local painter. They looked at Ann, who was sprawled across the passageway, hat off, apron in the gutter. Llewellyn told Field he should take Ann to his watch box, and Field bluntly spat out that he would see her damned rather than look after her. So Llewellyn suggested to Williams that the pair of them carry Ann home. Williams declined and instead offered Field a shilling to do it. All of a sudden Field was motivated and ready to assist. They got Ann to her feet, but she was too heavy and they dumped her back in the street. Field concluded that he needed a wheelbarrow, which was the cue for people to start disappearing.

The watchman left to find a barrow. Hedges and Champ went inside their house and Llewellyn wandered off. Now 12.30 a.m., it was left to Harriet and Williams to

New Inn Hall Street, 1836, showing New Inn Hall to the right and St Peter-le-Bailey at the far end. (OCCPA)

tend to Ann. But Harriet was impatient and went off to find Ann's landlord, who she had decided should be brought to take Ann home. A drunken Harriet staggered off, but passed out in the middle of New Inn Hall Lane, only to be woken some time later by a watchman. It was the end of the evening's exertions for Harriet; the watchman took her back to her lodgings and Harriet had no recollection of what happened after she had left Williams.

In his wanderings, Field met Anthony Cromwell, another watchman, as well as Esther Simpson and Maria Burley, two ladies taking the night air . . . and possibly some customers along the way. Simpson and Burley were the first to go rubbernecking and found Williams with Ann, who was comatose with her petticoats up around her knees.

A moment later Llewellyn turned up again. The girls only stayed five minutes and when they left Llewellyn went with them. Time passed and Cromwell turned up at 1 a.m. Williams told him that he had been alone for twenty minutes. Making a second pass at 1.30 a.m., Cromwell found Williams exiting via the High Street some 150yd away from Ann. Williams was beating a retreat, saying he had had enough and was going home. Minutes later Cromwell was back with Ann, still unconscious. As there was no change the watchman left.

Field returned about 2 a.m., but without a barrow; Ann had not regained consciousness. When Field left he bumped into Cox, yet another watchman. The story of Ann was related to Cox and the men departed. But minutes later Cox came

The eastern end of the High Street in the nineteenth century showing University College, left, the spire of All Saints (now Lincoln College library), centre, and the spire of St Mary the Virgin. (OCCPA)

running up to Field yelling that there was blood – Ann was dying. Field finally located a barrow and ran back to Ann. Somewhere along the way Cromwell was collected. Now soaked in blood and lifeless, Ann's rag doll of a body was lifted by the men into the barrow. They were assisted by Ebbin, another watchman. Ann was wheeled home and left in front of the fire for her landlady Mrs Cox to care for, but Cox retired to her bed.

Ann's groans brought Mrs Cox downstairs. She noticed Ann was bleeding and had lost a great deal of blood. Field, concerned for Ann's well-being, had awoken Mr Dickeson, a doctor. Field saw Dickeson leave for Ann's at 4 a.m. and watched him as he returned home at 5 a.m. Ann had been a bloody mess for hours by now, but it took twenty minutes of hammering on the Coxes' door for Dickeson to get a response. Hanging out of a bedroom window, Cox asked Dickeson what he wanted. To see Ann, of course, but Cox said Ann was only drunk and anyway she was usually brought home in that state. When Dickeson left, Cox went to Ann and asked if she had been 'misused'. Ann told Cox she had, by a man, but she did not know who it was. Well, who would after a pint of brandy?

It was not until 8 a.m., when Ann's condition had worsened, that Cox sent for the doctor. Dickeson saw Ann, but he could find no external wound to account for the massive blood loss. He was puzzled. Ann was conscious, but weak, so he left and returned that evening. Dickeson's diagnosis was poisoning. Ann's symptoms, however, were more attributable to a hangover and blood loss. Leeches were applied, medicine given, but Ann died the following morning at 2 a.m. Dickeson carried out a post-mortem and found two 2in internal cuts in a very delicate area. The wounds had been delivered with a strong thrust.

At the coroner's inquest held the next day, a verdict of 'murder against an unknown person' was pronounced. The finger of suspicion had been pointed at John Williams, and at one point he was dragged in off the streets and into court to answer questions. The magistrates sat on numerous occasions to hear witnesses. The papers were rife with the story of Ann's murder and a reward of £100 was offered on 15 December. Somebody suggested that Ann had died after a blood vessel had ruptured as a result of drinking brandy. This 'interesting' idea led to confusion; could this have been the cause of Ann's death? To answer the question the best medical minds in town were consulted and Ann's body was exhumed, but nothing altered. Meanwhile Williams had been held in gaol. The University offered a further reward of £100 on 22 December. There was no doubt that if the case went to court there was insufficient evidence to convict Williams, but the magistrates had to try something and so they questioned Williams repeatedly.

The examinations continued throughout December, but nothing new was found. The magistrates thought they had a breakthrough when Henry Bell came forward. Bell was a juror at the original inquest and his mother washed for John Williams.

£100 Reward.
CITY OF OXFORD.

AT a MEETING of the MAGISTRATES, holden This Day, it appeared that a Coroner's Inquest was taken yesterday, in the parish of St. Thomas, on view of the body of ANN CROTCHLEY, a young woman who died on Saturday last, at her lodgings, whither she was conveyed by some Watchmen at an early hour on Friday morning, from a passage in Blue Boar-lane, being found there apparently in a state of intoxication, and bleeding profusely. The Jury found a verdict of Wilful Murder by some Person or Persons unknown; and it appearing, upon the testimony of two Surgeons, that the death was occasioned by a wound inflicted with a sharp instrument on the body of the deceased, a Reward of ONE HUNDRED POUNDS is hereby offered to any person who will give such information as shall lead to the discovery and conviction of the atrocious offender or offenders, to be paid by the Treasurer of the City of Oxford.

JOHN HICKMAN, Mayor.

Oxford, Dec. 11th, 1827.

A reward notice for information leading to the conviction to Ann Crotchley's murderer or murderers was advertised by the city authorities in 1827. (Jackson's Oxford Journal)

Henry had noticed a shirt of Williams's at his mother's that had red marks on the cuffs, which he thought was blood. Everyone was called back in front of the magistrates. Mary Bell was brought in, but she told the court that Williams, who was a painter, often left shirts with her which had coloured marks on the cuffs and that she thought that the shirt in question just had red paint on it. This was not the only possible explanation, as Williams wore a red band around his wrist for support, having previously strained it, which might have accounted for any marks on the cuffs. It was a further blow to the prosecution. On the evening of the murder Williams had been involved in a punch-up at the City Arms, which can only have added to the prosecution's case to bill Williams as the murderer. Eventually bail was set at £500 for Williams with an additional two sureties each for £250.

The final act was played out in court on 14 January 1828 when all the evidence was heard again and the witnesses re-examined. Although the murderer was still at large and never to be found, the case did report one gem concerning the caution which should be exercised when accepting the testimony of the 'lower classes'. Mrs Cox said she had seen Williams in her house a week before the murder, and had just seen him in court. In fact, it was proved that Williams was not in court that day and the man she had pointed out was a London reporter who had just arrived in Oxford.

Williams seems to have been a convenient target, but there were occasions when he was alone with Ann and could have murdered her. There was also the strange behaviour of Llewellyn, who returned a second time and left rapidly. Did he return undetected one final time and murder Ann?

14

TRIALS, PUNISHMENTS AND LARKING AROUND

BONE OF CONTENTION

During the 1650s Mr Addison was a student at Queen's College when, as a joke, a bone was thrown at him during dinner and he 'had his eye accidentally struck out'. Later, as Dean of the college, he was shunned for the unwise social move of marrying a chef's widow who had neither money nor beauty or status.

Maybe love was blind, but the college authorities were not and Addison ended his days in a low-paid job as the clergyman for Hampton Poyle near Oxford.

JUSTICE, THE SIDESHOW

Two Richards, Mansfield and Dancer, aged 20 and 19 respectively, were about to be executed on the morning of 21 March 1755 for the theft of 2*s* and a brass counter-weight. The prison cart that would take the men to their destiny waited outside the gaol.

What was to be the thieves' most notable hour was hijacked by a dog. As the men stepped out of the gaol, a bulldog wrapped its teeth around the carthorse's throat and the frightened animal bolted, bulldog still attached, crashing through the crowd that had assembled to see off Mansfield and Dancer. The men were sidelined and all that was reported were the casualties caused by the bolting horse; none was spared: the elderly, women and children were all bruised and battered.

THE THIEF FINGERED

At the foot of Folly Bridge, in 1768, lived Mrs Parker who having lost several fowl, lost her patience as well. As a preventative measure she placed tenterhooks where she supposed the thief must climb over into her garden. Looking at the hooks the following morning, Sunday 3 January, she found the little finger of a man and a considerable amount of blood. She went into town to see if anybody had seen a man requiring medical assistance for a missing finger, but came back empty-handed, presumably as did the thief.

CLATTERING THROUGH THE STREETS

As dusk fell on 3 March 1770 Henry Brown was sitting in his cell. Brown was incarcerated in the Castle gaol awaiting transportation. When the time came to lock up, it was the governor's daughter who went round the cells, her father being absent. Brown saw his chance, grabbed the keys and forced them from the girl's hand. With his cellmate in tow, he used the keys to break out of the prison. There was only one problem: the noise he made as he clattered through the city streets in his iron fetters. Brown was finally jumped outside Wadham College and promptly taken to gaol; his accomplice, presumably less noisy, escaped. Brown, much to his chagrin, was clamped in heavy irons on his return to a cell.

TOO MUCH WIFE TO BEAR

In June 1775 Thomas Hilborne was serving a six-month sentence in the Castle gaol for assault and had been indicted to stand trial for aiding a fellow prisoner in her escape from the Bridewell. Hilborne was a man obsessed with escaping; he had cut his way nearly through the walls when confined in the dungeon before being caught. On other occasions Hilborne had forced a window frame on the north side of the prison and had knocked through the wall in a gatehouse room in order to fix a rope and climb down the outer wall.

This time he was confined in St George's Tower, a tall building. In order to escape, Hilborne needed to know how far down it was from the cell. So he bet his other cellmates as to their height from the ground and 75ft was fixed upon. Hilborne managed to buy pieces to construct a 60ft-long rope and figured this would be enough. With the rope fixed in place, he broke out and began his descent of the tower's outer wall. In broad daylight he moved downwards, watched by several locals, but after 8 or 9ft the rope snapped and Hilborne plummeted into a neighbouring garden. The onlookers rushed to the house and into the garden where he was found to be conscious, but his limbs were a tangled mass. Having sustained major internal injuries, Hilborne did not see the day out.

His reason for being so desperate to escape? He had two wives, still both alive and well. Hilborne had previously told a fellow prisoner that escape was his only chance to avoid being hanged. Perhaps he was hoping to evade conviction for bigamy to add to his ever-increasing list of crimes, or maybe he just wished to avoid both his wives.

A TIGHT SQUEEZE

On the night of 14 October 1776 Elizabeth Boswell and Rebecca Hall waited at their window. Outside, the iron bars to their cell were cut away by accomplices atop a ladder and the two women, one after the other, were dragged out through the 17in by 12in gap. It was a particularly remarkable escape because the 21-year-old Hall was heavily pregnant at the time. An advertisement for their return was placed in the local paper with a reward of 10 guineas for Boswell (who stooped) and 5 guineas for Hall (who was missing several teeth). Boswell had been previously sentenced to death along with her common-law husband, James Corbett, for a robbery at Beckley. Upon James's execution Elizabeth had been upset that she had not been put out of her misery at the same time, having had her sentence commuted to fourteen years' transportation.

Boswell was captured by locals in Tetsworth on 3 February 1777. She was returned to Solomon Wisdom, the governor of the Castle gaol, who duly paid her captors the 10 guineas' reward. But Hall was never found.

On the night of 2 February 1778 Boswell escaped a second time. The escape was even more audacious than her first attempt, since this time she was assisted by two highwayman prisoners. Their long premeditated plan was put into effect. Boswell was confined alone in the sickroom, next door to where Thacker and Jones, the highwaymen, resided with four other prisoners in the condemned cell. This group was heavily secured by two sets of doors to their cell, both of which were fastened with two bolts, and the outer door also had a strong lock. Thacker had for some time feigned illness in order to be close to Boswell's cell, where he had sawed almost through the staple of the lock to her cell. Likewise he had sawn through the box staple on the outer door to the condemned cell. Both these he had plastered over to prevent his handiwork being discovered by the prison guards. Soon after being locked up Boswell forced her own cell door. She moved rapidly to the condemned cell and unbolted the outer door. She forced the lock and finally, unbolting the inner door, released Thacker and Jones. As they dashed out they bolted the inner door to prevent them being inconvenienced by their cellmates, who no doubt would have been happy of the chance to escape.

Sitting on the floor, they cut their fetters away, then began work. They chipped away at the wall until they finally forced their way through the tower on the west side of the felons' yard level with the high outer gaol wall. Knotting the bed sheets they had removed from their respective beds, they lowered themselves down and over the iron-spiked outer wall into a garden adjoining the Castle ditch and got clean away.

Again, a reward for their capture was advertised in the paper for the three of them, all in their 20s: 5 guineas for each of the men and 2 guineas for Boswell. Only 2 guineas? Boswell must have felt undervalued. On 26 February Boswell was again returned to the gaol. This time it was by a young man who had caught her at Wantage. Boswell related to the authorities that on the night of their escape she and her accomplices had slept in a haystack in a field near Wantage. Thacker and Jones had adopted cunning disguises: Thacker had tied his hair back with a false pony tail and Jones had tied his hair up in curls. This would surely be enough to outwit the police. And it did for about four months until Thacker was captured in London by two local policemen. He was finally taken to be tried at the Berkshire Assizes for robbing, with his former partner Richard Latham, the landlord of the Bear at Henley. Latham had been executed at the previous Lent Assizes while Thacker was still on the run. Ominously, as Thacker was transported back from London the horse-drawn carriage broke down as it went through Henley, directly opposite his prosecutor's house.

Though no more mention is made of Boswell, it can only be assumed that, further bungled escapes notwithstanding, he was finally transported. Jones was eventually captured and along with Thacker sentenced to hard labour on the Thames.

A BRIDGE TOO FAR

James Hanks, an Oxford labourer, was imprisoned in the Castle gaol on 14 August 1793. He was incarcerated on suspicion of having burgled the lodgings of the Warden of New Inn Hall. During the break-in he is said to have stolen 25yd of Irish cloth, 3 guineas, two silver shoe buckles and four silver spoons, among other items. He was also charged with having stolen two watches from Mr Denton in Oxford.

On 20 August Hanks was in the gaol's day room. He managed to break through the grating that enclosed the room. From here he scaled the boundary wall nearest the Castle mill. Dropping down into a garden, he ran across it and away. A reward of 10 guineas was advertised for his return. The escaped prisoner was caught at a pub in Woodstock on 12 November. He was returned to gaol the next day by the person who had recognised him in Woodstock.

Rather than disappearing while on the run, Hanks had stayed in the area and taken a job in the service of a local gentleman. Cheekily, Hanks had made regular visits to Oxford during this period. On the day he was caught he had travelled by coach to the city in the early morning. Eating breakfast at the Cross Inn, Hanks told people he was on his way to Worcester to disguise his real destination, Woodstock. This was a gutsy move since he was well known at Woodstock and it proved to be his undoing. Yet, when confronted there, he said he was Smith with such confidence that even his accuser doubted who Hanks really was.

But the man detained Hanks all the same. Mr Smith, an Oxford policeman, was sent for. Smith came quickly and identified Hanks before he was sent back to Oxford gaol.

Hanks was tried on 5 March 1794 and found guilty of robbing the Revd Mr Friend, Warden of New Inn Hall, and also stealing two watches from Mr Denton in All Saints' Parish. Hanks was then sentenced to be transported to Botany Bay for seven years and taken from the Castle gaol to the Woolwich hulks on Friday 23 May 1794 to await his cruise.

PERJURY AND PILLORY

John Tubb was sentenced to twelve months' imprisonment and to stand in the Oxford marketplace pillory the next market day for one hour. This was his punishment for making a false statement that he had been robbed of cash at Mr Beasley's, barge master, in Oxford, for which Beasley had been tried and convicted at the previous Assizes.

SAFE AND SECURE

On his usual rounds Mr Wyatt, governor of the gaol, went to lock up the prisoners. Awaiting his approach were four prisoners armed with bludgeons and, jumping out at the unarmed man, one swung a heavy blow. Wyatt dodged, turned and ran. The men followed in hot pursuit, yelling 'murder him'. Wyatt ran for his life. Ducking behind one of the heavy iron doors, he managed to close it, stopping the men's progress.

KEEPING THE FAITH

James Bannister of Shillingford was charged at the Oxford Assizes on 5 July 1815 with the murder of his wife. Bannister pleaded guilty. The judge coaxed him to rescind his plea. Bannister obstinately refused. He said he had made his peace with God and was prepared to die. He had a long history of depression, which is maybe why the judge urged him to reverse his plea; it would allow for leniency in sentencing. Bannister had suspected his wife had had an affair and passed on the clap to him. After brooding over this for many months he slit her throat on 19 June. Bleeding profusely and covered in blood, his wife had staggered out of their house. She died in the street a few yards from their front door in full view of passers-by. Immediately Bannister slashed his own throat, but it was a half-hearted attempt and he survived. A few days before his trial he was examined and was found to be weakened from blood loss. When the day of execution came he was examined one final time and was still very weak, but not so frail that they could not hang him.

On 10 July at 8 a.m. Bannister was executed outside the gaol and, after hanging for the usual time, his body was cut down and delivered to the anatomy school at Christ Church for dissection. He left two children to lament the death of both their parents.

HONOUR AMONG THIEVES

William Clack was born at Blackbourton, Oxfordshire, into a farming family, but on the death of his mother in 1822 they moved to Great Milton. It was his mother's dying wish that he look after his younger siblings of 3 and 7 years, which he endeavoured to do. At this time, having some surplus cash, they bought two horses and sold them at a profit, and William and his father decided to set up their own business. William attended the fairs and bought all he could. They prospered until, at one fair, William was robbed of £40 by a pickpocket. His father was furious and his anger was compounded by the fact that William was involved with a woman of whom his father disapproved, all of which led to a great deal of unpleasantness at home.

In the two and a half years that followed William's loss he found that his happier moments were away from home. Yet he still endeavoured to assist the family and worked hard in order to send his younger siblings to school, though he spent most of his time in public houses and even took all of his meals there. But the relationship with his father deteriorated and after returning on one occasion at 1 a.m. from a fair in Oxford a blazing row ensued.

The row must have preyed on his mind, for instead of going to a fair in Wales the next day he seemed distracted, arose late, and wandered around the neighbourhood all day and into the evening, when he sat down in the woods and decided to commit suicide. Just as he was about to slash his throat with his razor, a stranger walked up and distracted him. He drank his way through Eynsham and on to Witney. On a street in Witney he bumped into a man he recognised from the fairs and they went to drink together, but this fateful meeting was to be the beginning of the end for William.

It was not long before his companion steered the conversation to the business of stealing. William would have had an excellent opportunity to sell stolen horses, moving freely and widely among the iron works as he did, and the profits were much larger. He was hooked and agreed to take possession of a horse formerly belonging to one Mr Thomas Lewis. Soon after he formed a similar relationship with a man from Wales.

On 19 September in Abingdon Clack was prevented from selling a horse when someone said they thought it was stolen. He left the fair with Mr Edwards and spent the night at his house at Ramsden. The next morning, as he was standing on the doorstep about to leave, he was introduced to the young Mr Staley. 'Are you Clack of Milton?' 'Yes.' Mr Staley had an arrest warrant for him for the theft of his father's horse: He knew exactly where the horse was hidden; no one could know this save the man who had sold him the horse in the first place, the man whom Clack had met in Witney and entered into an agreement with to fence horses.

Clack was taken to Witney gaol that day and later traced by Mr Lewis. He was stuffed. The police found three stolen horses, one each belonging to Mr Lewis, Mr Staley and Thomas Bowen, and he was taken to Oxford gaol to await trial. Clack stood trial at the Lent Assizes on 4 March 1826 where he was charged with three counts of horse stealing. Found guilty of all three charges, he was sentenced to death. After his condemnation he was attended daily by the chaplain, but not by his relatives even though they all lived within a few miles of Oxford; not even his brother or sister whom he had worked so hard to support, nor the woman of whom his father had so disapproved who was now pregnant with William's child. It was left to an uncle, who came one Saturday, just days before his execution, to settle William's affairs, but finding he had no property the uncle left.

On 20 March, at a little before 7 a.m., Clack was taken alone from his cell to the waiting chaplain who gave him the sacrament and offered him consolation in his last moments. The chapel bell began to toll just before 8 a.m., when the executioner was introduced into the room. William thanked the chaplain and the prison governor for their kindness, was led out, and following the executioner ascended the gallows platform, where he read a pamphlet declaring his innocence. 'He then shook hands with the executioner, and all things being ready, the drop fell, and closed his earthly career.'

RUDE, CRUDE AND LEWD

During the first week of March 1826, Carl Joseph Ostwald was charged with offering for sale obscene pictures and paintings within the confines of Oxford University. The judge and Mr Cross, for the prosecution, both spoke of 'the enormity of the offence', talking at great length about the 'evil consequences likely to follow the dissemination of such vile productions'. There were three such charges against Oswald and he was sentenced to one year's imprisonment for each, and at the expiration of the three years to enter into his own recognisance for £100 for his future good behaviour. Possibly rather gallingly, Simon Rosenstein was acquitted on the same day for an identical offence.

REPEAT OFFENCE

Thomas Cavendish of Friar's Entry who, in 1826, frequently annoyed his neighbours with his drunk and disorderly conduct and who, moreover, was known to beat his wife when in this state, was finally tried on 30 September. He was found guilty of being drunk on the previous Sunday and fined 5*s*, but, not being able to pay this, he was committed to the stocks for six hours. Unfortunately the punishment did not quite have the desired effect, as he went directly home and took it out on his wife by giving her a good thrashing. The following morning he was taken to prison to stand trial at the next sessions for assaulting his wife.

A DAMNED GOOD LARK

On 11 September, during the St Giles's fair of September 1826, Mary Brown, niece to the landlord of the Eagle and Child, received half a sovereign in payment for a pot of beer from Mr Abbey. She was directed to take the beer and change to Mr Abbey's

Folly Bridge, 1829, with Friar Bacon's study at its southern end. The bridge crosses the Isis and links St Aldate's to Grandpont. (OCCPA)

uncle's booth at the fair and on her arrival there she asked who was to have the change. A man stuck out his hand and said, 'It is mine', taking 9s 5d and the beer. At 6 a.m. the next morning Josiah West bumped into Thomas Walklin by Folly Bridge. Walklin told West that he had had a 'damned good lark' the night before by pocketing the change and receiving beer into the bargain. Thereafter he and four mates went down George Street and spent the remaining cash. In court the evening's events were presented and Walklin was put on remand for further questioning, and that was the last that was reported of the case.

THE TABLES ARE TURNED

John West, a farmer from Northmoor, turned up in the Anchor Inn on Cornmarket at 10 a.m. one November morning in 1829. Beer was had and cards were introduced. West was plied with drink. He played with the landlord, John Wharton, and another man, who, in record time, managed to clear West out of his cash, his watch, coats, gun and even his silk handkerchief. West was none too happy and decided to get recompense, for which he went to the magistrates and gave evidence. A case was instigated against Wharton for illegal gambling, which came to court, but West failed to appear as a witness and the case fell apart, Wharton walking out of court a free man. The court was unimpressed and West was soon charged with failing to appear. He was convicted on 24 November and fined £10. West was unable to pay, and was sent to gaol for three months.

HARD LABOUR FOR BREAD

In February 1830 Charles Streick, a pauper in the workhouse, fancied he had not had his daily allowance of bread and went directly to the master. Berating and threatening the master, Streick left and set out about inciting the other inmates to mutiny. For this act of defiance Streick was taken to court on 22 February. The workhouse rule was that if any inmate was to refuse to work, be guilty of drunkenness or any other misbehaviour, he would be sentenced to twenty-one days' hard labour. Streick was led away to the gaol to begin his sentence.

A LUCKY ESCAPE

Mr Haldon Jr, was walking home at 9.30 p.m. on 22 October 1831. When he reached the bottom of Beaumont Street a woman came up to him and got his attention; she punched him in the face and poked her fingers in his eyes. Having his hands in his coat pockets and an umbrella under his arm, he was rather unprepared and the woman proceeded to rip off his waistcoat pocket, which contained 7s 6d. Collecting himself, he went to grab hold of her, but was struck from behind by a male accomplice and fell to the ground. The muggers ran off in different directions.

Haldon, assisted by Holloway, the University marshal, searched the streets for an hour before they found the woman. Spotting her near St Martin's Church, Haldon waited for her to pass him under a lamp so he could get a good look at her in the light. Unfortunately, no sooner had she noticed him than she made a break for it, running across the street and up a passage. Haldon now went for Clark, a University police officer, who eventually collared her on Cornmarket. Turning her pockets out, the policeman only found 1s 6d and a few halfpennies on her. On examination it turned out that her name was Ann Hurcomb and her defence was that she had been in a local pub the whole evening. The landlady of the pub was brought in, who said

St Martin's (Carfax) Church in 1827, of which only the tower remains, was situated on the corner of Queen Street and Cornmarket (right). (OCCPA)

Hurcomb had been there drinking brandy with a man. However, Clark stated that he had seen Ann on Beaumont Street around the time of the robbery and blew her alibi clean out of the water.

At her trial in the first week of 18 January 1832 Ann again stated that she was not in Beaumont Street and had never seen Haldon before. She stood charged with assault and robbery, but being found guilty only of the assault Ann was acquitted as the whole charge was not proved. All that the judge could do was reprimand and discharge her.

YOU CANNOT BE SERIOUS

George George was brought before the Mayor on 18 February 1834, charged with stealing a hat from the head of Charles Leach. On Saturday 23rd, as Mr Leach crossed Magdalen Bridge, George was with two other people when he turned, snatched the hat and ran away. The hat was later found in St Clement's churchyard.

Leach had walked after George and, obtaining a policeman along the way, eventually collared him. When stopped, George asked Leach if he really was intending to have him charged with stealing the hat. Leach said no, he had not yet, but immediately got the policeman to arrest him since he did not take it as a joke. At trial in April George was found not guilty, as his intent was not a criminal one. Obviously the court was more favourably humoured than Mr Leach.

NEGLECT

A coroner's inquest was held on 12 September 1836 in the Lamb and Flag in St Thomas's on the body of Maria Wright, who had died the previous evening during childbirth while at home. The case was the focus of media attention as the local residents were pointing the finger of blame not at childbirth, a risky business, but at Maria's husband Charles, saying she had died of starvation and ill-treatment at his hands. During the case it transpired that Maria had, on several occasions, applied for warrants against her husband after he had kicked, beaten and thrown her out into the street. Charles was an alcoholic, who spent what little money the family had on drink. Maria had been taken pity on by Mr Bossom, one of the guardians of the United Parishes. Bossom gave her money and food from the poor funds, and even on occasions listened to Maria's tales of brutality, even when her husband was present in the house. So inhumane was her treatment that on one occasion when she was confined to her bed because of illness, Charles had ordered his 14-year-old son to set the family dog on her to pull her out of bed, and she was forced to defend herself against the vicious dog with a candlestick. The jury's verdict was that Maria had died owing to the 'Visitation of God', but that her death was greatly accelerated by the ill-usage, brutality and neglect inflicted on her by her husband, saying that they regretted the fact that they were not able to punish him, excepting their ability to condemn his conduct.

DANGEROUS AND IDLE

Sitting in Mr Astley's pub in St Peter-le-Bailey at 3 p.m. on the afternoon of 8 October 1836 was William Hargrave. Placed on the table was a bundle of sixty pairs of stockings which Hargrave had been selling in the city's pubs that day. When John Weston came in he went up to Hargrave, and asked him how much he wanted for the lot. 'Nothing at all,' Hargrave said and Weston remarked, 'Well then, I'll go and sell them', picked them all up and left the pub. Five minutes later Weston returned and plonked them down in front of Hargrave before turning around and strolling out of the pub.

It was not until later when Hargrave came to sell another pair that he noticed that two pairs were missing. Thinking back, he remembered Weston's brother standing outside Astley's. The penny dropped and John was arrested. In court on 26 October Mr Astley, among others, said Weston was an honest man, but prone to 'larking' around. Even Hargrave said he thought John was just messing around, which is why he did not follow him when Weston took the bundle away. Weston was found not guilty, but the judge commented on his 'larking' and told him to 'leave off such dangerous and idle practices'.

A SMASHING TIME

Jane Jones and Drucilla Cox faced a charge of misconduct in court during February 1845. Their accuser was the master of the Headington workhouse. The two girls had been committed to the workhouse on an unrelated offence. They were confined to a cell without light, heat or a chair in a room with a brick floor. There they spent ten hours before panic set in. They thought they were near the morgue and being frightened tore the plaster down from the walls with their bare hands. The magistrates were particularly astonished by the fact that they did not even have a chair to sit on. Feeling that the girls had suffered enough, they were sentenced only to seven days' imprisonment, rather than the usual month.

ALL RIGHT JACK

Preston and Saunders, prisoners in the hospital wing of the Castle gaol, were discovered missing on 21 August 1846. The men had cut up sheets and bedding and let themselves down into the yard. An immediate search was made and Preston was found wandering around the exercise yard. It seems that Saunders, having been helped over the boundary wall by Preston, had legged it across Mr Tawney's garden and away, leaving Preston stuck on the other side.

Men were dispatched to find Saunders. They searched all the lodging houses and brothels in St Thomas's and even the drains and sewers. Meanwhile, Preston was returned to his cell and clamped in irons. Nothing more was heard of Saunders, though presumably he now had one less friend.

WHAT'S MINE IS MINE ALONE

In June 1849 Thomas Stone who worked for Mr Johnson, the wheelwright in George Street, was charged with beating his wife and stripping her of her clothes. The couple had been married a year and a half and Stone did not deny the charge. He considered he had the right to do what he wanted that which what he owned, i.e. his wife, and if he thought beating his wife would improve her manners he would do so. Likewise he felt equally at liberty to take away her clothes should he choose, as he considered that what was his was his and what was hers was also his. The magistrates told him he was wrong, that it was unjustifiable that he should beat her, and only a brute would strike a defenceless woman. They bailed him in the amount of £26 to keep the peace for twelve months, to which he strongly objected, saying that it was harder still to swallow that 'he could not thrash his wife, when he thought she would be all the better for it'.

THE AGE OF FLOGGING

A stout pauper named Willis was charged with flogging two boys who were over 14 years old in the workhouse on 24 September 1849. The flogging was ordered by the master, but he was not present when the punishment was meted out. For this the magistrates reprimanded the master, and for the fact that the flogging was so severe. The regulations required that the master or the schoolmaster conduct any flogging, and only with instruments 'approved' by the board. Willis said that he was ordered to flog the boys by the master as the schoolmaster said that he could not flog them severely enough. The regulations also stated that corporal punishment should not be administered to a boy above 14 years of age. The magistrates pronounced it a disgraceful case that they could not turn a blind eye to, as they were determined not to allow boys of such a tender age to be flogged in such an unmerciful manner. They fined Willis 20s and costs, which seems to miss the point slightly, since it was the master and the schoolmaster who imposed the punishment of flogging and it was only incidental that Willis was the person to actually carry it out.

A LITTLE WARMTH

David Roberts, an inmate of the Headington workhouse, was in court on 29 January 1848 charged with breaking down the door to his room. Roberts was in the lock-up for twenty-four hours and in his defence said he was kicking the door to keep himself warm.

The cell where Roberts was confined had a stone floor. It was too small to lie down in and with no roof was open to the elements. Roberts said he was perished, but the workhouse's master said there were enough blankets 'to make one comfortable'. Dr Harrington, an expert witness, disagreed, saying that the master had strange notions of 'comfort'. The defence commented that the master would have been placed in an 'awkward' situation had Roberts died during the cold winter's night.

The bench remarked that the cells were unfit for confining inmates, describing the room as a 'hole' and, noting that somebody had died recently at the Slough workhouse under similar circumstances, recommending leniency. Roberts, however, was found guilty, but sentenced only to one week's hard labour in gaol. Perhaps this kept him warmer.

IN THE CALL OF DUTY

During the Assizes of 12 July 1849 Mr Rogers, a hall-keeper for the Town Hall, headed for the court's public gallery to open the windows. On reaching the top of the stairs he found the door shut. Pulling it ajar, Rogers saw a javelin-man (a foot soldier who carried a javelin or light spear) and Mr Powell, who had his hand firmly on the door. Rogers asked to go up as he needed to open the windows, but Powell refused and a determined Rogers yanked at the door three or four times before it flew open and he went sailing backwards down to the bottom of the stairs. Rogers then rushed back up and argued with Powell, who put his hand on Rogers's chest, and shoved him back down the stairs a second time. Rogers flew at Powell and it took a policeman to separate the men as they took each other to task.

In court on 24 July Powell said he had his orders and was merely complying with them. The judge said that Powell had seen it was the hall keeper who wanted access and suggested that Powell make an apology, which Rogers should accept to end the matter. Rogers said he was happy with that, but Powell refused to apologise, saying it was Rogers who was at fault and he could prove it. The bench said that Powell had exceeded his duty and as he refused to apologise they ordered him to pay a fine of 5s plus 11s costs.

15

BODY BEHIND THE TOILET

John Wheeler was a shepherd to Mr Costar, a farmer at Littlemore, and lived with his wife and three children near the Stadhampton road, about 1 mile from both Cowley and Littlemore. The cottage's nearest neighbour was Richard Humphry, about 1 furlong away.

At 7 p.m. on the evening of 4 March 1829, as dusk was drawing in, John Wheeler was at the end of his garden digging at the back of his privy with the intention of clearing it out. A ditch ran 5ft behind it. After half an hour the hole was 18in deep when, with a crunch, John's spade struck something wrapped and sewn up in cloth. Undoing the stitching, he unwrapped it, dropped the parcel back into the hole and ran back to the house yelling for his wife, Sarah. It was a few minutes before she arrived. John was alarmed, very pale and could not talk. Sarah asked him what was wrong, but he could not tell her. She told him to speak to his mother, Mary, who that evening was visiting from Dorchester.

John related his tale: he had been digging to clear the privy and struck a large bone. Putting his spade in again he discovered it to be a parcel. Mary went with him down the garden to the hole, and John again lifted the bundle; blood could clearly be seen. Mary was startled and said he should go for the parish constable, and that he should bring the bundle into the house and have somebody else present when it was unwrapped. John left the house.

When he returned he said he had been to Richard Humphry's, who was not at home, though he made no mention of trying to find Thomas Hedges, the parish constable. On entering the house, he was met by his mother and wife. He looked at his wife; her expression said it all. He said from the look on her face that she must have an idea what the bundle was and asked Sarah the same, saying that if she did know, he would leave her for good. John unwrapped the parcel before them to reveal the body of a new-born boy. Placing the body back in its shallow grave, he buried it and left it there until the following morning.

John told some other neighbours that night about the bundle and the next morning he dug up the body before John Castle and William Phipps and took it into the house to examine it further. He noted that the child was secured in a towel with brown paper wrapped round it. Wheeler suspected a woman who had visited with her husband on 24 February, a week before the discovery. He thought she was the mother of the dead child, as she had arrived with a mysteriously large bundle.

The couple in question were Hannah and William Cadel; Hannah was the sister of Sarah Wheeler. William had first met Hannah in August 1828 and John at around Christmas that year. John commented that she appeared to be 'somewhat lusty'. Hannah was 28 and single, but linked to William by this time and the two were married on 5 February 1829. They moved to the house of William's grandmother, Elizabeth Dickeson, at Toot Baldon, ten days later. It was when John had first met Hannah that he suspected she was 'in the family way'. Sarah had joked about it in

Hannah's presence. During her time in Toot Baldon, Mrs Dickeson said that she had not known Hannah before she arrived, having only met her once before in August 1828, and that Hannah kept to herself and did not go out among their neighbours.

On 24 February Hannah and William Cadel set out from their house to Hannah's sister, Sarah Wheeler, at Littlemore, William carrying a large bundle. Elizabeth and William had understood it to contain dirty washing, though neither had seen the contents. Elizabeth had advised Hannah to wash William's clothes, as they had been dirty for some time; the reason for going to Littlemore was seemingly that there was more space to dry them there.

William and Hannah arrived at the Wheelers' cottage at about 11 a.m. that morning to be met by Sarah; John returned home a little later. Shortly after arriving, William shook the bundle, depositing the contents on the floor of the cottage. Sarah observed that her sister looked pale; Hannah said the walk had tired her. William stayed for an hour while Sarah popped in and out of the house. John arrived home to find Hannah drying her cloak and was told by her that she was washing it, because she had fallen on her way to the cottage. John observed the bundle in the middle of the floor. Both John and Sarah were struck by Hannah's appearance, saying on more than one occasion that she looked pale and very slender, especially her belly, as compared to when they saw her last, two months previously. Sarah asked, but Hannah always denied being pregnant. Hannah told John she was unwell and had come to recover; Sarah had considered her sister to have been unwell for some time.

John had left them all together and had retired to his sheepfold by noon. William left shortly afterwards, but not before he had seen his wife soak some of the linen. In his opinion the bundle contained only sheets and shirts, but he did not know how many. William finally arrived back in Toot Baldon at 5 p.m.

The Littlemore Lunatic Asylum, opened in 1846. In 1998 the hospital moved from the original site to new buildings across the road. (Giles Brindley)

Shortly after William's departure some women visited Sarah and after an hour they, too, left. Sarah suggested to her sister that they go to Cowley for beer, though in the end Hannah remained behind with the Wheelers' children. Presumably Hannah had stayed to look after them as they were aged 5, 3 and an infant. Sarah departed at 2 p.m., returning with the beer almost an hour later. Hannah continued with the washing, taking the rest of the clothes out to soak them. Sarah had not seen the full contents emptied, as something remained in the bundle, though, oddly, she testified to seeing no blood on any of the items.

William again visited the cottage the next afternoon and took tea. The washing was now hung out on the common to dry. Sarah was always by her sister's side, leaving her not more than three times during the entire stay.

Come 27 February, it was time for Hannah to leave and William came to collect his wife. The couple returned to Toot Baldon, taking the washing with them. On that night John finally got to sleep in his own bed, having slept in another bed while Hannah and Sarah had slept together; in fact, John had been engaged at his sheepfold those nights, often not returning home until 5 a.m. As John went to bed he discovered a napkin under the bed. He stooped down to pick it up and then threw it over to his wife; it had a large amount of blood on it. The cloth John had found was on the side of the bed where Hannah had slept; it was rolled up and covered in blood. He asked Sarah what it was and she replied that it belonged to 'our Hannah'. Sarah said that it was nothing that anybody would find of interest and she hid it under the bed where it remained, stating later that it had half a dozen spots of blood on it when she examined it by candlelight, but that she never showed it to anyone else, finally saying 'it was discoloured as issued by a female at a certain period'.

The coroner's inquest was held on 5 March at the Duke of Wellington pub at Littlemore. The post-mortem was conducted by Charles Webb from Oxford who stated that the child's skull was fractured and under it there was a great deal of blood; that the umbilical cord had been torn off close to the body and not secured; and that there were nail marks on the left side of the baby's neck. The boy was born alive and healthy, but either the skull fracture or the umbilical cord being torn off would have caused death. All this was corroborated by Joshua Love, Mr Webb's assistant. A verdict of murder was returned and the criminal investigation began.

A lot of time was devoted to napkins, the body having been discovered wrapped in one. Three napkins were produced as having been found at Elizabeth Dickeson's house, but she denied all knowledge, saying that they must have belonged to Hannah. These had been discovered by Henry Walsh, a policeman, when a search of the house was conducted on 16 March. One napkin was found in the cellar, one in the room where William and Hannah slept and one elsewhere in the house. A fourth napkin was also found, the one which Sarah had replaced under her bed at the Wheelers'. At first Sarah said she could not find it, but later, when she did, she said that she had washed it. This fourth napkin was produced at the inquest, when Sarah said it had been lent to Hannah during her visit. But why the fuss? The child's body had been wrapped in one, this now being in the possession of Thomas Hedges, the Littlemore policeman.

At the Assize trial on 1 August 1829 Hannah was charged with concealing the birth of her bastard child, and both she and William were charged with murder. The napkin found wrapped around the body was compared with the three found at Toot Baldon. They matched in size, shape and make, as if all had come from one piece of linen. Furthermore, the loop of cloth found tied around the child and the loop of the napkins also found at Dickeson's house corresponded perfectly.

William had heard no teasing of his wife in respect of a suspected pregnancy, stating that he had slept with her, but saying, 'I think it impossible my wife could have been with child and I not have know[n] it.' Three doctors disagreed: Charles Webber, William Rusher and John Freeman Wood all independently examined Hannah and stated that she had recently given birth, though both Sarah and Elizabeth were convinced that no child had been born in either of their houses.

The trial finally came to a head Mr Cross for the defence stated that the Coroner's inquest was flawed in that it did not state that the child discovered was Hannah's. The judge agreed that the exact charges against the Cadels were therefore incorrect and directed the jury to acquit. Hannah and William both then walked free from court.

Before the trial commenced, the judge lectured the jury: 'It frequently happens that children are born under circumstances where no assistance can be obtained at the time, where without meaning to do anything criminal, at the time of delivery an act of violence may have been committed . . . that children in birth have received injuries in the head, or have died from effusion of blood, where the woman has not had the presence of mind to prevent the effusion of blood, which terminates in the loss of life.'

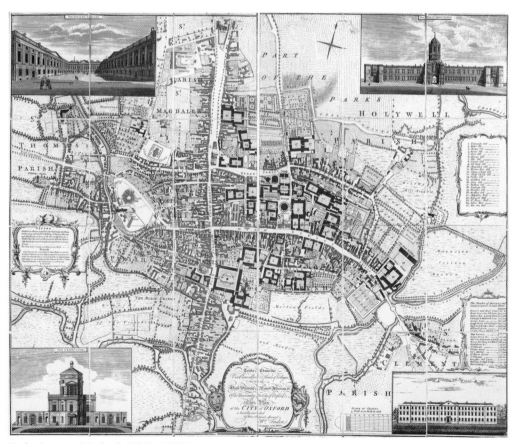

Faden's map of Oxford, 1789. (OCCPA)

16

MOTHER'S RUIN FOR FATHER

James Grainger returned home on 10 January 1877 from his job in the china dealers on the High Street. At 7.30 p.m. he walked through the front door on Randolph Terrace, Cowley, to be met by his drunk wife who demanded gin. James refused to go and get any, but said he would get some stout if she wanted some for dinner. This was not good enough for Marion Grainger. She wanted gin and argued bitterly, but since she was not going out to get it, James left and returned with the stout.

Things cooled and they sat down to eat dinner. James told his wife how bad it was to be drinking spirits, which led to another argument and Marion threw a glass at him. Dinner came to an end, but not Marion's temper. She was still furious and James stood up and put his hat and coat on. Grainger told his wife he thought it was better if he left, which infuriated her further and, grabbing a knife, she squared up to James. He had turned to go, but the glint of the sharp instrument had caught his eye. Now in close contact they argued and Marion thrust the weapon back and forth at James, saying 'Would you like some of this?' James felt a sharp prick in his left buttock.

Enough was enough and James exited by the front door and walked 50yd to the house of his friend Robert Hawes at 115 Cowley Road. It was the banging at his door

Cowley Road Workhouse, 1865. It was situated off Cowley Road opposite Randolph Terrace. All but the chapel was demolished after the buildings were vacated in 1981. (OCCPA)

that brought Robert downstairs to find James leaning against the doorpost standing in a pool of blood. James was not the most coherent, but told Robert that Marion had stabbed him. It was now after 9 p.m. and James refused to come inside; he wanted Robert to return home with him. Hawes agreed, but after only a few yards Grainger collapsed in the street.

Things started to happen very quickly. A crowd of neighbours gathered to help James onto a chair that had been fetched, while others went for another neighbour, Alfred Purnell, a policeman who lived at 113 Cowley Road. As Purnell made his way to the Graingers' home he passed the crowd as they lifted James onto the chair. Purnell was the first person Marion saw and, as the group struggled to get Grainger back home on the chair, Purnell arrested her. Marion said, 'He has got no more than what he asked for.' She said James had called her a 'bloody whore'. Mrs Grainger said she would not stand for any man calling her a whore, then boldly stated that she never touched him.

It was 9.30 p.m. when the neighbours turned up with James in tow. He wanted Robert to help him to the toilet at the end of the garden. James showed his friend the stab wound and tear in his trousers, but it unnerved Hawes to find that James's trousers and shirt were soaked in blood. Medical assistance had been called and it came in the guise of Mr Druce. As he entered the house he met Purnell. Marion stated she would have a word with the 'good doctor', but Purnell did not have time for that sort of nonsense and carted her off to the police station. Grainger was on his way back from the toilet when Druce caught up with him, but as the wound had stopped bleeding there was not much more the doctor thought he could do. James had his workmate, Charles Sims, called, and he came and stayed the night. James insisted on going to work the next day.

James told the police he did not want to press charges: Marion's threats meant nothing and he felt he had suffered little.

Returning from work the day after the stabbing, James was walked home by his son-in-law, Marmaduke Pratt. They discussed the evening's events and Marmaduke was worried: James was very weak and limped. Marmaduke did not think James would last long. Later, Pratt was party to a verbal rally between Marion and James. James complained of Marion's brutality, she retorting that she was sick of nursing him. James was indignant, snorting that she had recently jumped on him during the night and beat him in her sleep as if deranged. James added, 'Good God Lou, you slept like a pig.' James showed Robert Hawes the knife with which Marion had stabbed him. It was a meaty 8in-long blade and a full inch wide. Marion was in a state of confusion, probably owing to drink, and didn't remember the incident; during moments of clarity she said that she could not live with herself for what she had done.

James was brought before Edward Hussey, senior surgeon at the Radcliffe Infirmary on 18 March. The swelling in Grainger's buttock was about the size of an orange and the surgeon wanted to operate to repair the severed artery, but Grainger refused. By this time James had sent his son Charles as well as Marmaduke to collect his possessions from Marion. When the men arrived Marion worked herself up into a hysterical state, threatening to punch her son through the door. Charles said that if she tried, he would knock her brains out and claim self-defence. Marion squared up and said, 'Would you?', telling him not to come near or else, saying, 'I'll serve you worse than I did the one that's in the Infirmary, I'll run you through with a carving knife.' Charles was taken aback and looked to Marmaduke for support, saying he would go and give a statement to the police. Marion said, 'Go for it', telling him she would say it again just so he could write it down. The men managed to leave with James's possessions . . . and their lives.

By 27 April time was running short and James was committed to the Infirmary because of the swelling underneath his scar, the result of internal bleeding. Two days later Hussey performed the operation that he hoped would save James's life. The swelling was now three times its original size. The operation went well, but there were complications. James contracted an infection and finally died at 3 a.m. on 2 May, just two weeks after the operation.

Marion was charged with wilful murder and brought into court on 3 June 1877. At the trial Hussey stated that James's operation had been essential, for without it the swelling would have continued to enlarge until it burst, killing James as he bled to death. By all accounts Marion was lucky; she was found not guilty and released. Maybe if the guilt did not kill her, the drink would.

17

HOW TO WIN FRIENDS AND INFLUENCE PEOPLE

FRIGHT NIGHT

Having been drinking all night at the Mermaid pub in Oxford on 21 December 1683, three students of All Souls College, Thomas Baker, John Aldworth and Ralph Olive, had not finished. At about midnight they banged on the shut doors of the Mitre Inn on the High Street, whereupon the door was finally opened by a serving boy who was still up. They said they wanted to eat something, and the boy told them everybody was in bed, but the students were unimpressed and asked where was Mrs Lasenby, the landlady. The boy pointed to a ground-floor window and the students all staggered out to it. Hammering on the window, they awoke the landlady and told her that they wanted meat. She told them it was late and she was not getting up. This annoyed the students further and they yelled at her that she was a bitch and a whore and that she deserved to have her throat cut. Mrs Lasenby was reportedly so frightened that she fell into fits and died at 3 a.m. that very morning.

NOT ONLY, BUT ALSO

Dr Lancaster, the Vice-Chancellor and Fellow of Queen's in the early 1700s, was not universally loved and there were rumours of his embezzlement of funds from the University chest. Fellows and students alike were fond of the high-life and Dr Lancaster was no exception. In November 1710 he was returning home to Queen's drunk, so drunk that in passing the new buildings being constructed at Queen's he fell into one of the recently dug cellars. This was just one of many similar incidents – some weeks before, drunk in charge of his horse, he had jumped into one of the pits at Headington Hill and nearly broken his neck.

BEER LIGHT

April 1706 saw Dr Charlett fire his servant Davis for being unprofessional. The final straw had come when Davis got drunk one night in New College and had guided his master home by the light of a silver tankard as a substitute for a dark lantern.

MAN OF THE CLOTH ... AND GLASS

Dr Gardiner, Vice-Chancellor and Warden of All Souls in 1714, a 'stout man at a glass', caught some students in an ale house in March that year. He said he would allow them to drink and spend money in taverns, but not in downmarket ale houses.

PROLIFIC DRINKER

James Newlin, Yeoman Beadle of Arts and steward of Corpus Christi College, both of which jobs were well paid, died on 25 March 1716 in debt, despite having also married two rich wives. He was a good-natured but hard drinker and must have spent most of his time inebriated in order to have died penniless. The next day his body was buried for fear that his debtors would seize it; perhaps they had intended to sell it to the anatomy school in an attempt to cover some of his debts?

MUSICAL CHAIRS

There was outrage at the scandal caused when women were allowed, by the Warden Dr Butler, to attend a music concert in Magdalen College hall on 17 April 1725. Women in college . . . where would it all end?

WRONG EXIT

Mr Watkins, who lived near St Giles's Church in 1725, fell backwards down the stairs when drunk, beer in hand, and cracked open his skull, dying soon after. It was said that his wife was foul-mouthed, loose and plagued him constantly, and that he was driven to drink in the knowledge that she had slept with half the town.

ANOTHER LITTLE DRINKIE

Philips, a servitor at Exeter College, had been drinking all day in town on 4 October 1725, returning to college for evening prayers. At 10.15 p.m., after the college doors had been locked, Philips decided with a companion to go out drinking again. They attempted to get over the college wall between Convocation and the (old) Ashmolean. Philips went first, but slipped and landed on the iron-spiked railings below. One spike went clean through his thigh.

Philips was thrown out of Exeter and entered himself into St Edmund Hall – the practice of swapping college or hall was common at the time. He was not the luckiest:

The front quad of St Edmund (Teddy) Hall at the beginning of the nineteenth century. (OCCPA)

he had lost his brother who had drowned in the Cherwell near Christ Church Meadow a couple of years before. This drove him to excess. He slept with all who came his way and committed several robberies, among other things. Despite maintaining a demure exterior, Philips was expelled from St Edmund Hall in August 1728, whereupon his father, a Welshman and governor of the Cardiff gaol, came to collect him and dragged him off to Cambridge, intent on having him entered at that university instead.

A LITTLE MEDICINAL

Diagnosed with 'Gout in his head', Dr Gastrell, Canon of Christ Church, was told in November 1725 that if he drank a whole bottle of port, would sort it out. Gastrell said he would rather die than drink the stuff, which he presently did, that very night in his rooms at Christ Church.

NOT A LOVER OF THE TURF

Since the beginning of time people have been caught in criminal and sometimes downright weird activity. In 1747 Thomas Tobby was tried for felony for the unlawful, wilful, malicious killing, maiming and wounding of four mares priced at £6, £7, £8 and £14. For this he was found guilty and, having no possessions, he was sentenced to be hanged, though luckily for him he was reprieved at the summer Assizes in 1748 and merely transported to America for fourteen years.

THE COST OF MARRIAGE

Pritchard was formerly a waiter at the Cross Inn, but in October 1768 he lodged with a shoemaker in St Ebbe's. His leisure was spent making love to a young woman who

St Thomas the Martyr was built by Oseney Abbey in the late twelfth century. After the dissolution it passed to Christ Church and became a parish church. (Giles Brindley)

lived, conveniently, on the opposite side of the street. But the usual time and effort involved in such a traditional relationship being too tedious, this youth had other ideas. On 14 October he suggested to his landlord that he buy the landlord's wife from him. The bargaining began and a deal was struck. Pritchard would give his watch (worth 6 guineas) in exchange for his landlord's wife, whereupon he demanded his purchase.

An argument ensued between the two men, and finally a resolution was reached for 5 guineas more. Unfortunately, and by chance, Pritchard's lover had heard of the men's negotiations and came over to lay her claim. She was ignored by Pritchard since he had already bought a wife. After all, why would he want two?

The next morning Pritchard again tried to claim his purchase, but the landlord refused and instead lent him a guinea to enable him to see some friends at Deddington. When Pritchard returned the landlord gave back the remaining cash and the watch, refusing to yield his wife to Pritchard.

Days later, on the 20th, Pritchard, having dispensed with purchasing a wife, gained one in the old-fashioned way and married his lover Sarah Deakin in St Ebbe's Church. As the couple exited the church they were saluted by the assembled shoemakers with a peal made upon their lap shoes – a ceremony reserved for none but the most important occasions.

DO NOT MESS

Mrs Crawford, landlady of the Jolly Tar pub in St Thomas's Parish in July 1768, noticed one of her customers had left without paying. She went after the man, collared him near Nettlebed village and dragged him all the way back to Oxford. He tamely agreed to pay rather than face the consequences. She was one woman not worth messing with.

THE BEER WALK

A labourer working on the Radcliffe Observatory accepted a bet on 19 June 1776 to drink three quarts of ale (6 pints) in less than three minutes. This he readily achieved, in two and a half minutes, but finding himself somewhat drunk, decided to walk round the building to sober up – and instantly keeled over dead.

HORSEPLAY

A young boy at Marston was in the habit, with his friends, of playing with an elderly horse. At 7 p.m. on 17 April 1778 the child's body was discovered by his father and sister hanging upright with the horse's tail wrapped around his neck. Despite having a child hanging from his tail, slowly being strangled to death, the old horse had made no noise, nor had he kicked the boy.

BAD TEMPER FOR A HORSE

An unruly and restive horse bolted on 1 November 1794 complete with its rider and galloped down Cornmarket to the corner of George Street where it ran straight into one of the huge stone bollards that were there to prevent carriages mounting the pavement. The stone was ripped out, the rider thrown off and the unfortunate horse was found to be so mangled that it died where it came to rest.

The Radcliffe Observatory, 1835. It now forms part of Green College on Woodstock Road, just above St Giles's. (OCCPA)

DIY POLICING

Arriving at Mr Tallant's house, the White Hart Inn on the Cornmarket, at 7 p.m. on 23 November 1814, Amelia Franks brought with her a small trunk and requested a room for the night. She intended to leave on the 8 a.m. Birmingham coach the next day. Before going to her room she spent a little time in the bar where she left her trunk under a table. Arising early the next morning, she went to her trunk and half an hour later was screaming that the leather hinges had been cut and that she had been robbed of clothes and a small caddy which contained £16 in notes along with several gold rings. When Mrs Tallant came downstairs Amelia accused her of being the thief. Amelia made a deposition before the Mayor and a search warrant was obtained, but the police found nothing. Mr Tallant believing, as the innkeeper, he was liable, engaged a friend to estimate the loss and make good the damages. Amelia was given £18.

Nothing being found on the first search, Amelia demanded she go with the policeman and search a second time. However, before she left the town clerk's office, having obtained a new search warrant, she was seen to take a small article from her trunk — a cap. The party went back to the inn and Amelia was anxious to search the Tallants' bedroom, saying her property would be found there. Opening a drawer, she darted her hand in, exclaiming, 'Here's my cap — that's all I want', thereafter not being interested in continuing the search, which by now must have seemed rather farcical.

Amelia promptly left, but the Tallants' friends were suspicious and enquiries were made. During her time with the Mayor, Amelia had told him that she had lived in service with Lady Ormond at Ditchley and only recently left her, that her husband had been a butler and had died there two years previously, and that her brother-in-law belonged to the 5th Regiment at Windsor.

Amelia's luck ran out and she was dragged back from Birmingham to face trial on 13 January 1815. It is slightly strange that having so readily been compensated for her loss that Amelia still tried to prove that the Tallants were guilty of theft. The truth came out at trial when she was charged with fraud. The Tallants' servants stated that at 7.45 a.m. on the morning of the robbery they saw the trunk open, where it had been since the previous evening, hinges intact, with Amelia busily engaged in it. Amelia finished and was seen to lock and stow the trunk and head off into town. On returning ten minutes later she screamed that she had been robbed. The witnesses proved that Mrs Tallant did not come down until Amelia started screaming and therefore could not have robbed her. It was likewise shown that Amelia had at first claimed to have been robbed of £5, which had rapidly risen to £16, and that she had also changed her story about which clothes had been stolen.

Further nails in her coffin came from the housekeeper at Ditchley and a sergeant from the 5th at Windsor. The housekeeper proved that what Amelia Franks had said concerning her and her husband's residence with Lady Ormond was bunkum. Similarly, a letter had been sent to Colonel King, the commanding officer of the 5th, detailing Franks's appearance and claims. The reply to the Mayor was that Colonel King had no doubt she was the woman he had forbidden to enter his barracks on account of repeated charges of theft having been made against her, the sergeant had by this time positively identified her on 8 December 1814 at her examination as the woman on whom he had found stolen property while she was at the barracks.

At the trial, Mr Tallant was praised for his 'active exertions' and commented that he had spared no expense or effort in bringing Franks to justice, which was hardly surprising since he had paid £18 in compensation and had had his wife branded as a thief. Amelia stood before the jury, who stated that her whole story was false and fabricated from end to end and was of 'the most wicked and infamous nature'. They found her guilty, but sentencing was reserved until the next session when it was decided she should serve a further nine calendar months inside.

CASH, A WOODEN LEG AND THE GARTER

Two men, hawkers, were brought into court on 24 July 1824 charged with highway robbery and the rape of 16-year-old Martha Hopkins in a field near South Hinksey.

The women in court were ushered out before Martha was sworn in. Martha said that having been in Oxford on 17 July she had left for home in Abingdon at 11.30 a.m. She was followed by two men, Nash and Casey. Nash asked her which way she was going as they came up to the first turnpike gate, 'Abingdon' was her reply. Crossing the footpath, the men continued to follow until the next stile when they asked if she would 'go with them'. 'No,' she replied, whereupon Nash grabbed her legs and Casey her arms and they threw her into the ditch. Casey climbed over the hedge and Nash went into the ditch after Martha, grabbing hold of the dazed girl and heaving her bodily over the hedge to the waiting Casey. Casey pulled at her and forced her to the ground and attempted to rape her, but she managed to break free and run across the field, rounding a hayrick. Casey was faster. The man cornered her and ripped the pocket from her, examining the 2s contents in his hand while she watched. Martha's bonnet had been torn to pieces and Casey in grappling with her had kicked and repeatedly punched her. Martha stated she thought she would have been killed, but for an elderly man who was passing. Casey had pulled a knife on her and told her he would cut her arm off, drawing the blade across the back of her hand. Martha displayed her wound to the courtroom.

The well-dressed Nash and Casey were also facing charges of selling contraband, but worse was to come when Mr Holyland, head of the Reading police, came on the scene. He said that Nash had recently been tried for defrauding someone of a large sum of money in Hertfordshire, but was acquitted for want of evidence. Casey's real name was Dick Bowers, a notorious thief who had been in custody more than fifty times for numerous offences.

Robert Hunt, the elderly man Martha mentioned, was sworn in. He was returning home to South Hinksey when Martha overtook him and the two men caught up with her; one clapped his hand on her shoulder and they walked off together. Martha went willingly with Casey, a man with a wooden leg. Later, passing a yard with a hayrick, he heard a woman squeal, there was a lot of talking and Martha came leaping over the hedge and, running to Hunt, told him that she had been abused. Hunt told her she had no business to be in there with them, but all Martha said was that she was off to her parents who would have the men arrested.

Another witness, John Fletcher, was brought in. He was also returning home from Oxford and bumped into Hunt after Martha had walked off with the men. Having seen the three together, Fletcher commented to Hunt that there would soon be a fight. Arriving at the yard ahead of Hunt, Fletcher surprised Nash, who came out and was asked by Fletcher what business he had. Nash said, 'As much business as you.' Nash asked if it was Fletcher's premises, 'No', but it was his uncle's, which prompted Nash to threaten to blow Fletcher's brains out. Casey joined them and all three marched off, Casey complaining he had been robbed of his sovereign.

The defence said Martha had gone willingly, had even invited the men's attention and that she had an infamous reputation. Nash and Bowers had met her at Oxford market, where she had winked at them and said they could accompany her to a field near South Hinksey as a 'convenient place'. On the footpath she stopped to show them her garter, taking it off in front of them. Casey had money, 90 sovereigns, and she went off with the one-legged man, leaving the cash-strapped Nash to stand guard while the couple 'retired'. A short while later a brawl ensued after Casey refused to 'give her satisfaction for favours granted', which led to the afternoon's excitement witnessed by Hunt and Fletcher. The case was stopped as among further witness statements it was stated that Martha was a known prostitute. Nash and Casey were duly acquitted which, considering how dodgy they were, must have been something of a novelty.

FAMOUS LAST WORDS

In 1827 Joseph Smith was a travelling jack-of-all-trades: chair bottomer, razor grinder and chimney sweep. He was 36 years old with a wife, Jane, of thirteen years and several children. During June of that year he, along with his wife and five of their children, were travelling with another family. Robert and Sabrina Bagley and seven of their children, along with Joseph Smith Jr were camped on Marston Lane on 30 June 1827 when the Smiths arrived at 9 p.m. They collected their son, luggage and donkey and set off. Not so fast, Sabrina and her son Thomas Bagley followed. Sabrina exploded at Joseph Sr; her son had helped Smith to bottom chairs that very day, but had not received any money for it. In her opinion Smith was 'a bloody thief', in his she was 'a whore'. They yelled obscenities at each other for another quarter of an hour, Sabrina goading Smith to hit her with his stick, saying she would kill him if he dared. So he did, on the arm and head, but he being drunk the stick was wrestled from him by Sabrina and she gave as good as she got, smashing him in the eye with it. Running 6ft away to a pile of stones at the roadside, she flung them at Smith. All of this was watched by the merry band. She missed with all of them and yelled for her son to fling stones as well. The first one he threw weighed 2lb, which cracked Joseph on the right temple and as he fell to the ground Joseph hit his head on another stone. Mrs Smith and son Joseph ran up and held him. Joseph told his wife that she should wrap the children in blankets and he would get up, but as he did so he passed out. Meanwhile, Sabrina was screaming repeatedly, 'If he gets up, I'll kill him!'

Mrs Smith ran for help while Joseph's son stayed with him. A group of milkmen coming from Marston and passing them at 10 p.m. also said they would go for medical assistance. It was slightly macabre that Sabrina was still there. As the milkmen remarked on the desperate state of Smith, Sabrina said he could be 'damned and die'. But help never came, and Joseph died in his son's arms on the roadside at 8 a.m. the very next morning.

The same day, Thursday, an inquest was held at the White Hart in Marston: Charles Wingfield, surgeon, performed the post-mortem. Smith's skull was fractured and large amounts of blood were found underneath. The jury returned a verdict of manslaughter against Sabrina and Thomas Bagley and they were remanded until the next Assizes. At their trial on 28 July Thomas was found guilty of manslaughter and Sabrina of aiding and abetting. Both were sentenced to one month's hard labour. This seems to have been rather a lenient sentence, maybe because nobody of importance had been killed.

FOR BETTER, OR NOT AT ALL

At the church of St Peter-le-Bailey in 1826 a fond couple, having attained a marriage licence on 9 March, were to be married the next day. At the appointed time the bride, her brother and bridesmaids, waited with the clergyman and clerk in the church. They were anxious for the arrival of the bridegroom who had 'only nipped to the pub on business'. They waited and waited and eventually sent somebody out to look for him. The man came back and told them that the bridegroom had jumped on the Star coach and was now several miles down the road to London.

UNUSUAL PET

John Beasley was a cattle and sheep dealer living in Headington. In April 1830 it was suspected that John was heavily involved in stealing animals and selling them on. Not only did Beasley have a cottage in Headington, but he rented a house at Noke. When the police raided the Noke house they found it completely empty except, in an upstairs room, for one sheep and its dead companion. It seems that this was Beasley's storage facility, where he kept animals until he had the opportunity of selling them to some unsuspecting person.

But even better was to come when the police turned up at Beasley's cottage in Headington with Mr Hurst of Cowley. Hurst had lost several sheep, which were found among Beasley's flock. Despite having had their markings removed, the sheep came to Hurst when called for. Amusingly, one of the sheep was so docile that

Beasley's children used to feed it. The woolly quadruped had become their 'pet lamb' and they had named it Betty. Beasley was rapidly charged and taken to gaol on 10 April to await trial. He was found guilty and sentenced to death for his crime.

BEER, SWEEPS AND THE POLICE

Mary Guy, John Furby and Christopher Furby of St Peter-le-Bailey were charged on 15 February 1831 with allowing people to drink in their houses after time (10 p.m.).

Mary Guy was visited by Keats, the policeman, on the 9th at 10.30 p.m., who found two people in her house with cups in front of them. But Keats was unable to prove whether there was any beer in them and Guy was acquitted and let off with a warning.

Keats had visited John Furby's at 10.40 p.m. On knocking, the locked door was opened and there were seven people smoking with cups in front of them. The defendant stated that no beer had been drawn after 10 p.m. George Best and Henry Bunting were brought in for the defence, who stated there were no cups on the table when Keats entered, and in particular that Best had stopped drinking at 9.50 p.m. The magistrates, seemingly happy to accept that two people could be sitting around, said that seven people would not be sitting around at that time of night without any beer to drink and summarily convicted Furby, fining him 40s and costs.

But this was not an end to Keats's activity that night. He had then gone to Christopher Furby's at 11.30 p.m., where twelve people were found, including at least four sweeps. Christopher Furby was fined 40s and costs.

The magistrates commented that the Furbys had been let off lightly as the penalty for each and every offence of drinking after time was 40s, so John should have faced seven counts and Christopher twelve, which would have made their fines a staggering £14 and £24 respectively.

WHERE THE TRUTH LIES

Henry Edwards, a private in the Oxford militia, was charged with the rape of Sophia Bridgewater, aged 16, on 10 October 1831. Sophia was a servant to Mr Chaundy at the Robin Hood pub and had gone to bed at 10 p.m on the 10th. Five minutes later Edwards came into her room and, she stated, raped her. Under cross-examination she did not waver, but said that she did not cry out louder than when she was talking; which was not more than a whisper. Her mistress and a lodger did not hear her cry out and stated that she did not say anything until she was accused of being 'too intimate' with Edwards. The recorder was not allowed to sum up; the jury duly acquitted the prisoner.

ANIMAL CRUELTY

Elizabeth Williams and her husband made a living selling sand and kept a donkey for transporting it. The donkey, loaded with sand, stood in Mr Cole's yard in St Michael's Parish on 25 June 1832. Mrs Williams stepped inside the shop to deliver some sand, returning to find that turpentine had been poured all over the poor donkey, which had driven it nearly mad. William Halsey was caught red-handed at the time, turpentine bottle in hand. He was tried before the Mayor later that week. The animal paraded before the court could still be seen to be in great distress. Halsey was later convicted and fined the full penalty of £5.

HAND IN HAND

An advertisement appeared in *Jackson's Oxford Journal* on 8 September 1832 addressed 'to all drunkards and revellers, and to the thoughtless and imprudent of both sexes'. After two months of deaths from cholera, the paper stated that Oxford's inhabitants were being told for the third time that death and drunkenness went hand in hand during epidemics and that those who had suffered the most from cholera were those who indulged too freely in spirits. The Board of Health implored people to abstain from all types of intemperance and imprudence, such as staying up late, dancing, revelling and overindulging and mixing in crowded or unknown company. Infection was thought to last a long time in stone and brick buildings. People were told above all, to beware of drunkenness as it 'bit as a serpent and stung as an adder'. The paper gleefully stated that many who had happily drunk suffered in agony for their excesses, saying that their deaths were to be their legacy by way of a warning to all drunks. It concluded, 'Death smites with its purest and swiftest arrows the licentious and intemperate – the rash, fool-hardy, and imprudent.'

FROM NOUGHT TO DRUNK

William Higgs was released from gaol on the morning of Sunday 26 January 1834, but by the time Sunday morning service was under way that day he was already in a state of 'beastly drunkenness'. Higgs was happily flashing anyone who walked past him, while he stood outside St Giles's Church. He was not so merry when two policemen tried to arrest him; he violently beat them about and all three ended up rolling in the mud with their clothes torn. The policeman finally manhandled Higgs into a barrow and carted him off to gaol. The next day Higgs was found guilty in court and sent back to prison. After only tasting freedom for a day, Higgs was facing another three months of hard labour, which would leave plenty of time for him to sober up.

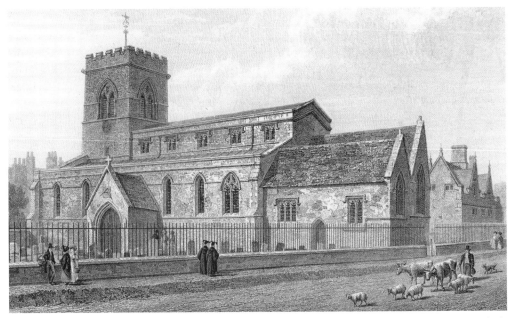

The medieval Church of St Giles's, pictured in 1833, dates back to 1086 and lies at the northern end of St Giles's outside the original city walls. (OCCPA)

DOGGY IN THE WINDOW

It is often claimed that we live in a litigious society, where the most trivial of disagreements can escalate beyond all proportion and end up in the courtroom. The archives of Oxford University's Vice-Chancellor's court suggest that this has long been the case. The following is a description of the events which led to an accusation of assault brought by the butcher William Coles against William Pigott (of New College), heard in the Vice-Chancellor's court on 16 December 1835.

One day in the autumn of 1835 Coles's son was followed back to his father's shop around midday by an unusual-looking dog. Coles, believing the dog to be of value, tied it up and began to make enquiries about its owner.

Pigott, the owner, appeared at the shop later that afternoon. How he first heard of the dog's whereabouts is unclear. He and his servant, Richard Swallow, both alleged that a milkman had told them the dog was with Coles. However, a Fellow of New College, Henry Holloway, reported that he visited the butcher's shop that afternoon, informed Coles that the dog belonged to Pigott and subsequently brought Pigott to the shop.

What could have been a straightforward handover turned sour. Perhaps Coles had expected some kind of reward for his trouble? Perhaps he threatened to make use of his professional skills on the dog unless he was adequately compensated? The records are inconclusive. Coles claimed that he asked Pigott's name and Pigott refused to answer, punching him instead in the face. George Neele Jr, a witness to the fracas, stated that Pigott had in fact answered Coles, but confirmed the punch. Another witness, William Lewin, testified that Pigott did not give his name and Coles had therefore refused to hand over the dog. He also stated that when Pigott attempted to seize the dog, he was pushed out of the shop protesting as he retreated that he would not take the animal unless it followed him once released. Holloway and Swallow testified that Pigott had accused Coles of wanting to keep the dog. Coles replied 'I will not call you a liar' and used force to eject Pigott after being punched.

In reply to the charge of assault, Pigott argued that he had struck Coles only in self-defence. He alleged Coles had refused to give up the dog unless he produced a reputable person who could confirm that the dog did indeed belong to him, so Pigott had fetched Mr Blackwell. The dog was then handed to a servant of New College. Pigott claimed that even after he had been established as the dog's rightful owner, Coles followed him into the street and shouted abuse.

The Vice-Chancellor listened to the evidence from all parties and dismissed the case.

GET YOUR OWN BREAKFAST

Sarah Duncomb lived with her husband Thomas, a tailor, in St Thomas's Parish. On the morning of 16 July 1838 Sarah went upstairs. Thomas asked her if his breakfast was ready, but she said 'No.' 'Why have you not done it?' he asked. Sarah told him that if he was in a hurry he could do it himself. He said he would hit her and Sarah said that if he did she would hit him in return. Sarah turned her back and Thomas threw a large table knife which stuck in her back. Sarah could not remove it, but her husband assisted. They went next door where the bleeding was stopped and the wound dressed.

When the case came to trial in September 1838 Sarah said that they had never quarrelled before. She asked the recorder to be lenient with her husband, hoping that the trial would caution him in future and that they would live happily ever after. But the recorder had Thomas transported for life.

NAVVIES

A group of navvies were drinking in the King's Arms at the end of Broad Street on 25 March 1844, but when it came to paying the bill they said they had no money. This did not please the landlord, Mr Thomas, and James Stone, one of the men, was forced to leave his waistcoat as security. Later, when Stone returned and demanded the waistcoat back without paying the bill, the landlord refused to hand it over, so Stone beat the landlord about and took the waistcoat anyway. The next day Stone was in court and, being found guilty, was sent to gaol for fourteen days for his 'ruffianly' conduct. During the case it turned out that the King's Arms was not the only pub the men had drunk in that day and walked out of without paying.

DOWN BUT NOT OUT

Mr Dodson, the landlord of the Star in St Giles's, called Lewis, the policeman, to have George Daly thrown out. It was March 1847 and Daly, a man with only one leg, was drunk and abusive, in which manner he continued as Lewis frog-marched him outside. This annoyed Daly and he beat the policeman with his crutch and bit him. It took two more policemen to subdue him. In court Daly was fined 40s and costs but, failing to pay, was imprisoned for twenty-one days instead.

HOW DRUNK IS SOBER?

The Revd Dr Whorwood instigated the prosecution of William Ward for being drunk in Oxford on the afternoon of 14 October 1849. Whorwood wanted to break Ward of the habit of going to Oxford on Sundays and getting drunk. This was because Ward's family was poor and needed his weekly earnings, which he always blew on drink.

In his defence, Ward said he was neither drunk nor sober, which threw the magistrates into confusion, as they were unable to decide what the difference was between not drunk and not sober. Deciding he was drunk, they fined Ward 5s 6d or to sit in the stocks for six hours. Ward objected to such a large sitting and elected to pay the fine if given a fortnight to do so. Dr Whorwood offered to pay the fine if Ward would stay sober for six months, but this was just too much and Ward could not be convinced to agree to such a rash undertaking.

18

In the Hunt for Medals

Under the staircase in the Ashmolean Museum, John Peter Le Maitre awaited his chance. Once everybody had left for the evening, he crept out of his hiding place and up the darkened staircase, stepping into one of the rooms and over to the cabinets. The original Ashmolean had been built in 1678–84 to house the collections of the antiquary Elias Ashmole, and by this time in 1776 the building was no stranger to light fingers, but this was something different. It was 3 February 1776, and a full moon lit the room. Le Maitre skilfully prized open the cabinet while the world outside happily slept oblivious to the work going on inside the Ashmolean. Le Maitre began to remove and conceal about his person a variety of objects from a cabinet, fifteen in total, including gold and silver medals, several gold and silver chains and a large gold coin. The haul was valued at around £200. Laden down, he moved through the shadows cast as the moonlight streamed through the windows. It was at one such window that Le Maitre now worked, pulling a bar from it and levering the window open. Unseen and unsuspected he made his escape.

Le Maitre made a hasty exit, climbing aboard a post coach bound for London early that morning, cheekily offering the post-boy payment in gold medals – two to be exact. It took a while for the theft to be discovered since it was a weekend, but

Broad Street in the early nineteenth century, with the Ashmolean, Sheldonian and, in the distance, Clarendon buildings. (OCCPA)

The Ashmolean Museum on Broad Street, 1834. The building was completed in 1683 to house the collections of Elias Ashmole and is now home to the Museum of the History of Science. (OCCPA)

thereafter news of it spread fast and the trail soon led to Le Maitre. Information came back from one of the policemen at Bow Street police station that Le Maitre was with a friend in Whitecross Street, London. Mr Bond, who had been sent from Oxford to investigate the theft, now went to Le Maitre's friend only to find that Le Maitre had sold some of the medals to Richard Morrison, a jeweller in Cheapside, for £7. Bond had missed Le Maitre and, to add confusion, for the next two weeks all the newspapers were rife with stories of Le Maitre absconding to France. In fact, Le Maitre had left with the same speed with which he had arrived, heading for Colchester, where he sold another medal, and then for Norwich.

Information was distributed throughout the country concerning the robbery. Le Maitre was described as 'a short thin man, squints very much, his hair tied back, marked with the small pox, stoops a little . . .'. Conspicuous at the best of times, he had, so far, been able to evade the police. A letter was delivered to the authorities dated 19 February from a Norwich jeweller and goldsmith named Richard Hutchinson who, when Norwich doctor Mr Rigby vouched for him, had bought chains and two medals from Le Maitre. Rigby knew Le Maitre from his days at Warrington Academy where Le Maitre taught French. It was only when he saw the wanted notice and description that Hutchinson went to Norwich's Mayor to give evidence. Unfortunately the notice had arrived a week after Le Maitre had left. So cocky was Le Maitre that he had stayed in the city a full three days and had even attended a concert in Norwich wearing one of the stolen metals around his neck.

Unknown to his pursuers, Le Maitre had visited Lichfield, selling yet more items, then gone to Liverpool, where one of the medal's gold chains was melted down and

A True and Authentic Account of the Trials of

JOHN PETER LE MAITRE,

For Robbing the Museum at *Oxford*;

AND

JOHN the PAINTER

For setting Fire to his Majesty's Dock-Yard at *Portsmouth*.

The TRIAL of JOHN PETER LE MAITRE.

ON Thursday the 6th of March, 1777, John Peter Le Maitre was tried upon a Bill of Indictment found at the last Summer Assizes at Oxford, for robbing the Museum in that University, and in consequence of which the Prisoner was removed by Habeas from Newgate in Dublin, in which City he was apprehended, for robbing the Ashmolean Museum in this University of divers Gold Medals, a Queen Anne's Five Guinea Piece, and two Gold Chains, together intrinsically worth upwards of two hundred Pounds.—Previous to the Examination of Evidence, Le Maitre harangued the Court for a considerable Time upon his own Situation (with some Ability, and no small Degree of Confidence) praying his Lordship to indulge him with the Use of Pen, Ink, and Paper;—not to be offended at his Ignorance of the Laws of this Country, being himself a Foreigner;—expressing his Hopes that he should have the Assistance and Protection of the Court; and, having no Council, be permitted to cross-examine the Evidence. The Use of Pen and Ink was readily granted.

The Trial then proceeded: The first Evidence deposed, that between the 3d and 5th of Feb. 1776, the Museum, of which this Witness had the Care under the Keeper, was robbed of Gold Medals, in Number from thirteen to sixteen, and likewise two Gold Chains.—A Silversmith from Norwich was next called, who produced two Medals and a Couple of Gold Chains, purchased by him of the Prisoner, upon the 8th, 9th, and 10th of February, 1776.—The Lord Mayor of the City of Dublin (for the Year preceding, who voluntarily attended this Trial, was not sworn, and deposed, That having received Letters from the late Vice-Chancellor of Oxford, and from Sir John Fielding, signifying the Loss sustained by the University, describing the Prisoner, and giving Information that he had embarked for Ireland with some Part of the Property, due Attention was had, and in Consequence thereof the Prisoner soon after his Arrival was apprehended, and brought to the Mansion-House, where he was familiarly accosted by his Lordship on his first Appearance, with " How do you do, Mr. Mara?"—to which he replied, *That is not my Name;—My Name is Matthews*.—At this Examination, nothing satisfactory being found upon Le Maitre, his Lordship went in Person to search his Lodgings, where he found two of the Medals concealed in the private Drawers of a Bureau, of which Le Maitre had the Use.—Upon the Evidence of this Discovery his Lordship committed the Prisoner to Newgate; but finding from his Landlady that a third Medal had been seen in Le Maitre's Custody, his Lordship went to the Prison, and found the other Medal buttoned under his Waistcoat, upon a blue Ribbon round his Neck.—This Medal, with those found in the Bureau, the Chains and Medal purchased at Norwich, and two other Medals sold in Oxford being severally delivered into Court, were afterwards all positively proved to be the identical Pieces stolen from the Museum; and here the Evidence closed for the Crown.

The Prisoner, in his Defence, occasioned the Examination of two or three Witnesses, in no wise to his Advantage; and dwelt for a considerable Time upon the following Circumstances,—That the Indictment was laid for his having committed the Robbery between the 3d and 5th of February; whereas it had appeared to the Court and Jury that

two of the Medals had indisputably been disposed of prior to the Time the whole were sworn to have been stolen; and this he hoped would totally invalidate the Charge with the Jury. The Prisoner was then informed by the Court, that he must not rely upon evasive Quibbles; that the only rational Means of serving himself with the Court and Jury would be to shew that he came honestly by the Things thus found in his Possession, and to account for quitting Oxford at so critical a Juncture.—In attempting this, many embarrassing Difficulties were apparent, which the Prisoner attempted to remove by alledging, that a Person who wanted him to assign a Legacy had discovered his Residence by an Application to our Post Office; because he refused to execute the Deed unless proper Compensation was made to him;—that his Creditors were to be let loose upon him, &c. &c. and to authenticate this Narrative, he desired Mr. Oliver Parsons might be called, who, upon Examination only proved, that there had been an Enquiry by Letter, Whether such a Person resided in Oxford? and that having answered the Letter, soon afterwards a Stranger called at the Post Office, whom he conducted to Le Maitre; that afterwards, at the Cross Inn in this City, he was privy to a Conversation in which the Person threatened the Prisoner, that if he refused signing the Deed, he would make Discovery of a Forgery of which he had been guilty.—The Prisoner, after this, rested his Defence upon a most impudent and iniquitous Assertion, That he first received two of the Medals from a Member of the University, who stood indebted to him for Tambour Waistcoats; that he had very inadvertently been thus entrapped; but that upon remonstrating with the Gentleman when they came to settle Accounts, he was held in Defiance, and threatened with the Consequences; that finding the deplorable Situation to which he was reduced, he had afterwards received from the same Person all the Rest; yet, that though he should suffer whatsoever the Law could inflict upon him, he was firmly resolved never to divulge the Secret.—His Lordship then summed up the Evidence with great Candour, yet with just Indignation reprobated the horrid Insinuation with the Prisoner had suggested, in hopes of deluding the World into a Belief of his own Innocence.

The Jury, without withdrawing from the Court, returned their Verdict GUILTY.—He was afterwards sentenced to hard Labour on the Thames for five Years, and then to be discharged.

James Hall, for stealing a Great Coat; and Richard Smith, for stealing Blankets off the Tenters at Witney, were severally found Guilty of Grand Larceny, and ordered to be sent to the House of Correction and kept to hard Labour for three Years, pursuant to the late Statute.—Sarah Merrick, for stealing Apparel was branded in the Hand.—Benjamin Reader and John Hatter were acquitted; and the other Prisoners ordered to remain according to their former Sentences.

At these Assizes was tried, a Cause brought by a Tradesman of this Place against a Gentleman for Necessaries provided for his Son during his Residence at this University, wherein the Judge expressed the clearest Opinion that the Father was in general, responsible for every necessary Article, found for his Son whilst a Minor and a Member of the University, and accordingly directed the Jury to find for the Plaintiff in this Case, which they did much to the Satisfaction of a very crowded Court.

The TRIAL of JOHN the PAINTER.

AT Eight o'Clock on Thursday Morning the 6th of March, 1777, James Hall, alias Hill, alias John the Painter, was put upon his Trial at Winchester, before Mr. Justice Ashhurst and Mr. Baron Hotham, upon an Indictment for wickedly, maliciously, traiterously, and of Malice aforethought setting Fire to his Majesty's Dock-Yard at Portsmouth, to which Indictment the Prisoner pleaded *Not Guilty*: And for his Delivery put himself upon God and his Country.

No less than nineteen Witnesses were produced and sworn in support of the Charge alledged against him, from whose Testimony a great Variety of Circumstances were made known to the Court, and were given with so much Clearness and Connexion, that all who were present felt a full Conviction of the Prisoner's Guilt. It appeared from the Evidence, which was as strong as Circumstantial Evidence could possibly be, that the Prisoner had himself originally planned the destroying of the King's Dock-Yards, that he had imparted his Intention to Mr. Silas Deane, employed by the Congress at Paris, had received Bills of him in Consequence, drawn on a Merchant in the City, for 300l.; that he had invented the Form of the Tin Cannister found in the Hemp-House at Portsmouth Dock-Yard, had prepared all the Combustibles, and had finally perpetrated the Fact, without the Assistance of an Accomplice.

The Jury pronounced him GUILTY without going out of Court; and Baron Hotham instantly (which is not usually the Case) passed Judgment upon him, prefacing his Sentence with one of the most solemn and awful Speeches ever addressed to a Prisoner in a similar Predicament. The Judge warned him to make a good Use of the few Days he had to live, declaring that it was not in the Power of Words to aggravate his Crime: That its Enormity was so great, and the Evidence which had been heard against him so full and convincing, that he must not flatter himself with Hopes of Mercy.

The Prisoner said he was totally indifferent with regard to his Fate, and was willing to live or die, as the Laws and Justice required. In the Course of the Trial he asked the Witnesses several very shrewd and pertinent Questions, and changed his Defence into an Animadversion on the Conduct of a principal Witness, resting chiefly on an Appeal to the Judge, if Evidence given under such Circumstances ought either to be credited, or to be a sufficient Ground of Conviction. His Argument on this Point, though short, was artful, and managed with all the Casuistry of a practised Barrister.—During the Trial his Behaviour was singular; he appeared not at all affected with his Situation, and yet his Manner wore not the Air of Audacity or Sullenness, but rather appeared to be the Effect of Ignorance and Enthusiasm.

Lord Sandwich was on the Bench the whole Time of the Trial, which lasted till near Three in the Afternoon.

In the Course of the above Trial it came out, that a German, who is now Abroad, and an American, who is a Painter, and came over in the same Ship with Dr. Franklin, were both concerned in the above diabolical Transaction.

A pamphlet was printed about the trial of, among others, John Peter Le Maitre in 1777 for the robbery at the Ashmolean Museum. (ORO) sold to a goldsmith in order to pay his bill for board and lodgings; then he departed for Ireland. In fact, two days before the Norwich jeweller wrote his letter, the local Oxford newspaper said that Le Maitre was bound for Liverpool and Ireland, but nobody believed this as it was still resolutely believed that he had gone to France.

Now the tide turned against Le Maitre. On 24 February the Mayor of Dublin received the wanted notice and a letter from the Mayor of Lichfield detailing Le Maitre's recent presence. The floodgates had opened and Mr Bedford, the Dublin magistrate, scoured the city until he collared Le Maitre two days later in Grafton Street. On being questioned before the Mayor, Le Maitre said he was called Matthews. The Mayor did not believe him and had him searched, but nothing was found. He sent Le Maitre to gaol and then went to the prisoner's lodgings in the city, where he found two medals concealed in a bureau. Le Maitre's landlady said she had seen more than two medals and the Mayor went directly to the prison, where he found another medal under Le Maitre's waistcoat, hung around his neck on a blue ribbon. Most of the medals were recovered, but some pieces like the gold chain had been melted down. In total it cost the University nearly £186 to buy back what was left of the stolen goods from the various goldsmiths, silversmiths and jewellers across the country.

Le Maitre, originally a native of Switzerland, had been a resident in Oxford for some time. An advertisement had appeared in the Oxford newspaper publicising his services as a drawing tutor; it had also been known that he gave private French lessons to members of the University. Shortly before the robbery he had moved with his wife to a house on the south side of Broad Street behind Exeter College, which was later demolished to make way for the college's new buildings, rather close to the Ashmolean. Le Maitre had ingratiated himself with William Milnes, a servitor of Corpus Christi College and one of the Ashmolean's caretakers, whereupon Le Maitre was left to 'his own studies'. Le Maitre did this too frequently for comfort and aroused suspicion in his overenthusiasm to view the gold and silver medals, even being ushered out on the very day the robbery was committed by Milnes himself under the pretence that there was a group of special visitors who wished to see the exhibits. Thus Le Maitre was well acquainted with the museum before he actually set about pillaging it.

Le Maitre, having been incarcerated in Newgate prison in Dublin for six months, was transported back to Oxford and gaoled on 1 September to await trial at the next Assizes in March. Hence Le Maitre had time on his hands and wrote his autobiography. He even advertised it in the local newspaper, though no trace of the book survives.

Le Maitre had waited a year for his trial, which finally took place on 6 March 1777. Even before the trial started he harangued the court, pleading ignorance of the laws as he was a foreigner, demanding pen, ink and paper and even, rather stupidly, defending himself and asking leniency for it. He called for the whole case to be dismissed and certainly did not lack confidence. The charge stated the robbery happened during 3–5 February, but Le Maitre was not in Oxford on the 5th and therefore could not have still been burgling the Ashmolean on that day. Technically he was right, but the court ignored it as an evasive quibble and told him he would need to prove he came honestly by the medals found in his possession and give a good explanation of why he fled Oxford so fast. Though understandable, this does smack of guilty until proven innocent.

Again Le Maitre played the victim, saying he had refused to witness a will because it was a forgery and was blackmailed with having his creditors let loose on him. He reported an argument between himself and another in the Cross Inn concerning the will. Perhaps Le Maitre was trying to suggest he was a scapegoat. In fact, he claimed John Griffin, Fellow of Worcester, had given him two of the medals in payment for embroidered waistcoats (Mrs Le Maitre taught needlecraft). Le Maitre said he had later objected as they were stolen, but was blackmailed since he was now equally complicit, having received stolen goods. This backfired, as the University was indignant as it would never consider one of its own as having been responsible. Le Maitre said that later he had been given the rest by Griffin, who must have had a room full of waistcoats considering the medals' intrinsic value.

The judge summed up, commenting on Le Maitre's 'horrid insinuations' in trying to convince the world of his innocence. The jury did not retire, but pronounced him guilty. For once luck was on Le Maitre's side: he escaped the noose because an Act of Parliament had just been passed which resulted in him being sentenced to five years' hard labour on a hulk at Woolwich, dredging the Thames for sand and soil.

But Le Maitre had other ideas. Barely a month later he and four others, were involved in a little do-it-yourself. He was imprisoned in the Castle gaol awaiting transportation, where he was locked up with Jones, a highwayman, Maggs and Bradbury, both deserters, and Hall, a thief sentenced to three years' hard labour for stealing an overcoat. For some time they had been digging away at the earthen floor of their cell, using sticks and a clamp from a pump, to create a hole next to the wall. They threw the soil down the toilet on their regular visits. The hole was covered daily with old mats to disguise it. Eventually, they could see light under the wall and their work was complete. Armed with tools to cut away their fetters, they waited for dusk and the time before lock-up when they could make their escape. But they were discovered before they ever got the chance to break out when their guards removed the mats and saw daylight clearly coming from under the wall. They were handcuffed and guarded at all times.

Finally, at 2 p.m. on 15 April 1777, Le Maitre was taken out of the Castle, secured and guarded, and delivered the same evening aboard one of the hulks at Woolwich. After serving his time he became a bookseller in Bristol, but ended up in the debtors' prison. He was freed by a former Warrington pupil acting for the Society for the Relief of Prisoners for Small Debts.

There has been speculation that Le Maitre was one and the same as Marat, leading light in the French Revolution, since they were both of Swiss extraction and in England at the same time. But when Le Maitre was in Oxford in 1776, Marat was a physician in London, and barely two months after Le Maitre was taken to Woolwich, Marat took up a position attached to the French court. The idea that they were the same person is a romantic notion rather than fact.

19

TO KILL A MOCKING RAT

Charles Blackstone, a student and scholar of Corpus Christi College, was found dead in his rooms on the morning of 6 February 1849. The University coroner held an inquest the same day in the college bursary telling the hushed audience that such a death in the University was rare. This was a miracle, he said, considering how many 'in the rashness and impetuosity of youth, were daily tempting their fate on the water, as well as riding, and in the use of deadly instruments'. Blackstone was no exception, as he had died from a gunshot wound. His death was not only felt in the college, where he was well liked, but throughout the University, particularly because he had won the prestigious Newdigate poetry prize. Blackstone looked as if he had been transfixed by the immediacy of his death; his appearance still retained the same calm and placid demeanour he had held during his life.

Throughout the day the story unravelled. On 29 January, along with another student, Godfrey Faussett, Charles had gone to Mr Pether, the gunsmith, asking for a

Corpus Christi College on Merton Street, with Merton College in the background, 1792. Corpus Christi was founded in 1517. (OCCPA)

pistol, powder and bullets. He was exceedingly annoyed by a rat that he had heard and seen in his rooms. He wanted to hire a pistol to blow the rodent away and end his problems. Little did he know that the gun would lead to a very permanent solution, not just to the rat, but to all his problems, current as well as future. Pether suggested shot, but Blackstone wanted bullets because shot would only fly around the room. Pether sent the weapon and ammunition to college later the following day.

The previous term another Corpus scholar, Mr Kirkpatrick, had heard a rat in Blackstone's rooms and the pair had crawled around on their hands and knees, hunting high and low for the dreaded foe, but had not found it. Relating the tale of how he had once come eyeball to eyeball with his nemesis, Blackstone told Kirkpatrick that if he had had a gun he would have disposed of the rat. A trap had been set on many occasions, but Blackstone revealed to his friend that he had failed to catch the rat and spoke repeatedly of his grand plan to get a pistol and shoot it.

Mr Walsh, a student of Balliol, was next to be lectured on the benefits of handguns. He had visited Blackstone in Corpus in early February and saw the pistol for himself. Blackstone told Walsh that he kept the loaded gun to kill a rat, pointing out a bullet hole near the door where he had previously missed. At this meeting Blackstone was cheerful, and talked of his hopes of becoming a college fellow. It all seemed plausible until Blackstone pointed the loaded pistol at Walsh. His fellow student was horrified and told Blackstone not to be so stupid.

On the evening before his death Blackstone had dined in Exeter College in Mr Southwell's rooms. He had left sober shortly before 11 p.m., declining to stay longer because he said he wanted to be up for chapel in the morning: Charles had only attended on Sundays during that term. Before Blackstone departed he accepted an invitation to breakfast on Thursday. He spoke at length of his intention to vote for a new president in the forthcoming elections at the union. Later, knocking at the front gate to Corpus, Charles was let in alone at 10.45 p.m. by the porter, Robert Barnes.

Days previously, in the rooms above Blackstone's, Mr Fort had heard two shots ring out at 11 p.m. Rushing downstairs, he had flown into Charles's rooms only to find Blackstone and Mr Haverfield conducting target practice against a candle, which they had propped up on the sofa. So clueless was Blackstone about guns that Mr Fort had taken the pistol to pieces in front of him to show him how it worked. Earlier that evening, between 6.30 p.m. and 8 p.m. Mr Blayds had been with Blackstone among others.

Having staggered back into college alone, Blackstone had headed for bed. In the rooms above, Fort had gone to sleep at 11 p.m., only to be woken shortly afterwards by a noise. Thinking nothing of it, Ford had gone back to sleep. Just before midnight, Blayds had looked into Blackstone's rooms to see if Faussett was there. He saw Blackstone, by a light burning in the room, lying on his sofa, as if dozing and, not wanting to wake him, left and went to his own rooms.

Blayds had heard on several previous occasions that Charles had hired a gun to eliminate the rat. But the reality was more shocking, as Charles was known to waft the loaded pistol at people. When Blackstone had pointed it at Blayds, Blayds had told Charles precisely what he thought. The list of people who were none too pleased with Charles's laissez-faire attitude included his good friend Faussett, who told him it was dangerously foolish to point a cocked and loaded pistol at people.

At about 12.30 a.m., Blackstone's friend Faussett looked in to say goodnight. He saw, so he thought, Charles peacefully asleep on the sofa. He shook the furniture in an attempt to wake him, but nothing happened, so he took Charles's hand. It was stone cold and in it was clasped the pistol. Faussett raced back to the college rooms he had just left, those of Mr Slater. The two men returned for a second look and decided that Blackstone was indeed dead. Slater saw that the left side of his shirt was soaked in blood, something which Faussett had missed. The porter had gone to bed at 12.15 a.m. and had heard nothing, but now Barnes was awoken by the concerned students. All three returned to view the body. Unmistakably, Blackstone was dead. Barnes left the college to find help, but before he did, he carefully removed the pistol from Blackstone's hand.

It was only in the early morning when the alarm was raised that Fort realised that what had woken him earlier was, in fact, a gunshot. Mr Martin, the doctor, was raised from his bed at 1 a.m. and went to Corpus to examine Blackstone's body. He found that a single bullet had penetrated Charles's chest and passed through his heart and left lung. Death would have been instantaneous. Later, Martin removed the bullet from Charles's back. At the inquest the Warden of Corpus said Charles was to sit finals the next term and ruled out any possibility of suicide. The jury's verdict: 'That the said Charles Blackstone caused his own death by accidentally discharging a loaded pistol, which he, as has been satisfactorily proved to the jury, had been in the habit of incautiously handling in his room.'

<h1 align="center">20</h1>

<h1 align="center">THE TOWN VS GOWN QUESTION</h1>

OVERREACTION

Perhaps one of the first noted town versus gown riots, at a time when they were exceedingly violent, bloody confrontations, was in 1209, when a student accidentally or otherwise killed a woman in Oxford. The town, in retaliation, saw that two University students were hanged, even though they had nothing to do with the original event. This must have not at all pleased the students, after this all hell broke loose in Oxford, which led to many students fleeing. Since members of the University were answerable only to ecclesiastical law, hanging would have been rather a surprise to the students; this was reserved for the common folk. The most the students would have expected, even if they had been found guilty, was a penalty or possibly a short stint inside.

ANOTHER BRAWL

After four days of fighting in 1298, which included the death of at least one student, the town was eventually fined 200 marks (one mark = 13s 4d) and 'excommunicated' for seven months by the University, though little was done to tighten up University discipline itself. In effect, excommunication usually meant the withdrawal of rights to trade with University members.

ST SCHOLASTICA'S DAY

The most famous of all medieval town-gown riots originated in a tavern called the Swyndlestock, at the corner of Carfax. In 1354 a group of scholars called at the tavern for wine. The landlord brought it, but the scholars disliked it and words were exchanged. The landlord vouched for the quality of his wine. Naturally he maintained a healthy disregard for the students. Unfortunately this resulted in the vessel being pitched at his head. The dispute gathered pace, and the bell of St Martin's Church was rung to call the townsmen into the affray. The Vice-Chancellor of the University endeavoured to stop the tumult, but was shot at and fled. The ringing of the University church's bell brought the gownsmen out in numbers with weapons of every kind. Both sides let fly with bows and arrows, swords and practically anything that came to hand.

The following day 2,000 men from the surrounding countryside entered Oxford to reinforce the townsmen and the tide turned. The scholars retreated to their halls, hostels and lodgings. The battleground moved locations and many of the buildings were broken open and sacked. The fighting continued into a third day, and the number of student deaths rose to more than sixty. The Bishop of Lincoln took the drastic step of placing the town under an interdict, King Edward III sent the Mayor and bailiffs to the Tower of London, the Sheriff was dismissed and 200 townsmen were arrested. The King increased the University's powers over the town, ordering that the Mayor and chief citizens, among others, should attend mass on this day each

St Mary the Virgin on the High Street is both the University church and serves one of Oxford's parishes. It is shown here in 1810. The earliest part of the current church dates from 1280. (OCCPA)

year, thereafter known as St Scholastica's Day, to pay penance and give an offering of one penny per student killed. So deep was the wound that the University only consented to the disbanding of the ritual nearly 500 years later in 1826, much to the jubilation of the townsfolk.

WORKMEN MADE OFF WITH THE BOOTY

It would seem that articles of value grow legs and walk when we least expect it, but especially when our guard is lowered. This was certainly true in Merton in October 1655. On the 17th part of the chapel's roof in the south transept fell to the floor, inflicting damage on several of the monumental stones. The workmen brought in to repair the damage did so, and at the same time made off with the 'loose' brasses.

SAUCE FOR THE GOOSE

Visiting Wolvercote on 29 September 1662, several students were out to plunder geese. They were discovered and chased off by the none too pleased locals. One student was lanced in the arm by a prong and another was captured. This student hostage was dragged back into the village and placed in the Wolvercote stocks, resplendent in his gown, for they were to be worn at all times. The students rallied forces in the town and forty of them charged into Wolvercote and succeeded in rescuing their colleague, stealing a goose into the bargain. The students marched back into Oxford in triumph with the bird rammed on the end of a pole.

A QUICK BOOK

Several Christ Church students were returning to college in December 1663, having been to Mother Horwood's pub on Catte Street. They were staggering drunkenly, but saw a light on in Convocation House as they passed. Thinking it was some sort of covert religious meeting (a conventicle), they went off in search of help to arrest the members of the meeting. They called on Dr Tomkins of All Souls, and returned with him and several other students. Listening outside under the window, they heard one say, 'Oh the Bible! I had almost forgot the Bible', and burst open the doors to find Mr Davis, the bookseller, with his wife and son rifling through the volumes in order to take the best for sale in London. Davis had, some weeks before, been taken into Convocation to make a library from the books.

MORE PLEASE?

A northerner who came to the Angel Inn in July 1668 was reported to have died after students fed him too much drink and meat.

VIOLENT TEDDY BOYS

An argument ensued between Lord Norris's servant, mounted on a horse, and two students of St Edmund Hall in

Convocation House, left, and the University Court Room, right, are located behind the Sheldonian Theatre on Broad Street. (OCCPA)

front of University College on 16 December 1674, whereupon the students whipped out their knives and killed the horse.

MURDER MOST HORRID

John White, a Balliol servitor, took his coat to Thomas Hovell, the tailor, to mend in 1679. In conversation, White made the mistake of telling the tailor that he had just received a parcel of money from his father in Devon which was to pay for him taking his bachelor's degree the next day. Having worked several years for it, this should have been a happy time, but White foolishly told Thomas where the money was in his rooms.

The temptation proved too much for Hovell. He knew it would not be easy, but under the pretence of returning the coat, Hovell went to the student's rooms when he knew White would be due to leave to serve in college. When Hovell arrived, White was in rush to go to his work. He let the tailor into his rooms and showed him to a chair, saying he would be back soon. White rushed out and Hovell set to work. Pulling a hatchet from his coat, he smashed open the closet. But White returned all too soon and caught Hovell in the act; they fought and White fell to the ground. As

A simple gallows where the condemned would have been left to asphyxiate to death. The 'long drop', causing a broken neck and instant death, was not introduced until 1872. (ORO)

Below: All Saints Church was rebuilt at the beginning of the eighteenth century. It was declared redundant in 1971 and since 1975 has housed Lincoln College's library. (Giles Brindley)

he got up, Hovell hit White repeatedly about the head with the hatchet and bludgeoned him to death.

Hovell panicked and fled the scene, but was shortly arrested and executed on gallows specially erected in Balliol College forecourt, hanging all day until 2 or 3 p.m. The next day his body was hung in a gibbet at Bullingdon Green as a warning to all, but it was not until 1686 that his body had finally rotted and been eaten away.

IN THE FAMILY

At 10 a.m. on 16 March 1716 a young woman was hanged at Green Ditch on the edge of the new park in Oxford for killing her bastard daughter. Let's call the mother Ann. Ann was illegitimate herself and twenty years earlier her mother had wreaked havoc in Exeter College by claiming that Ann's father was a member of that institution. This was a scandal indeed, and as a result of an extensive investigation Dr Bury was expelled, but then Mr Colmer was suspected. Eventually the real father was found out to be a townsman named Mr Smith, but it was too late for poor Bury who had been given the boot. That should have been the end of it except Smith later had a son and it was that son who had fathered Ann's child. So that would mean Smith's son had slept with his own half-sister.

BUNDLE OF JOY

Mr Elyot was a student of University College and his love was Jenny Barnes. Jenny, like the rest of her family, was a chandler to the college. In 1717 celibacy was, and had long been, the key to college life for all but the heads of houses. Once Jenny was known to be pregnant, Elyot had his scholarship removed and Jenny lost her business with the college. Two months before the birth of their baby son in August 1717 they were married. Mr Elyot died of smallpox less than two years later.

JUVENILE DELINQUENT

Mr Payne, a wealthy brazier of All Saints Parish in 1727, had two sons. The youngest was apprenticed to him, but as he was wicked and wild Payne had him committed to the Bocardo prison. His eldest son was an MA, but so dull that nobody would allow him to be ordained. Before the committal, Payne indulged his elder son, but made the younger one wait on them and have his dinner after them. The younger son had burgled a few houses and had even attempted to rob his own home. But this was a little tame when you consider that he had also tried to kill his mother.

On Saturday 27 December, while in the Bocardo, the son stabbed himself with a knife and languished in agony for the whole day until he died at midnight. He was buried the following night at All Saints Church. Strangely, his father had wanted to have him released from prison before this, but, unsurprisingly, his mother had been terrified by the idea and set against it, which is why the son had remained where he did.

A TAIL OF TWO CITIES

On 4 April 1727, at a bull baiting in Headington, a quarrel arose between some students and two or three Headington locals. The argument concerned a cat, that the students had brought for the specific purpose of tying to the bull's tail. Fists flying, the students were beaten black and blue and chairs had to be sent for to convey them home.

What happened next must have been an impressive sight as several hundred students rounded the top of Headington Hill in pursuit of revenge for their compatriots. At the time this must have comprised the majority of the University's students.

As the Headington inhabitants either fled or hid, the students proceeded to take the place apart, smashing almost every window there. The locals who remained had the living daylights beaten out of them. Their possessions were thrown around and even the houses' window bars were ripped out. It was only the intervention of one of the University Proctors that stopped the students from sacking the whole town, including the church. Finally the victorious students returned back to their rooms in Oxford to celebrate while Headington began the process of repairing the damage.

THE HONOURABLE THING

Sarah Adkins was a laundress to Hart Hall and, falling pregnant, gave birth to a boy in the summer of 1727. The father was Mr Hunt, a clergyman and tutor at Hart Hall. Hunt later married Adkins, it being considered that this was the least he could do for her.

TAKE A WIFE – ANY WIFE

In January 1728 Mr Brasier returned home to his father's house in St Peter-in-the-East with his wife and Mr Leaver. At 1 a.m. they were walking down the High Street, while on the opposite side were two students from Magdalen College. One student took a fancy to Mrs Brasier and said to the other, 'We'll have that woman', and they raced across the road, just as the party reached their home. Leaver told the students to calm down and be civil. They punched Leaver to the ground and grabbed Mrs Brasier. In the struggle Mrs Braiser was bundled through her front door. Mr Brasier whipped out his pen knife and stabbed one of the students, named Pescod, in the stomach. Pescod collapsed in a pool of blood and was carried to the Greyhound Inn at the corner of Longwall Street, but that was the last that was heard of him.

Leaver's moral stance was not all that it seemed. Before she married Mr Brasier, the young lady was Leaver's servant. Leaver had slept with her while she was employed by him and continued to sleep with her on a regular basis even after she married. Rumours were rife that he had slept with a great number of his past and current servants.

SORRY LIFE

At the beginning of May 1728 Sarah Jackson, daughter to Ralph, a victualler and farmer at Iffley, died of tuberculosis at her father's house. She was a very pretty young girl who was admired by many, particularly Mr Rich, gentleman commoner of Queen's College, who was once engaged to her. When Rich's friends found out about the engagement he was forced to break it off and thereafter edged out of the University. This wound him up so much that he married one of his father's maids to taunt them. He died soon afterwards. Meanwhile, Sarah pined away for him.

Time went by and Sarah become pregnant by a Merton student. She went to her grandmother at Littlemore to undergo a back-street abortion (abortion was to remain illegal for another 200 years), but died shortly afterwards, aged 23. She was buried at Iffley church on 8 May.

Sarah had lived a rather sad life, during which she had loved and lost more than once.

BODIES A-GO-GO

Richard Fuller of Caversham was hanged at Oxford on 28 July 1730 for murdering his wife. This in itself was not unusual, but at the time the students could not get their hands on enough bodies to dissect. So frantic were they at the execution that, when Fuller's body was cut down and placed in a coffin, brought by the family, the students ran in and, smashing the coffin tried to make off with the body. Family and locals attempted to wrestle the body from them, but the students finally ran off with it to Lincoln College. The Proctors made the students return it and took it to a 'safe house' in Bullocks Lane.

A second coffin was purchased by the family and the body placed in it. The students discovered the hiding-place and breaking down the doors at the Bullocks Lane house; they destroyed the second coffin and removed the body. Once more the authorities intervened, but the students had by this time cut off Fuller's head. The body was returned to the family in two pieces and placed in a third coffin.

No house in the town was considered safe from the students, so the body was taken to the Castle. At 11 p.m., while all was quiet and still, the authorities moved the body quietly by water in a boat. The students lay in wait for them, ambushed the boat and coffin and all were thrown into the water. Great numbers of students dived in after the coffin and dredged the stream. Eventually they managed to raise the body and made off with it to Queen's College where they reduced it to hunks of flesh and a pile of bones. It is not known whether the remains were first delivered to the man's family before burial.

GROUP WORK

Following the Port Meadow horse races in September 1730 a woman, whose name was Cradock, spent the evening flat on her back on the meadow having sex with at least thirty men, while people stood around and watched. In the repercussions, three students of Exeter College were expelled along with two from Queen's. One student from Queen's returned north and committed suicide by hanging himself. In contrast, one of the expelled Exeter students returned and set up in St Edmund Hall in February 1731.

EIGHTEENTH-CENTURY MAFIA

In a room next door to the Magdalen College buttery, burglars walked away happy on the night of 11 January 1780 after removing silver, including half-pint pots, pepper boxes, mustard pots, spoons, a salt cellar and a brass candlestick, along with four room keys.

Two weeks later, on the 27th, light fingers were at work again, this time in Christ Church, where silver beakers, candlesticks, candle snuffers and stand, a punch stirrer, salt spoons, teaspoons and even the tops of a cruet set were removed from the Fellows's common room.

Magdalen had advertised a reward of 20 guineas for a conviction and now Christ Church offered another £20 for the arrest of the criminals. It was too much for Moses Cohen, the criminals' fence, who told the police that William Best and James Slatford had offered him as much silver as he could carry, three times over. The only problem was that it would need to be melted down before it could be sold, as it was engraved with college crests and other arms. Best and Slatford were gaoled on 2 February to await trial.

The names of Best and Slatford were synonymous with crime in Oxford and appear throughout the court records – and more than once in this book as well. But this time it seems they may well have got away with it, as no record can be found for their being tried for this crime.

SUING AT WESTMINSTER

The University was assiduous in asserting the right to oversee its members, so much so that all cases concerning its members and those considered privileged persons were conducted in its courts and nowhere else. However, the time taken for cases to be heard was long and often frustrated anybody who wished to proceed against one of the privileged few.

An example of this and the often almost hypocritical stance taken was displayed during a case in January 1817. University rules meant that students were not permitted to hire gigs, but instead of the students being taken to court it was the stable-keepers who, more often than not, were taken to court for hiring them out to the students. With this in mind, the University brought an action against Isaac Austin, an Oxford stable-keeper. Meanwhile, Austin was suing James Worsley in one of the Westminster courts for non-payment of a debt. When the University brought the case Austin confessed to suing the student. The University threatened to 'discommon' Austin, i.e. to prevent him from conducting business with members of the University, unless he withdrew his suit from the Westminster court. Presumably he did as he was told, as there seems to be no more mention of the case against him proceeding any further. However, in July of the same year Austin was 'discommoned' for two months for another similar offence.

THE VALUE OF HONOUR

In Miss Stevens vs Mr Stavely, on Saturday 22 July 1820, an action was brought by the plaintiff for a breach of promise of marriage that the defendant had made to her. Miss Stevens, of course, had dragged Mr Stavely into court to defend her honour and not to seek compensation.

Stavely was a student of University College and Stevens was described as a young lady of great personal beauty and considerable accomplishment. The couple had come together and been engaged, but when Stavely's father found out he told his son to break it off, saying that he should not marry until he had finished his education and settled down. The verdict was for the plaintiff, for which she received damages of £210. It would seem that honour still had a price.

PICKPOCKETING DEBATE

The University proceeded against William Kwin for picking the pocket of Mr Reyner Casues, of Queen's College, in the Town Hall on 3 March 1825. At trial the judge, Mr James thought the evidence was not sufficient to warrant a charge of felony unless the prosecutor could prove the handkerchief was removed from the bottom of his pocket, which Reyner could not. So Kwin was charged with misdemeanour instead but, still unsure, Mr James called the counsel for the prosecution who agreed that the lesser charge would be the safer bet. The prosecution, however, decided to press both charges of felony and misdemeanour. Kwin was eventually found guilty of a misdemeanour (the lesser charge) and sentenced to three years' imprisonment with hard labour.

KNACKERING A HORSE

The undergraduate Henry Mitchell of New College was sued in the Chancellor's court by William Payne, a stable-keeper, for £18 on 7 June 1833. Payne put in a claim against Mitchell for this sum, which was the cost of the horse Mitchell had recently bought; failing that, Payne wanted £10 for damage caused to the horse.

It transpired that the horse had originally been hired by Mr Godfrey of St John's and was injured to the point of being considered useless. Mitchell acknowledged riding and then returning the horse, but pleaded that the horse was unsound at the time of the injury and consequently was not worth the £18 claimed. The plaintiff then brought forth witnesses who testified that the horse in its current state of disrepair was not worth more than £8 to £10. Payne proved to the court that the defendant had previously agreed to pay £18 for the horse following its injury. The judge decreed that Mitchell should pay Payne £10 and the court costs before Mitchell left Oxford for the vacation.

LOCK JAW

James Holland, an Oxford gardener, died on the evening of 23 October 1833 from lockjaw, having been stabbed in the hand. It seems that day he and two others had been walking up St Giles's when they met three gentlemen of the University. There was an altercation between Holland and one of the students which led to blows, Holland afterwards complaining of an injured thumb.

The surgeon attending Holland said that the man had been stabbed by a dirk or dagger. This was embedded in a stick that had been aimed at Holland's head, and in putting his hand up to protect himself he had received the injury to his thumb. A verdict of manslaughter was returned at the inquest on 1 November against an unknown person. The jury expressed their detestation of the practice of carrying such covert weapons, which was considered all too regular an occurrence.

Enter Mr Davenport of Brasenose College, who, on the night in question, had returned from a walk in the country with two companions and met Holland's group. He voluntarily stepped forward to be examined by the Vice-Chancellor. Davenport left the two unremarkable walking sticks that the company had with them on the night in question. The student said that no blows were dealt out with the sticks, but that Holland advanced alone from his companions and walked into Davenport, at which point blows followed and Holland, falling, had injured his thumb.

Both the apothecary and the nurse who had between them dressed the wound said that it was lacerated. Therefore it had not been caused by a sharp object, but something more like a nail.

It was considered a justice to add that Holland had before his death admitted that he was in the wrong, similarly that no blame was to be attributed to Mr Davenport, although a bond to guarantee Davenport's appearance at the Assizes was taken, should any charge be laid against him.

STUDENTS RULE

William Woodcock, Richard Higgs and William Hedges were charged with riot and assault by the Revd Mr Dyer, the Senior Proctor of the University.

On 7 May 1834 a large group of undergraduates accompanied by many townspeople were parading through the streets of Oxford. Mr Dyer, with a number of policemen, was out that evening clearing the streets, as all good Christian gentlemen ought to have been in bed by 10 p.m. Having already taken one student into custody, Dyer and his companions ran into a mob on Turl Street, who rescued

There has always been a special relationship between town and gown, and riots, especially during the University's early history, were renowned for being violent and even fatal. (OCCPA)

their fellow student. The Proctor was pushed about and in the process lost his cap and was forced to run into a shop on the High Street to seek refuge.

The prisoners, on recommendation of the judge, pleaded guilty and were bailed to appear, when called for, to receive judgment. It is not mentioned what their punishment was.

A RIDE IN THE COUNTRY

On 18 June 1834 Charles Hesketh Case, a student of Brasenose College, was in court having hired a horse from Thomas Barratt, an Oxford stable-keeper. Unlike other cases, it was not a question of whether the student was allowed to do this, but more that, having gone to Cottisford races, Case returned late at night and jumped the horse over several heaps of dirt. The horse eventually fell and damaged its knees as well as suffering further injuries.

Mr Barratt sued in the University court for the loss of business caused by the horse being out of action for more than three weeks. Case was eventually found guilty and ordered to pay £3 13s 6d in compensation, plus the costs of the court case.

DO NOT ARGUE WITH THE UNIVERSITY

On 6 July 1838 the University proceeded, in its own court, against George Cooke, an Oxford policeman, for violating the statutes and privileges of the University by removing and retaining the goods of a member of the University, David Durrell, without authority from the Chancellor's court.

Durrell lived with his family in Oxford and had been appointed as an overseer for the Parish of St Michael by two of the city justices. He had declined the position because, as a Member of Convocation, he was neither obliged to serve the office nor was he subject to the jurisdiction of the city magistrates. Both these objections were valid, as members of the University were subject to its rules and its court alone.

The overseers, as well as other churchwardens, were bound to collect the poor rate, but as Durrell had not taken up his position the poor rate had not been collected and

The Chancellor's Court heard cases relating to matriculated persons from the twelfth to the twentieth century. The central door leads to Convocation. (Giles Brindley)

The University Court occupies a small but attractive room. (Giles Brindley)

Durrell faced a penalty of £10. The fine was demanded by the Guardians, but Durrell refused to pay and a warrant was issued by Oxford's mayor to remove Durrell's possessions to this value. The policeman dispatched had entered Durrell's house and removed a silver cruet stand which was considered to be worth £12.

In court the University waved several charters asserting its rights and contended that the seizure of goods was illegal, as was Durrell's original appointment as an overseer for that parish. Since the original warrant was signed by the Mayor it bound Cooke, the policeman, and he had no alternative but to obey or he was liable to be charged by the city court for neglecting to execute it.

The University met the Mayor to discuss the matter and the goods taken were restored to Durrell. Cooke was made to apologise for the inconvenience he had caused the gentleman.

However, an action was still lodged in the University court, but when it next came up the prosecution asked that the case might be dismissed, to which the judge agreed, and no further action was taken against the Oxford policeman.

LACK OF MANNERS

On 27 February 1740 Robert Craddock, a grocer of the Parish of St Mary Magdalen, was in court over a certain business concerning the 'reformation of his manners'; it was as a result of his refusal to open the door of his house at night-time to admit the Revd Richard Lydiatt, one of the University Proctors, so that he could search for errant students. Craddock used 'contemptuous words and expressions' towards the said Proctor for which he confessed in the University court, was fined 20*s* and forced to make a public apology for his offence before the Vice-Chancellor and the Proctors.

POWER LIFTER

If it is not nailed down somebody will have it away, and even if it is, that is no guarantee. At the Lent Assizes of 1746 William Wall was charged with ripping up and making off with 26lb of lead, valued at 2s 6d, from the roof of Magdalen College on the night of 7 January that year.

THEFT OF SILVER SPOON

At the Lent Assizes of 1756 Sarah Whorwood (alias Horrod), described a desperate criminal, was convicted of grand larceny, for which crime she was liable to be marked and punished by branding her hand.

The judge in his leniency, however, commuted the sentence to transportation to one of His Majesty's colonies and plantations in America. Her crime: theft from the Warden and scholars of New College on 16 January 1756 of one silver spoon valued at 5s.

TREE LOPPING

On 8 March 1775 it was recorded that William Hyde was confined in the Castle gaol. He was serving a sentence of six months for lopping a young tree on 19 December 1774 which belonged to New College. Unfortunately for him, things went downhill from there: following his release from the Castle he was finally executed on 22 March 1779 for housebreaking.

PORT WINE COLLECTION

Some people have a taste for the high life and James Brucker was one such person. He was brought to trial at the summer Assizes in 1788. Brucker had managed to make off with 600 quarts of port (150 gallons or approximately 682 litres) and 600 glass bottles of the same, with a total value of 50 guineas, from Brasenose College. In April of the following year he was eventually transported for life to Botany Bay.

ARGUING THE TOSS

Sarah Stevens of the Vine tavern proceeded against Edward Mastyn Wade, a student of Trinity College, for trespass on 9 December 1841 and damages to the value of £10. It was shown in the University court that in November 1840 Wade with others had gone to the Vine where, in a riotous attack, they broke down the door to the bar and smashed glasses, among other things.

Wade was again present when they did the same in March 1841. Since Wade was the only person Stevens could identify, she had collared him and asked him for compensation, for which he had promised to speak to his friends. The group of friends objected to the £10 asked for, considering it to be extortionate, and had therefore gone to court. Here many witnesses proved the damage, for which the total came to £3 12s 6d. On being found guilty, Wade was induced to pay this adjusted amount.

ROUGH JUSTICE

Eights Week is one time when college rowing crews meet to race each other on the Isis. It is an occasion which is attended by thousands of spectators. But in June 1842 one boatman did not care for the spectacle. As the boats came up the river he charged down the towpath, knocking people over with his towing rope. The crowd argued with the man, but he would have none of it. So they grabbed hold of him and hefted him into the river, much to the amusement of the assembled crowd.

THE FAMILY BUSINESS

On 9 February 1844 George Bleay was charged and convicted of assaulting William Davis that day and fined 40s. The same day he was charged with assaulting his own brother, James. During the day James had made his way to see the Vice-Chancellor in Turl Street to give information against University members for riding on Port Meadow. As he passed the Maidenhead Inn his brother hit him from behind and James ran away, afraid to return. This scene was witnessed by George Cook, who heard George say, 'that if that long *** came there to give evidence he would knock his brains out'.

It transpired that the men riding on Port Meadow were gentlemen of Christ Church, among them several noblemen. The town clerk had gone to the butler of Christ Church for the students' names, but was refused. The clerk thought better of asking the college Dean for the information and never returned. James Bleay was happy to provide this information; however, his brother did not share his enthusiasm. It is not clear what George had to gain by stopping his brother, though it is possible that it was the Bleays who had hired the horses to the gentlemen of Christ Church in the first place.

No verdict was recorded against George for beating his brother and the case against the students was not taken any further. The Vice-Chancellor said he hoped it would act as a warning to students to treat the meadow with respect and not to inconvenience the freemen who had the rights to the land.

STEALING TROUSERS

One William Bull, aged 35, a groom, was convicted at the Assize court of felony for breaking and entering the cricket pavilion of New College on 22 May 1908 and stealing Cecil Ernest Wells Charrington's trousers. Bull confessed and was sentenced to six months' hard labour.

21

THE GENTLEMAN'S SECRET IDENTITY

Arriving on the Abels' doorstep in Bridport Street, St Ebbe's, at the beginning of June 1839, Mr Martin knocked. Sarah Abel answered the door and Martin, a surgeon and apothecary, asked if she would take a child in to be nursed. Martin said he would make payments as and when necessary. Sarah agreed and collected a 3-month-old baby the next week from Mrs Drew in St Clement's. Barely ten days later Sarah had another visitor, a well-dressed young woman. The woman said she had come from Abingdon and was the infant's aunt. When the woman saw the baby she clutched it in her arms, kissing and cuddling it. It was soon after that two parcels of baby clothes were delivered to Sarah by the Abingdon courier. When Martin next visited Sarah commented that the 'aunt' was so fond of the child that Sarah thought she was in fact the mother. Martin said flatly, 'No, it is not.'

Many months passed and no one visited, then on 4 October the aunt called again, but this time she was shabbily dressed. She made it obvious that she did not want to be recognised, but wanted to see the baby girl. Sarah told her that the child was asleep and a long conversation ensued, but the woman refused to go into the house. She said she was a servant and had only fifteen minutes, telling Sarah that there was somebody who wanted to see the child. She waited in the passageway until the little girl was brought out. The baby looked up and smiled at the visitor. The woman asked what her name was and Sarah told her: Mary Ann, the name which the woman who stood before her had given her. The visitor looked stunned, but asked Sarah for a further list of clothes the baby needed. She was told there was little the child wanted for and then left with the child in her arms.

Aunt and baby returned half an hour later. Sarah noticed the child had been crying and the woman agreed. Now to business the christening expenses were outstanding. Martin had previously told Sarah that the parents would pay for them when they called. So Sarah asked. The woman panicked: who was Mr Martin? Sarah explained and gave his address when asked, and the woman left.

Sarah saw that the baby's chin was spotty and very red. This was odd. The child's breath smelt pungent, but it was not beer or spirits. Sarah took the infant to a neighbour for her breath to be smelt, after which the child grew more and more restless. The baby was laid in a cot and although dozy was unable to sleep.

The baby began to struggle in a fit and foam at the mouth, so Sarah ran to the neighbours who told her to send for Mr Martin. He arrived an hour later at 6.30 p.m. Sarah was sure the baby had been poisoned and Martin criticised her because she had not called him sooner, saying he would have been able to do something about it if she had. Sarah related the story of the woman visitor. Martin thought it was odd that after asking for his address the woman had not come to see him.. But there were more pressing matters. The doctor prescribed a warm bath and emetics, saying Sarah should keep whatever the child threw up.

What little the baby vomited ended up on people's clothes. Martin called the next day and so did Mr Field, who also gave the child an emetic. It was Mr Abel's efforts, after he had run around Oxford, that had brought two doctors to the house. But neither was aware of the other having visited, which is what led to the baby receiving such a thorough flushing out.

Another day, another visit and more emetics. This time Martin managed to collect two spoonfuls of vomit at 2 a.m. the following morning, which were placed in a saucer for safe keeping, but a dog in the house licked it all up. Ever alert for an opportunity to advance scientific knowledge, it was recorded that the dog's subsequent health was fine. Martin left, saying, 'The mischief is done, and I cannot do anything more,' for 'it cannot last long, for you may expect that every breath will be its last.'

Three days after the mysterious visit of the child's aunt, at 6 a.m. on 7 October, the baby died. The inquest held the next day at the Bull Inn in St Ebbe's considered the death of 8-month-old Mary Ann Greenaway. Sarah had pointed out a stain on the baby's frock to Martin which she thought was laudanum. However, the post-mortem found no signs of poisoning or anything else untoward. After hearing several expert witness statements from doctors the jury returned a verdict of natural death.

That evening, the jury's foreman went to see the coroner. He had new evidence and a statement signed by the whole jury requesting a second inquest. The coroner told them that the case was closed and he could not reopen it nor instigate a second inquest. However, the coroner called on those who could and the Mayor and magistrates met to further examine the witnesses. They issued an arrest warrant for the child's mother, Mary Ann Greenaway, the namesake of her daughter.

Mary Ann was brought before the magistrates on 18 October and even though she admitted to being the child's mother and visiting in June she denied visiting again in October. She was remanded and brought out of gaol a week later for the second inquest. The evidence and the conclusions arrived at were the same, with one exception. Martin revealed that he knew the identity of the child's father, but would not release the name. There was a public outcry. Martin wished to 'prevent injury to a professional man'. The magistrates and coroner said that they also knew the man's name and were prepared to release it should it prove necessary. Finally, the prosecution admitted that there was just not enough evidence to send the prisoner to trial. The jury again returned a verdict that the child was not poisoned, but had died of natural causes, and Mary Ann was released.

Mary Ann's freedom did not last long. A further twist to the tale was added when she was again in court on 20 October. This time; she was charged with stealing from Mr Copeland of Abingdon. In court it was shown that it was not only Copeland who thought Mary Ann had stolen from him, a Mr Williams thought so, too. Mary Ann had been in Williams's service from April until September 1839. After she left, several items were found to be missing. A search warrant was obtained and five large boxes of Williams's property were found, one box in Wantage and four at Mary Ann's father's house in Steventon. The boxes were a treasure-trove of Williams's possessions, including clothes and table linen.

Copeland was prosecuting over his losses incurred on 29 September, including a child's silver-mounted coral and bells. This was the very same item which had arrived in one of the two parcels of baby clothes at Sarah Abel's shortly after Mary Ann's visit and had obviously come from the young woman's lootings. Mary Ann had stolen to clothe her baby and possibly herself and the jury felt sorry for her despite the impression that Mary Ann was more of a kleptomanic. The jury returned a guilty verdict but recommended, without giving a reason, leniency. The judge said at the time that had it not been for the jury's recommendation he would have had Mary Ann transported; instead she was sentenced to twelve months' hard labour.

22

THE EARLY DAYS OF MOBILE BANKING

On 18 March 1844 the Defiance coach left London carrying a box which contained 1,500 sovereigns, bound for Messrs Robinson, Parsons and Thompson of the Old Bank, High Street, Oxford. On reaching Oxford it was discovered that the box, which had been placed in the front boot by a porter of Coutts Bank, was missing. Confusion reigned at the time of the discovery and it was considered that the theft was the result of a cleverly contrived plot, put into effect by several individuals, members of a 'swell mob'.

At 10 a.m. on the 18th the Defiance coachman, Hobson, called at Coutts and signed the receipt which would release 1,500 sovereigns to be paid to the Oxford Bank, handing it to Mr Hare who was to prepare the consignment. Hare, at Coutts Strand office, weighed out the coins, placed them in a tied bag and handed them to Richard Quint, one of the bank's porters.

Criminals often made their getaway by coach. (Neil Storey Archive)

Quint placed the bag in a wooden box and nailed shut the lid, which bore the address of the Oxford Bank, and placed it inside a blue bag. On the inside of this bag a label read: Coutts and Co., 59 the Strand. The bag was tied and Quint set off to the Gloucester coffee house in London to meet the Defiance at noon.

Quint waited in a side street next to the coffee house. Hobson had only left the Belle Sauvage on Ludgate Hill at noon, collecting several passengers along the way. By the time he reached the coffee house the boot was almost full of luggage and parcels for Oxford, but Hobson took the consignment from Quint and placed the heavy blue bag near the bottom of the front boot. Taking on another passenger there he made sure the bag was safe and set off for Oxford at 12.40 p.m. The passenger list stated this person to be a 'gentleman'. He was a big man in a dark blue greatcoat and hat which obscured his face, who climbed aboard and sat next to the coachman on the box. On nearing Knightsbridge horse barracks, he said to Hobson that there was somebody who wanted to get on the coach, but there was nobody waiting there. He pointed to a gin shop from where the person wished to board, but no one was seen, though the coachman obligingly stopped. There was no one at the door or in the street. Then Richard Elliott stepped out of the shop and raised his hand as if to hail the coach, but the coach had already stopped. Elliott turned around, went back into the shop, returned a few minutes later and climbed on the back of the coach. He was wearing a large, drab-coloured coat. Hobson asked where he was going. Elliott said 'Benson', was informed that the fare was 6*s*, and they set off.

The Crown Inn on the High Street in Benson was a coaching inn and continues to offer accommodation for travellers. (Giles Brindley)

The horses were changed several times along the way. Hobson checked on the bag at Longford and they arrived in Benson at 6.45 p.m., immediately before dusk. The passengers disembarked, some going for a walk, others going into the Crown Inn, outside which they had stopped. The horses were changed while the coach was in the charge of the Crown's ostler and his assistant. Hobson and Mr Scrubb, the coach proprietor, went in to discuss the passenger list and bill with Mr Costar the innkeeper. William Chapman, Scrubb's servant, watched his master and Hobson go into the Crown and then saw someone come down from the back of the coach and climb up on the splinter bar, with one foot on the wheel, and open the lid of the boot from the off side. Chapman was taking his master's bags inside and the man had his back to him, but Chapman did notice he wore a light-coloured coat, the same as Elliott's. Richard Carr, the ostler, likewise observed a man in a light-coloured coat standing on the splinter bar, leaning over and doing something in the boot.

Inside the Crown, Costar, having met Hobson, then saw Elliott walk in and look out of the front window, where he could see the coach, as if keeping watch. Elliott eventually came into the passage between the front door and the bar and asked Hobson for change so that he could pay his fare. Outside, Martin Mountjoy, another passenger, returning from stretching his legs, came within a short distance of the coach when he observed the man who had sat on the box with the coachman apparently pulling the luggage about in the front boot of the coach on the near side,

The Old Bank Hotel, 92–4 High Street. Number 92, left, was home to Messrs Robinson, Parsons and Thompson in 1844. (Giles Brindley)

where the coachman had been sitting. Mountjoy watched, worried in case his bag was taken away. The man merely removed a large blue bag, but Mountjoy did not see what happened to it. Inside, Elliott had tipped Hobson 1*s* and offered a beer; Hobson declined saying he had already had his beer, but Mrs Costar had already drawn another glass of ale and Hobson reluctantly said he would drink some. He left Elliott at the bar and headed back to the coach. The coach had remained at the Crown for less than ten minutes.

The coach set off, stopping for the last time at the Harcourt Arms at Nuneham for its lamps to be lit before arriving in Oxford. Hobson pulled the coach up outside the Old Bank where Mr Parsons was waiting, and on opening the boot the blue bag containing 1,500 sovereigns was not there. A lamp was brought and Hobson turned the coach upside down, but was left to explain to the waiting Parsons that the bag was 'missing'. All Hobson could now do was drive the remaining passengers to their final destination at the Vine Inn, where they alighted, including the man who sat upon the box – he left the way he had arrived, luggageless. Hobson quizzed his passengers before they finally departed, asking if they had seen anyone touch the boot. The box man said, 'No', tipped 1*s* and disappeared into the night.

That night Elliott stayed at the Crown in Benson. He called for tea and some dry toast and when it was brought to him he was found wandering around the house, but eventually went to bed at 8.25 p.m. taking his empty carpet bag with him.

Thomas Lucas, a policeman, had received information concerning the theft which pointed to it having occurred at Benson, so off he went to visit Richard Elliott, arriving sometime before midnight at the Crown Inn. Here Costar joined Lucas and the two men went upstairs to see Elliott. They found his bedroom door unlocked and called to him as they entered. Elliott was awake, and Lucas explained that he had come to make enquiries. The policeman got Elliott out of bed and the room was searched. They found not only clothes, but a fair amount of money including, suspiciously, nineteen sovereigns in various pockets. Having turned the room upside down, Lucas and Costar remade the bed and Elliott climbed back in, finally revealing that he was a cigar dealer and tobacconist of Bell Street, Paddington, London, and on his way to Box, near Bath.

Elliott often remained silent while Lucas questioned him, only yielding information after several attempts at asking, though he had been very keen to find out what the policeman knew. Lucas gave little away. He wanted to take Elliott to Oxford for further questioning. Elliott was unwilling to go as it was 'out of his way', but Lucas said that he would be just as close to Box. Elliott refused to go unless Lucas insisted, which he did, and Elliott dressed. On going downstairs, Elliott had the cheek to ask for his money back. Again, he protested about going, this time saying that he had promised to meet people at Eton and Windsor. Lucas merely noted these discussions in his pocketbook and took Elliott directly back to Oxford. The policeman made one concession: he allowed Elliott to wear his overcoat, which Lucas had confiscated along with all the man's other possessions.

On the night of the robbery William Burgess, innkeeper of the King's Arms, was on his way home to Sandford from Nuneham when he passed the Defiance coach and shortly afterwards came upon an object lying in a ditch. It was a blue bag, containing a heavy deal box filled with sand, stone and bricks, which he then proceeded to deliver to Mr Thompson's house in Oxford, Thompson being one of the Oxford

The Justice's Residence on St Giles's was where the judge would stay when he presided over the city's Assize court. (Giles Brindley).

Bankers. But when and why the bag was dropped from the coach or thrown away would forever remain a mystery.

On 29 March Elliott was brought before the magistrates for examination. Mr Ballantine and Mr Robinson applied to be present on behalf of Elliott, but the judge refused counsel or attorney to be in attendance, or for them to hold any conversation with Elliott. Likewise Elliott's wife was refused permission to see her husband. On 15 April Elliott was again brought before the magistrates and bail was set at £500 and £250 each for two sureties. Ballantine complained bitterly that the bail was exorbitant, saying that they would appeal.

Elliott faced trial at the Assizes in the week leading up to 20 July 1844. During the trial, the following was conjectured to have been what actually happened. The man on the box seat had joined at the Gloucester coffee house; two more of the gang joined at Knightsbridge, one of whom was Elliott. Shortly before they arrived at Benson a stranger dressed as a 'fashionable sporting character' turned up looking for some 'Marlow ale', saying he would catch the coach to Oxford. Though he may have met the coach, nobody saw him nor did he ever actually travel to Oxford. When at Benson, Elliott had looked in the boot and gone into the Crown to distract the coachman. His accomplice on the box had removed the blue bag, concealing it from view with his coat and handing it to, they supposed, their 'sporting' friend, who was well known to the London police. The 'sportsman' had the bag taken to Wallingford station. In fact, by the time the robbery was discovered in Oxford, the coins had already reached London by train. But there was no proof and only Elliott stood charged. There was enough confusion in witness statements that the defence managed to seed doubt in the minds of the jury, who finally acquitted Elliott and he walked out of court a free man – and possibly a little richer to boot.

23

WORKING, ROBBING AND OTHER PROFESSIONS

A LONG DROP

Insider information is essential in any well-planned robbery, but it pays to reward your sources. In November 1675 two thieves carried out a daring raid on New College. Smyth and his unknown accomplice learned that Henry Nobes, the New College butler, had died two days previously. It was an unremarkable death, but it left a significant gap in New College security; until a new butler was appointed, the buttery wall would be unguarded at night. The thieves saw their opportunity and seized it. On 6 November, at the dead of night, they scaled the buttery wall (at the time the buttery wall was the external college wall; the buildings along Holywell Street were constructed at a much later date). Out of earshot of the sleeping college staff they were able to make off with the majority of New College's plate, valued at the time at £200.

Aware that any attempt to sell the stolen items in Oxford would arouse suspicion, the thieves made their way to London where they sold the plate for £90 to a fellow named Dogget, a petty forger posing as a goldsmith. Dogget then melted the plate down and sold it on to a goldsmith for an undisclosed, but presumably far higher, sum.

It is unlikely that the thieves' identity would have been discovered had they not reneged on their deal with Ingram, the person who had given them information about New College. He had alerted them to the possible route into the college and in return for this information was to receive a share of the spoils. When his share failed to materialise, Ingram betrayed the two men and in so doing so triggered a chain of allegations. While on the run, Smyth was incarcerated in Carlisle gaol; Dogget was caught and imprisoned and in turn supplied evidence which implicated the goldsmith. There is no record of what became of the unknown accomplice. Both Dogget and Smyth were sentenced to hang for their involvement in the robbery. However, Dogget was granted a royal pardon and escaped execution. Smyth was not so fortunate. He was brought from Carlisle gaol to Oxford and hanged for his crimes in March 1677.

The robbery fuelled an angry debate about policing in Oxford. At a meeting held between the time of the theft and Smyth's hanging several townsmen accused the Mayor and bailiffs of not patrolling the city. The University justices said this was the case, but asserted it was their right to patrol the city at night. In response, the City Council said it was their right and demanded a trial to prove it. Whatever the outcome, what is certain is that if there had been a patrol on the night of 6 November, the New College plate would not have been stolen.

THE DIRTY DOZEN

Twelve men entered Gloucester Hall (now Worcester College) on the night of 19 October 1687 between the hours of midnight and 1 a.m. They had arrived at the main gate and were let in by an accomplice who had entered before the gate was shut at 9 p.m. The accomplice forced the bars of a ground-floor window, wrenching it open to allow the group through. With lighted candles, they went to the sleeping occupants of the hall and woke them, binding the hands and feet of each one except for Dr Eaton, the Warden. They proceeded to loot the hall of all its silver, including everything that belonged to Dr Eaton himself. Not only that, they took rings, jewels and clothes belonging to the Warden's daughters. Then the men went downstairs and ate whatever they could find, polishing off three or four bottles of wine while toasting the young ladies until about 4 a.m. when they finally left.

Dr Eaton's loss was about £300. Considering that he had been robbed twice within the last two years or so, he managed to remain in good humour.

BOOKS WITHOUT WORDS

There was a time when books were very rare and expensive and they were chained to the library shelves. In October 1705, despite the chains, Christ Church found several of its books had gone missing. A cunning servitor of the college had cut the pages away from the bindings, leaving the covers on the shelves so it looked as if the books were still there. It was only when the cheeky student went to have the pages rebound in order to sell them that he was reported to the college authorities by the bookbinder.

To add to his crimes Taylor, the servitor, had recently managed to con a gentleman commoner out of 120 guineas. That was one way to fund a University education!

PAINT A THOUSAND WORDS

Old John Pricket, of University College, was caught in July 1716 stealing candles from the college. This he had done for many years, fencing items through another old rogue, Tonser Gilman.

So infamous were they that above the buttery door had been painted a scene depicting the theft with Gilman standing in the pillory and Pricket riding to hell on the devil's shoulders.

LAST WORKING DAY

Mrs Stone, formerly kitchen assistant at Brasenose College, had later taken up the profession of laundress. As she entered University College in September 1723, aged 70, she keeled over and died.

FAMILY JEWELS DAMAGED

On 22 September 1760, as the third floor of the Radcliffe Infirmary was under construction, one of the labourers was carrying a stone block up an outside ladder. As he neared the third floor his companion below, likewise with a stone block, started to climb the ladder. As the first reached the top of the ladder he let slip the block, which, gathering momentum, headed downwards towards the man's companion. The lower man was now twenty rungs up the ladder and moving well, though soon to be airborne, as the stone missile hit his load. The blocks landed safely, but the unfortunate man crashed with legs astride, his loins bearing the majority of the impact upon the stones. Despaired of, he was taken home to die. But after medical attention a recovery was expected. Earlier that summer he had had another airborne adventure when he had fallen from a rookery and broken both arms.

A SACK OF SILVER

Having slept soundly, the family of Sir Banks Jenkinson awoke in their Headington house on the morning of 13 September 1778 to find that a huge amount of silverware had been stolen: £600-worth to be exact. The finger of suspicion was soon pointed. The family had employed a man on 8 and 9 September to take apart and clean all the locks in the house. This had been carefully done by a travelling locksmith named Thomas Storer, who was noticed by the family to pay a little too much attention to the lock on the butler's pantry, where all the silver was kept. Storer had been out in Oxford in the days between his visit and the robbery casually questioning a silversmith as to the price paid for old silver.

The police raided Storer's lodgings and his girlfriend told them that they had had an argument on Saturday evening and that Storer had left. They searched the house, but found nothing. Unfortunately for Storer, the police caught up with him and he was arrested only two hours later. At this point the police also discovered that a young boy had seen Storer at 6 a.m. on the 13th, the morning when the robbery was discovered. He had been spotted lurking near the Cherwell, on its eastern side. Storer was slapped in gaol while the police looked for evidence.

Experts were brought in from Reading and London. They decided it would have been nearly impossible for Storer to have dragged such a large amount of booty all the way back to Oxford. Therefore a fingertip search was made of every hedge, ditch and bird's nest in Headington for the property. This drew a blank, so the police headed to the river where Storer had been seen the morning of the heist, and drained the Cherwell until a sack was revealed, held under Nappers Bridge above Holywell Mill. The sack's contents yielded all but three silver spoons from Sir Banks's house.

The sharp-witted detectives were not finished yet. The Headington robbery was rather similar to one perpetrated on Dr Smith's house in Oxford on 23 July and a tip-off led them to Storer's mother's house in Fulham and also his brother, a silversmith. Storer's brother, Joseph, was apprehended and confessed that he had sold a load of silver belonging to Dr Smith to a Mr Perkins for £20, and the rest of Dr Smith's silver was found at their mother's in Fulham. The local paper kindly commented that the servants of both Sir Banks and Dr Smith must have been happy since the robbers had been arrested, as servants were usually the first to be blamed for all such losses.

By now both Thomas and his brother Joseph were sitting in the Castle gaol awaiting trial on 3 March 1779. At the trial Thomas was charged with the robbery and found guilty, for which he was sentenced to three years' hard labour on the Thames, but no record is found of Joseph being charged, so he must have walked away from gaol a free man.

A LITTLE MIDNIGHT GARDENING

Mr Walker, who lived near George Street, was fed up, as his garden had been robbed of plants and vegetables throughout the month of August 1788. At 2 a.m. on the morning of the 10th, Walker's servant watched as two men climbed over an adjoining wall. Walking to the far end of the garden, the robbers looked round to check that nobody was watching before they began to pull up onions. Back in the house, the servant was loading a gun with ball and shot. He took aim and blasted at the men, who legged it back over the wall the way they had come, disappearing towards the cover of the Oxford streets.

DON'T I KNOW YOU?

John Hanks, owner of Osney Mill, stopped at the pub at the corner of Bullocks Lane on Saturday 27 October 1792 for a beer on his way home. Drinking there were William Barrett and some companions. They all, Hanks included, left the pub at 11 p.m. As Hanks passed through St Thomas's Parish he noticed Barrett and two others following him 25 to 30ft behind.

The pursuers disappeared and minutes later Hanks was walking down Kite Lane and nearing home. A man, stripped to the waist, rushed him and demanded cash, making violent threats that if Hanks did not cough up within five minutes he would be a dead man and that the ditch would be his grave. Hanks thought it was a joke. The threats were repeated and Hanks said that if this was the case he would have to fight first. The men grappled, struggled and pushed apart. The miller's assailant continued to make threats and Hanks handed over a guinea. Bizarrely, the mugger whistled and yelled that all was well and he was not known. Surprised, Hanks asked if he should know him and farcically the robber said 'Yes'.

Despite being the dead of night, it did not take much for Hanks to work out that it was Barrett who had robbed him. Barrett had stripped off his shirt and thrown away his black handkerchief, which was found the next morning on Kite Lane. Hanks remembered that Barrett had been wearing this handkerchief around his neck when the two had met earlier that night in the pub. Barrett was promptly arrested by Mr Smith the policeman and charged before the magistrates, where Hanks identified him. Barrett had already tried to launder the guinea that evening by changing it in another pub at around midnight.

Barrett was tried on 17 and 18 January 1793, found guilty and sentenced to death for the highway robbery. On 7 February, while in the Castle gaol, he was reprieved and his sentence commuted to fourteen years' transportation to the eastern coast of New South Wales. Barrett was taken the next day to the hulks in London.

GETTING ONE'S JUST DESERTS

Somewhat after 7 p.m. on 23 November 1796 the Bicester mail coach, driven by John Heritage, was stopped on the road by the parks by a highwayman who presented a pistol. The nervous highwayman demanded money and said to be quick about it or he would shoot. Heritage reached for his money, but the man, seeing a horn in his hand, supposed Heritage would resist and struck first, hitting Heritage on the hand. The horse took fright and bolted with the wounded Heritage at the reins, running down the highwayman and grinding him into the mud.

Heritage, ever attentive to duty, dropped off the mail in Oxford before going to Smith the policeman. Smith returned with others and went after the villain. He apprehended a suspicious person lurking near Worcester College. The man, David Jones, was covered in mud and had in his pockets something pistol-shaped; the weapon was stained with blood and mud. Heritage was brought in and identified the man, and Jones was committed to the gaol to await his trial. Jones was found guilty on 12 January 1797 and sentenced to be 'transported to parts beyond the seas', for seven years.

AN EXPLOSIVE OCCUPATION

Mr Bayne, a cutler on the High Street, was at work grinding a kitchen knife on an 18in spinning stone behind which he sat on 3 June 1817. With an almighty bang, the fast-spinning stone split into three pieces. One piece, weighing at least 7lb, crashed through the window, removing five of the glass panes and the wooden frame. It continued on its trajectory, soaring across the High Street and landing on the other side 50ft away. The other two pieces had simultaneously headed for Bayne and, together with the spindle, sent him flying out of his seat and into the middle of the shop. Badly bruised in the shinbone, Bayne seemed otherwise unhurt except for the fact that he was in such a state of shock that his whole body shook.

STRIP THE BEDS

A man arriving at the Dog and Partridge in Broad Street said he was a gardener and needed a room for a few nights. It was 4 October 1818 and he stayed for two nights. Leaving early, he took with him sheets, pillowcases and even flannel petticoats. In fact, he took whatever came to hand, presumably neglecting to pay his bill as well.

SHOEMAKERS' CARTEL

John Weston appeared in court on 18 November 1818. Weston had prevented Mr Bradstreet from employing two other travelling shoemakers in Bradstreet's shoe shop. For a long time past the city's travelling shoemakers had held regular weekly meetings and were so well organised that they had complete control over their employers. In court it was proved that Weston and another man had gone to Bradstreet as delegates from this body and insisted he fired two other travelling shoemakers from his employ as they were 'obnoxious' because they would not conform to the body's rules and regulations.

Bradstreet had been left with a choice: either fire the two men or his work would not get done. At the end of the trial Weston was convicted and sent to gaol for three months. At the same time the magistrates said they would not renew the licence for the public house where the cartel of shoemakers held their regular meetings.

FUMBLING FOR GOLD

At midnight on the night of 28 May 1819 the Revd Mr Bardgett of Merton College was returning to college from Headington. When he was about 50yd from Marston Lane he was jumped by three men. Since it was dark, he had not seen them until it was too late. One grabbed him by the waist and threw him into a ditch, falling with him. Kneeling on top of Mr Bardgett the man searched his pockets. The thief removed three gold seals – gold keys; one with a mariner's compass – cash and an ivory snuffbox, as well as another bunch of keys.

While this was going on Mr Bardgett managed to locate his pocket knife. He hoped to cut his fob to at least save his watch. But a fight ensued, each man having hold of something. The villain had the watch chain and when it broke the watch disappeared into the reverend's trousers. The robber followed it with his right hand. The scholarly gentleman was none too pleased and in return stabbed the man's wrist. For this Bardgett was rewarded with a violent punch to the face and some foul language.

The men ran away and Bardgett was left to pick up the pieces. The fellow found that his hat had been taken and a very old one stuffed with straw had been left in its place. Bardgett made for Oxford, later returning to the scene of the crime with his brother. By the light of a lantern they viewed the gate on the opposite side of the lane from where he had been mugged. This was the last place he had seen his assailants as the men legged it. They found a great deal of blood on the gatepost, indicating that Bardgett had cut the man to a fair extent.

It was suspected the men were boatmen. Why? When one boatman, with his hand tied, was told of the robbery he seemed rather agitated. Mr Bliss, the University policeman, teamed up with a boatman who was acquainted both with the canals and the prime suspect. They set off at 10 p.m., three days after the robbery. They found two of their main suspects: Richard Ayres at Fenny Compton and Thomas Smith, the man with the cut wrist, at Longford, near Coventry. The men were brought back to Oxford on Thursday at 2.30 a.m., and examined before the Vice-Chancellor that very day.

The third man remained at large, but it was not long before he was brought in. Samuel King, alias Bandy Sam, was committed to gaol on 19 June. King confessed that he, with Smith and Ayres, had robbed Bardgett. Smith and Ayres went to court on 24 July 1819. King had turned evidence on his former accomplices. Smith and Ayres were found guilty of highway robbery and sentenced to death; Ayres was reprieved before they went down. But Smith had committed such an atrocious offence that he was told to expect no mercy. However, on the day before his execution was due, he was given a week's reprieve until 10 September.

Smith finally suffered his sentence and was executed on the 10th. Ayres was sent to the *Leviathan* convict ship at Portsmouth on 6 November 1819, thereafter to start his life transportation sentence.

THE CRIMINAL MARK

Mr Taylor was on his way home to Holywell Parish at 10 p.m. on 29 November 1821. A man, without a hat dressed in a striped jacket ran up and grabbed Taylor's gold watch chain complete with gold key and gold seal. The chain broke at the watch and the villain ran off up Lincoln and Brasenose Lanes. He was described as a young man who had been seen in company with another begging in the streets – both without hats, which must have been one way of identifying a criminal.

AT THE END OF THE PARTY

Mr Kerby's, on the north side of Holywell Street, was broken into during the night of 4 October 1822. The raiding party entered the back garden from the parks. They broke a pane of glass in the back-room window, which enabled them to get into the house. Here they cleared out the silverware and more, searching through all the bureau drawers. They even took a pair of clean stockings and left their dirty ones. Now came the time to leave; their footsteps were later tracked back across the garden and to a ladder up against the wall. Here they had jumped over into Miss Chapman's garden, where there had been a rowdy party that night.

The raiders had not yet finished. They entered Miss Chapman's via the back room and into the adjoining pantry. The pantry door was not locked and gave easy access to all her silverware, which had been deposited at the end of her party. The thieves removed bread baskets, knives, forks, table, dessert and teaspoons, cream jugs and a fair amount more. Miss Chapman offered a reward in the local paper for information leading to the conviction of the robbers and the return of her property, but the burglars had disappeared, never to be heard of again.

WORKING BOTH SIDES OF THE STREET

On the night of 23 April 1824 two men, James Cook and James Rose, sat together and drank in the house of James Cox Jr publican of St Thomas's Parish. The pair were then joined by Henry Lock and Thomas Smith and all four continued to drink until midnight, when Rose and Cook left. They were heading for Mr Webb's in St Ebbe's Parish on a mission.

Webb was a lamplighter and the men well knew he would have a ladder stored there. Swiping the ladder to undertake their night's work, they dashed across town. Using the ladder to scale two walls, they dropped into Mr Tagg's garden in Paradise Square. From here they propped up the ladder in the garden against the back wall of John Cook's house. John was James's father.

The son, accompanied by Rose, smashed a pane of glass in an upstairs window and, reaching inside to open it, gained entry and proceeded to burgle the house. Working quickly, they plundered what they could and departed the way they had come, returning with their pickings to Cox's house where James lodged.

Lock and Smith, who had been waiting for them, met the two robbers as they entered the house, and between them they divided the stolen items: clothes, money and silverware.

The next morning, having discovered his house broken into and his possessions gone, John Cook went in search of clues. The amateur sleuth discovered the footprints of two men which had left distinct impressions in the moss of his garden just below the house's wall. One set in particular stood out; the marks indicated that the front part of the boot was studded with two different types of nails and that the heels were metal-capped. Cook measured and detailed the precise dimensions of the shoe's imprint. When the authorities came to trace these distinctive hobnail boots they rapidly found them – attached to James Rose. After he had been caught 'red-footed' the boots were stripped from him and taken to be compared with the prints in Cook's garden. They corresponded in all respects to the impressions left and the net began to tighten; possibly too tight for James, as he had already squealed and confessed all. Having been taken to his father's house by Rose, he had been quick to point the finger, leading the police not only to Rose but to Lock and Smith as well. The police promptly arrested them too; unfortunately for Lock and Smith they were caught wearing some of the stolen property, including John's shirts.

James Cook now became the prosecution's star witness and proved his worth at the subsequent trial on 12 July. Rose was charged with robbery and Lock, Smith and Cox with receiving stolen goods. The finger of suspicion having been pointed at James Cox, the only evidence against him was that the stolen property was found in his house. Considering that Smith and Cook lived there, the police had no reason to suspect Cox of any involvement and he was found not guilty, as was Smith. Rose and Lock were not so lucky: both being found guilty, Lock was to be transported for fourteen years and Rose received the death sentence.

But James had not finished. Having turned once that day, he then gave evidence for the prosecution in another trial. This was for another burglary, barely a week after the first, on 29 April. This time the house in question was that of Christopher Corbett in St Thomas's Parish. One of the key players was none other than James Cook.

On the night in question there was a dance at the house of James Cox. Cook was there with his 'associate'. During the evening, leaving the festivities behind, the two men took a stroll together in the fresh air. Chatting away, the other man suggested they burgle Corbett's house. Cook agreed, and so keen was his friend that he dashed off to fetch his housebreaking implements before the two went to their intended victim's house. Having done some more plundering, this time of groceries and money, they went to Cox's house where it was divvied up. Perhaps Cox was not involved, but he seemed to have missed the fact that his lodgers kept acquiring new possessions . . . seemingly overnight.

As before, Cook was the star and practically only witness for the prosecution. But whom had he fingered this time? None other than Thomas Smith who had just escaped conviction only moments earlier. Smith was found guilty of robbery and sentenced to seven years' transportation. Having dispatched three of his former accomplices, Cook walked out of court a free man.

CAUGHT IN THE ACT

John Box was riding home to Henley just before 8 p.m. on 8 March 1825 and had reached the top of Rose Hill when two men rushed at him, one from either side of the road. The first smashed Box's head with a bludgeon, stunning him. This only served to frighten his horse who reared up and trampled one of the villains as it started off at full gallop, saving John from being robbed, though not from a battering.

WHO'S WATCHING THE WATCHMEN

Under cover of darkness on 29 November 1828, the lock to the front door of Mr Hopkins, coachmaker in the High Street, was picked. The contents of the nearby cupboard – cold meat, wine and so on – were removed and four burglars sat down to eat. In the dark one of the servant girls came downstairs to get something for her mistress who was ill. The men bolted, but she caught sight of the last man as he left through the front door, which she rushed to shut. One of the men had the cheek to tap on the door and, in a low whisper, asked to be let back in. The girl refused and ran to Mr Hopkins Jr who jumped out of bed, took a light and went downstairs. On entering the room where the men had been he found two sacks crammed full of meat, boots, shoes, in fact everything from the front rooms of the house that had not been nailed down. The owners later realised that some silver plate was missing from the back of the house. When they searched the rooms they found one pair of the robbers' shoes. It was presumed that when the servant girl went upstairs there were other men still in the house, and that they made their escape from the rear before Hopkins's son arrived on the scene.

After satisfying himself that there was nobody left in the house, Hopkins went after a night watchman. It was now 3.30 a.m., but he could not track down any of those 'faithful guardians of the night'. When he did finally find the parish watchman, the man was sound asleep in his bed.

It was commented upon at the time that the system of protecting the parishes was of little use as the watchmen were rarely at their posts and that, like buses, three or four could usually be found together; generally in the pub. This was blamed on the trifling wages the watchmen received and the fact that those in the 'big houses' did not give anything extra to the watchmen.

A COACHLESS COACHMAN

The Magnet coach ran between Cheltenham and Oxford. On 16 January 1829, when the coachman jumped down at the Hollybush pub on New Road, the horses bolted and galloped away. At full pelt, the horse and carriage turned the corner at St Peter-le-Bailey and careered up Butcher Row (now Queen Street), where terrified people dived out of the way. Several people tried to stop the animals, which only served to frighten them more, and they increased their pace until they reached Carfax. There, going at speed, the horses could not corner tight enough to turn down Cornmarket and the coach crashed into Mr Breakspear's shop. The one and only passenger inside was not aware there was any problem until the coach went crashing through the draper's window and he saw people running up to extricate the poor horses from the carnage.

The strange thing was that many people who saw the accident said that if nobody had tried to stop the horses, they thought the team would have taken the coach safely to its final destination at the Roebuck. This would not have been the first time a coach, minus coachman, had continued until it arrived safely at journey's end.

NINE MEN IN A PUNT

In October 1831 James Brooks lost his punt. When he located it at Mr Drewitt's paper mill in South Hinksey and asked for it to be returned, Drewitt informed him that the punt had floated into his waterwheel and caused a large amount of damage – estimated at £5. Brooks was amazed and said that if this was the case then the punt would have needed to have 'floated' 300yd upstream against the current and, anyway, £5 was more than the punt was worth, so Drewitt was welcome to it.

There were disputed versions of events that claimed Drewitt had later offered Brooks his punt back if he paid 5s. What is certain is that Brooks was determined to recover his property. However, there was one snag: the waterwheel had sunk the punt and it would have to be raised from the river bed before it could be carted away.

On 17 October Brooks, two of his sons and Mr Panton and Mr Surridge set out to the paper mill to reclaim the lost property. The five men walked into Drewitt's garden and over to the river bank where they proceeded to dredge for it. Drewitt looked out of his window and saw the men in his garden attempting to make off with the punt. In a furious rage, Drewitt flew out across the garden, yelling that they could not have it. Brooks said they would take it by force unless somebody stopped them and Drewitt went full steam back across the garden. Minutes later, while Brooks and co. were preparing to leave, Drewitt returned with six men, including four of the Holloway family, and a loaded gun. Marching forwards, pistol aimed and hand outstretched, Drewitt threatened to blow Brooks's brains out. Obscenities were soon followed by blows from every direction; many of the combatants were armed with poles.

The fight continued until Brooks and party climbed into the punt and tried to leave. Drewitt was not having any of that and jumped in after them with three of the Holloways leaping through the air after him. The heavily loaded punt rocked around as the battleground moved from land to sea. Brooks was pulled down and Drewitt banged Brooks's head against the side of the punt. Having finished with this punishment, Drewitt dragged Brooks half over the side of the punt and forced his head under the water in an attempt to drown him.

To avoid further roughing up, Brooks and his crew broke free, escaped from the punt and ran into the neighbouring meadow. Unfortunately the Drewitt posse had not finished and ran after them. Catching up with Brooks and his men, they meted out further justice, battering them some more. Drewitt pointed the pistol at Surridge and, in true desperado fashion, threatened 'to blow his heart's blood out'. In a final rescue attempt, Drewitt's wife and daughters surrounded Surridge, fearing that he would be killed, and took him back to the house for safety – though it does seem a little more like a move into the lion's den.

The trial came on 5 November when Drewitt and friends were charged with assaulting Brooks and his men. The same day all four Holloways were charged with assaulting a county court bailiff by the name of James McGraw. Armed with a warrant and men, McGraw had gone to the Holloways' house on 26 October to seize their possessions. One of McGraw's party had succeeded in forcing a window at the house in Grandpont to let the others in. Once inside the group worked quickly, collecting various articles, and were taking them away through the front door when the Holloways returned to their home. They were less than pleased to see their possessions walking out of the house before their eyes. They jumped the men and took back their goods, giving the bailiffs a sound beating before they could escape.

WORKING FOR DRINKING MONEY

Robert Barney, a 14-year-old apprentice to Mr Buckland, was making his way from New College on 27 January 1836. He had turned the corner at what is now the History Faculty library when John Williams and Charles Saunders stopped him. The men asked Barney if he had any money. He said he had none, whereupon Saunders punched him in the stomach, which made money rattle in a box inside his clothes. They gagged Barney with a handkerchief and forced him round the corner into New College Lane. Here they held him while they emptied out the box, which contained two half-crowns, a shilling and three sixpences. Considerately they gave Barney back 1s 6d and the box, having divided the rest equally between themselves. Then Saunders said, 'Come on, let's go to London', and the men ran off towards the High Street.

Barney cried, and making his way home past Brasenose and Oriel met William Wheeler, who, on hearing the lad's story, went with George Bossom, the policeman, and apprehended the men as they drank in a pub in St Thomas's Parish. At court in April the men were both found guilty and sentenced, each to be transported for seven years.

FOURTH TIME UNLUCKY

Mr Walker, solicitor of Oxford, had his clerk, named East, take a writ to serve on a grocer, Mr Eaton, in Queen Street. The young clerk called at the grocer's twice on the morning of 12 July 1836 and though Mr Bartlett, the shopman, was there, Eaton himself was not.

Returning later, the grocer left his house with some books under his arm and met the clerk in the street outside his shop. After popping into a neighbouring house, Eaton returned to the shop without the books and, hopping mad, told Bartlett that if anybody came from Walker's the shopman should kick them out of the door. At that point the clerk came in, placed the writ on the shop counter and rapidly exited. Eaton went after East, dragged him all the way back into the shop by his coat collar and proceeded to punch him about the head and face. He knocked him down and as he did so the clerk's head hit the counter. As East stood up the grocer grabbed his collar in one hand, the writ in the other, and endeavoured to ram the paper down East's throat, saying, 'I'll teach you to serve me with a copy of a writ.' Fearful of further reprisals, East said he would take the writ and went back to Mr Walker's.

At his trial on 2 January 1837 Eaton was found guilty of assault and fined damages of £10. A week later Walker entered another charge for the same offence, though what he hoped to gain the second time around could only be left to the imagination.

It would seem to have been an unprovoked attack, but was it? A final court case was to decide upon the events which premeditated the attack. Walker had given Eaton £10 to become a shareholder in the formation of a new company, the Oxford and London Coach Company. Having done this, Walker wanted an agreement to be drawn up between all parties, which he would, naturally, charge them £60–70 to do. The shareholders baulked and declined, because of the price, and Walker demanded his money back, saying he wanted nothing more to do with the venture. But the company had already commenced operations and likewise incurred costs. Eaton, as treasurer, considered that Walker was bound to bear his share of the profit or loss, having already entered into an agreement by giving his £10. The company ran for two to three months, but it was unsuccessful and finally dissolved. Not getting what he wanted, when he wanted it, Walker had issued a writ against Eaton to make him personally repay the £10. This final case on 27 February, brought by Walker to recover his £10, was thrown out and Walker left empty-handed.

FRINGE BENEFITS

A mother took her children to Mr Taplin, the hairdresser in St Aldate's, on 13 February 1836. Nothing unusual there, but as the hairdresser busied about his work the children's mother pocketed four combs and a small black book. The woman paid for the cuts and walked out, but Mr Taplin realised instantly that the items were missing and followed her home. When he caught her there she denied having taken anything, but eventually she reluctantly delivered the goods back to their rightful owner.

ALL THE TIME IN THE WORLD

During the night of 7 February 1841 Mr Parker's on Turl Street was broken into. The thief made his entry through the house, which belonged to the rector of Exeter College. Once inside Mr Parker's bookshop, the burglar headed for the drawers in the writing table where the money was kept. He worked away at them with a screwdriver, then anything else that came to hand, making his way to the kitchen for extra tools. Finally he took a poker from the fire to have one last crack. By this time he had mangled the drawers, and he gave up. But now he needed to get out. He decided to leave by the front door which led to Broad Street and, pulling up some classic literature, stood on it to unfasten the bolt, but fearing discovery from within he fled the way he came, never to be heard of again.

THE CHEEKY POET-ROBBERS

On 17 June 1843 robbers hid themselves in the house of Mr Brown, apothecary, on the High Street. During the night they came out of hiding and ate their way through lamb, bread and cheese. Having finished their dinner they left the house, taking a large quantity of silver: spoons, knives and forks, tea pots, cream jugs and mustard pots, as well as shoes, boots and clothes. Disappearing before daybreak, they wrote a note in chalk on the table:

>Never trust nobody out of your sight,
>We aught to have laid these on Saturday night.

LEFT FOR DEAD

A workman removing ash from Mr Castle's, the builder in Cowley Road, St Clement's, on 12 April 1844, found a tied bundle, which, from the smell of it, he thought was a dead cat. He asked Castle what to do with it and he said to sling it over the wall, which he did next. The package landed in Mr London's field. The next day London's son was passing through his father's field and, having his curiosity aroused, picked up the packet and took it to Mr Gunstone who lived close by and asked him to open it. Unravelling it, Gunstone found the decomposed remains of a baby boy. Mr Rusher conducted a post-mortem and an inquest was held on 15 April at the Black Horse Inn in St Clement's. Rusher stated that the child was born alive, but had been dead for at least two weeks, though there were no marks of violence on the body. The jury was forced to record a verdict that the boy was found dead, though the method by which he had died remained a mystery.

FROCK LIFTER

Thomas Jackson remembered going to a pub on Hythe Bridge Street at the end of July 1844 and drinking there. He sat at a table and pulled out some cash to pay for the beer and his lodgings when Thomas Wheeler came and sat next to him. Having paid his bill, Jackson dozed off while his new friend sat and watched. A while later the landlord woke Jackson; Wheeler was nowhere to be seen. The landlord then assisted Jackson up to his room and asked him if anything was missing, but Jackson thought not. A minute later, now wide-awake, Jackson came flying down the stairs yelling that he had been robbed of all his money.

At court in mid-October the landlord proved he had seen Wheeler lift up Jackson's frock while the latter was asleep and remove something from Jackson's pocket. Likewise several other people who were sitting in the bar that day saw Wheeler remove Jackson's purse from the sleeping man's pocket.

Hythe Bridge, 1822, with St George's Tower in the background, is situated at the junction of Fisher Row and Hythe Bridge Street, leading to Botley Road. (OCCPA)

The jury returned a verdict of not guilty. The judge asked them what they were doing and was in the middle of telling them to reconsider when the defence counsel pointed out that the verdict had already been recorded and could not be changed. The judge demanded to see the record, and it had indeed been written down. He was forced to concede defeat, indignantly told the jury that it was their verdict and not his and dismissed them from court.

DIY IS BAD FOR THE HEALTH

On 3 September 1846 James Walter, carpenter and builder, was taking down curtains at Mr Bandinell's house in Beaumont Street. While on a ladder in the drawing room James fell. Luckily a chair broke his fall; unluckily the chair embedded itself in James's side and ruptured his liver. The poor man died later the next night.

ONE SANDWICH SHORT OF A PICNIC

Augustus Robinson arrived at the King's Arms Hotel on Broad Street at 9 p.m. on the evening of 15 March 1847 and gave his address as Trinity Street, Dublin. Robinson, a well-dressed gentleman, asked Mr Stone, the landlord, if his friend 'Mr Smith' was staying there, as they were to meet, having come to see a mutual friend at Wadham. There was no Mr Smith, but Robinson agreed to stay for a couple of nights and await his friend's arrival. Robinson ordered cocoa, drank it and went to bed, but without asking for a candle; Mr Stone assumed Robinson had gone for a walk. This highly suspicious act of going to bed without a candle set Stone on his guard, and the servants were told to watch Robinson's every move.

The next morning Robinson went for breakfast and, having finished, tried several times to leave the room unseen. Each time, as he opened the door, he noticed he was being watched. He grabbed some silverware and jumped out of the window and into the street, but was spotted by Richard Harris, a servant at Magdalen Hall. Harris ran to the King's Arms, told the staff what he had seen and rushing to the breakfast room they realised what was missing. They went off in several directions in hot pursuit, but Robinson did not make it far and was caught by Harris and one of the servants on the Abingdon Road, near the road bridge. Robinson confessed all when the men caught him and readily returned with them. At the police station he turned out his pockets, which contained silver spoons, tongs and a fork, and was charged with robbery. He made no defence, only meekly mumbling that everything he was accused of was correct.

Our stout-hearted hardened criminal was tried at the Quarter Sessions on 29 March, found guilty and sent to gaol. After about a fortnight in gaol he was befriended by William Quartermaine, who said Robinson should come to his house when released and make it his home; he also promised to find his friend work on the railway. On 28 July Quartermaine, having been released, returned to collect Robinson, who had served four months, and took him to his house as promised, but unfortunately work on the railway had been completed a few days before his friend's release. Robinson stayed a week and, by his own admission, lived like a king. On the eighth day he went for an 'evening walk' resplendent in Quartermaine's boots; the man's wallet completed the ensemble. His host's wife requested the wallet before Robinson left, but he refused, went out and never returned.

The *Police Gazette* of 16 August advertised the theft, complete with a description and attire of the 20-year-old. On 24 September the *Police Gazette* announced that our friend, now using the name Henry Robertson, was wanted for stealing a silver spoon from an inn at Lynn. He described himself as 'Scottish' rather than Irish, but his accent still failed to convince. When caught, Robinson, or Robertson, had a forged £5 note on him. It was a piece of paper onto which were stuck several small pieces of paper with the words 'London and Birmingham, to pay the bearer £5, Mr Matthew Marshall' among others.

It seems Robinson had continued where he left off, and he was finally dragged back to Oxford for trial on 26 June 1848. Now Quartermaine was a witness for the prosecution. A man who defends himself has a fool for a client and Robinson was that man. The trial lasted nearly six hours, most of which was taken up by Robinson rambling on, cross-examining witnesses. His cunning defence case was that the Quartermaines had handed over all the money to him and he had total control over all their affairs, both domestic and commercial. But why had he disappeared so rapidly? The Quartermaines, he said, were the vilest of villains; their generosity in bringing him to their house was a ruse as they had designs to use him to carry out their evil schemes, which they had not the ability to do themselves.

One of the jurors had had enough and told Robinson he was repeating himself, to shut up and finish. Robinson stopped and sat down. Seizing the initiative, and before our friend could get up again, the jury returned a verdict of guilty and the judge sentenced him to seven years' transportation. Perhaps in talking for so long Robinson thought he could bore people to death and thus make his escape.

EATING THE EVIDENCE

In April 1848 two hungry-looking lads, John Gibson and Samuel Jones, were charged with appropriating two sponge cakes for their own use. They had gone to Mrs Horn's shop on the High Street one evening between 8 p.m. and 9 p.m. and asked for charity. She refused and told them to go to the police station. They returned ten minutes later and each grabbed a 1lb sponge cake. They proceeded to eat the cakes in the shop, where they were finally arrested by Cook, the Police Superintendent. They were found guilty as charged and sentenced to twenty-one days' imprisonment with hard labour. At least they knew where their next meal was coming from.

THE BUNGLING BURGLARS

On 16 January 1849, in the dead of night, a group of individuals gained access to New College with the intention of carrying out a daring robbery. The ambition of their plan and the incompetence with which they executed it are recorded in the diaries of Warden Sewell of New College and the local newspaper.

The thieves gained access to the college's garden quad over the wall at the corner of Queens Lane and New College Lane. Their plan was to steal the Warden's crozier, a valuable antique donated to the college nearly 500 years previously by its founder, William of Wykeham. This crozier is displayed in the college chapel. The thieves' route from the garden to the chapel entrance lay through the front quad of the college, and thus directly past the Warden's lodgings. They were planning to steal one of the college's most valuable antiques from under its Warden's very nose.

On reaching the chapel entrance, the thieves found the door locked (one of the porter's nightly duties was to secure all college buildings). The group – later described by the newspaper as 'well-versed in house-breaking' – was undeterred. They used a skeleton key to open the door. Once inside, they made their way to the crozier and found it firmly secured inside a recess in the wall in the chapel's chancel. The group's gaffe then became apparent. They had entered the chapel armed with only a knife. All

The front quad of New College at the end of New College Lane, with the Warden's lodgings, left, and Chapel, right. The college was founded in 1379. (OCCPA)

efforts to dislodge the crozier from its niche were in vain and so they were forced to make off with the more accessible, though huge, silver-gilt altar candlesticks.

The extent of the group's disorganisation was later revealed by a search of St Peter-in-the-East's churchyard which adjoins New College gardens and now forms part of St Edmund Hall. Hidden among the graves were various items of house-breaking equipment, including a well-made, 20ft-long rope ladder, a pair of woollen-soled shoes (presumably intended to quieten the footsteps of the wearer) and a small crowbar. In their haste to proceed with the audacious plan, the group had neglected to take along the very tools that would have enabled them to pull it off. They did not, of course, leave empty-handed, but the silver candlesticks would have been small bounty compared to the crozier. Happily, the latter survives to this day and is housed in its original niche at the far end of the college chapel.

WAGE NEGOTIATIONS

Charles Cooper was at work at the beginning of February 1849 with several other men who were digging a drain in Headington, when the parish surveyor, Mr Tew, turned up. Tew took them to task, abusing them for not working faster and telling them that they did no more work than washerwomen Cooper hissed that they did not even get paid as much as washerwomen. The exasperated Tew grabbed hold of him and dragged him out of the ditch.

In court, Tew said he used no more force than was necessary, commenting that 7*s* for six days' work was all the parish would allow him to pay the workmen. The bench

The Church of St Peter-in-the-East now forms part of St Edmund Hall and houses a library. It is pictured here in 1820. Sections of the building date from 1140. (OCCPA)

cleared the court to consider its decision and, on readmission, the judge said that the magistrates were of the opinion that Tew was guilty of assault and fined him 20*s* plus costs. Further, he commented that the men employed by Tew had been ground down to their lowest point, saying he could not believe that the parish would only allow 7*s* a week. The judge said that these were almost starvation to a man, let alone one with five or six children, as some of the labourers had, and was unable to comprehend how a man with humanity could even think of extracting a week's work for such a trifling sum. Continuing, the judge said it was no wonder that people were goaded into violence when they were treated so badly, saying he hoped the parish would realise that Tew was not fit to be employed as the surveyor.

A HURRIED DEPARTURE

The 18-year-old Thomas Myers was driving two coal carts over Magdalen Bridge on 23 May 1849 when a young boy tried to hitch a lift by jumping onto the back of the end cart. In order to prevent this, Myers bent down to pick up a piece of coal to throw at the boy and promptly fell out and under the wheels, which ran over his head, killing him outright. The inquest, which was held the next day, recorded a verdict of accidental death, but laid blame at the door of Charles Hamilton, the schoolboy who had tried to hitch a lift. The coroner chastised Hamilton for his conduct, which had resulted in 'hurrying a fellow creature, without a moment's notice, into the presence of his maker . . .', issuing the further ridiculously pompous statement that he hoped the affair would improve Hamilton's future conduct.

$$24$$

POLICEMEN'S PUNCHLINE

At a little before 6 p.m. on the evening of 15 November 1825 at Oxford city gaol, Thomas Gardner, the gaoler, met William Gardiner, a city policeman, and John Billing, constable for the Parish of St Thomas, at the gaol gate. The gaoler was expecting John Paine, having been informed by the Mayor of the arrest warrant out for him. Paine was well known to Gardner and his wife and despite being roaring drunk was coherent enough to tell the gaoler he had come to see him and offered his hand. Paine, without any complaint or fuss, was led away to a cell saying 'Tom, I will go with you.' When Gardner returned to Paine two hours later, Paine was lying on a bed of straw asleep. He loosened Paine's clothing, laid blankets on him and departed, Paine saying 'goodnight Tom' as he left.

The next morning, Wednesday, Paine was well enough to demand a pint of beer, which was refused. He was given an extra half-hour's lie-in before Gardner returned and told him to get up, wash and dress. But Paine, clutching his head, said it was impossible. Gardner and his wife thought he was suffering a hangover, but nevertheless called Mr Wentworth the surgeon, who sent his assistant Coulson. Coulson conducted an examination in another room, where a fire had been lit especially. Finding only a bruise on Paine's head, he cut the prisoner's hair away to reveal a small lesion. Thinking nothing of it, Coulson applied the latest in medical thinking: he bled Paine

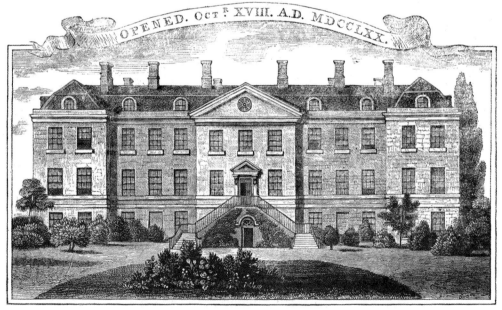

The Radcliffe Infirmary, 1838. The hospital opened in 1770 and is located at the northern end of St Giles's on Woodstock Road; the freehold is now owned by Oxford University. (OCCPA)

and gave him a strong emetic to make him vomit, both of which would have only made things worse. Coulson had Paine taken to the Radcliffe Infirmary where he was bled profusely and returned to gaol. Perhaps he had hoped to remove all the alcohol from Paine by removing all the poor man's blood. He noted that, not surprisingly, the man was delirious.

The next day, Thursday, Wentworth, Coulson's superior, bled Paine of a large amount of blood and gave him yet more vomiting powder. He noticed the bruise and cut on Paine's head, but also thought nothing of it. Ironically, he left orders for Paine's well-being. The prisoner told Wentworth how bad he felt. Later that evening Paine, again delirious, was visited by the surgeon who considered his wounds immaterial. By Friday Paine's condition had improved; he was lucid and told Wentworth that Billing had beaten him up. The next morning Paine was dead.

It would seem like an open and shut case, 'drunk dies of killer hangover', if one were to ignore his treatment at the hands of the doctors. The background was more complicated: William Gardiner had been out looking for Paine the previous Tuesday evening armed with an arrest warrant. John Billing had been called out because of a disturbance, coincidentally caused by Paine in St Ebbe's. Joseph Simmonds and Henry Chidley had gone to investigate noises in St Ebbe's and found Paine drunk and alone in the street. He had his shirt sleeves rolled up, was swearing and making an almighty racket, and was seemingly challenging a man to fight who was in the Bell near St Ebbe's Church, outside which he stood. This 'invitation' was accepted by most of the pub's occupants, who spilled out into the street. Paine was now ready to fight. His foe stepped up, but was pulled back by another 'tall' man who said that

St Ebbe's Church, 1835, is tucked away behind Queen Street on its southern side. (OCCPA)

Paine was drunk and did not really wish to fight. Gardiner and Billing arrived on the scene and the latter agreed to help execute the arrest warrant. Paine was collared by the two men and told there would be no fighting. What happened next was seen differently by many – Paine had drawn an audience of about fifty people.

The policemen, standing either side of him, grabbed Paine and dragged him down the middle of the street towards the gaol as he kicked and lashed out, screaming that he would fight. After struggling for 10yd, Gardiner let go. Later, the men said that Paine had fallen to the ground, but every witness called said that Gardiner had proclaimed to Billing that they would 'Have none of this nonsense' and told him to 'Pull him up and throw him to the ground.' Paine was thrown backwards over Billing's leg, with the policeman following, and a resounding crack was heard as Paine's head hit the wall of a nearby house then smashed against the ground.

Paine was unconscious. Gardiner sprinted to his own house, next door, but who knows why? Thomas Arrow, who was present, ran to Paine's wife at their house 50yd away, but she was out, so he returned. Billing was told by Mr Stevens, a bystander, that he had killed Paine, having cracked open Paine's head, but the quick-thinking Billing said it was his truncheon that had hit the wall. Elizabeth Winchester, whose wall Paine, or possibly Billing's truncheon, had hit, stepped outside with a candle, illuminating for all to see a pool of blood with more trickling from the back of Paine's head. Arrow noticed that Gardiner and Billing's attention was drawn to Paine's bloody and matted hair, but the policemen carried on as if nothing was amiss. Most people thought Paine might do better if he was taken to bed rather than to gaol and they told the policemen so. This was of little consequence to Paine who had been out cold for more than five minutes, while people stood over his lifeless body.

Gardiner said, 'Let me help you on with your coat, there's a good fellow. Where's your hat?' and Billing stepped in, pulling Paine up by his shoulders and, with assistance from Gardiner, clothing him. Paine had come round and was livid; so vile was his swearing that Mrs Winchester retreated inside, noting the bloodstain on her wall as she stepped indoors. By now Paine was rather subdued and was finally led away to gaol.

The inquest was held in the gaol on 21 November and caused serious 'excitement' in Oxford. The post-mortem was conducted by Mr Wingfield, who found Paine's unusually thin skull cracked wide open, a severed artery having caused the internal bleeding which ultimately killed him. The evidence admitted was damning of Gardiner and Billing. They both denied having been drinking that evening, though no one was quite sure; many witnesses had seen a bloodied Paine being scraped off the pavement after receiving some very rough treatment. The policemen's justification for taking Paine direct to gaol, rather than to the Mayor for questioning, which would have been the usual form, was that Paine made no complaints, was not injured and being drunk they thought that gaol was the best place for him, denying that they saw any blood on him. Despite the fact that the jury considered the men's conduct appalling, they did allow for some leniency as Paine was 'addicted to drink' and could be 'violently obstinate' when drunk. No matter, any attempt to condone their action skated on thin ice.

The most damning admission was that on Thursday evening, between 7 p.m. and 8 p.m., Billing was in the bar of the Three Cups and announced, unprovoked, to the three servants and a stranger sitting there that he, heroically, had been called to assist in a riot, and that the 'beggar' involved had collared him, whereupon he had 'kicked him up, and hammered his head'.

The trial lasted all day until 11 p.m. when the jury returned a unanimous verdict of accidental death, but expressed their disapprobation concerning the conduct of William Gardiner and John Billing. The jury sent a petition to the coroner recommending the removal of Gardiner and Billing, which was debated by the magistrates at their subsequent meeting two days later, when they stated that the men's conduct in apprehending Paine was 'so highly reprehensible and improper as to render them unfit to be continued in their respective offices', and they were both dismissed from their jobs.

2 5

THE SKY'S THE LIMIT

Arriving at the house of Esther and George Bennett in Holywell Parish on 8 October 1832, Mr and Mrs Butcher enquired after a house which they understood Mr Bennett had available to rent. They were let in by Mrs Bennett and she proceeded to tell Hugh and Charlotte Butcher that the house was on St John's Street and was a fine house, which seemingly met with the Butchers' approval.

They returned the next Tuesday and were told the rental was £1,000 per annum, but nothing more was discussed as Mr Bennett was not at home on this occasion either. Finally, the next evening they met Mr Bennett, who took the Butchers to view the property. They were impressed and returned to the Bennetts' house to discuss the deal over a few drinks. Mr Butcher fell over himself in an attempt to prove his wealth. He had a farm half a mile from Devizes which he had let for the next six years; he was to receive the money from the sale of the stock within a month, which was in itself worth £963, and £800 a year besides for the rent. Upping the ante, Butcher said that he had £30,000, £14,000 of which was in shares, the rest distributed among various banks. Naturally a man of this wealth would have had servants, and to explain why they were not present Hugh mentioned, unprompted, that his servants were to join them once they had served out their notice, presumably from the farm's new tenant.

The conversation moved on to the matter of furnishing the house. Hugh asked if Mr Bennett had any 'obliging friend' who could assist in fitting out the place in the style to which the Butchers were accustomed, suggesting that they would pay good money. The Bennetts recommended Mr Ellison. There was one snag, Ellison's was a 'ready money' shop – none of this old-fashioned credit malarkey. Hugh said, 'When the gentleman has brought his goods, I will pay his bill.' The next day the ladies went to the shop, Mrs Bennett regaling details of wealth to Ellison, who happily sent carpets, curtains, cotton goods, linen and furniture to the house, payment having been promised on delivery.

Setting up at least a dozen accounts over the next five weeks, the Butchers packed the new house to the rafters with chairs, beds, tables and more from Mr Collison the cabinet-maker in Holywell Parish; ironmongery from Mrs Mason in Lincoln Lane; and groceries from Mr Hicks in Holywell. They went back to Ellison's for Brussels carpets, gingham, calico, blankets, handkerchiefs, more furniture, as well as a clock and vases. Not stopping there, they obtained from other traders groceries, clothing, hats and wine.

Now the crowning glory: having ordered a French clock from Mr Steele, the silversmith and watchmaker was invited into the house when he delivered the timepiece and readily plied with wine. Casually Mr Butcher slipped into the conversation that he wanted a watch for his wife, in fact any watch she wanted, and rings, lots of them, and some chains, seals and silver pots. Steele could not believe his luck and, seizing the opportunity, tried to sell the Butchers one of everything he had in stock: 'An excellent clock suited to the dimensions of the recess in the house, completed the generous order . . .' for which 2 guineas was to be paid annually. Hugh could not resist the opportunity again to relate how wealthy he was.

When the furnishing was complete, Mrs Butcher presented Mrs Bennett with a scarf for all the help she had given at practically every stage. Mr Butcher had told Ellison that he would pay for whatever his 'old woman' wanted, returning to slip in the tale concerning his wealth and saying he would receive money for the farm in two to three weeks' time. Now it was Ellison's turn to call. Butcher explained to Ellison that he was collecting the money the next Saturday and would pay the bill then. Ellison had visited the house several times during his dealings with the Butchers and all had seemed well, but when Saturday passed he made enquiries: there was no Hugh Butcher who lived anywhere near Devizes. Hugh Butcher himself had, by now, not been seen in Oxford for several days; the penny was about to drop. Ellison was not the first to become suspicious: a butcher and an upholsterer were both unconvinced by the Butchers' conflicting answers when questioned and decided 'that their property was safest in their own shops'. Ellison went to the house one final time and to his horror it was almost empty. Panicking, he hired men to watch the house around the clock in the hope that the Butchers would return.

All remained quiet until 21 November when at 3 a.m., in the cold of the morning, as Ellison and his men, including Joshua Clarke the policeman, watched on, they were nearly taken by surprise when a cart laden with goods left the house. Emerging from their hiding place, they rushed across the streets of Oxford and caught up with the cart outside Trinity College on Broad Street. The cart was loaded with tables,

Trinity College, founded in 1555, opens on to Broad Street. The street was formed in the late seventeenth century when the city ditch was filled in. (Giles Brindley)

carpets, chairs, a clock and more, but none of the men they had stopped was Hugh Butcher. When questioned, two of the men, Henry and George Wingfield, said that it was their property. The goods were seized and the men arrested. This was much to the confusion of Aaron Brooks, whose cart it was. All he knew was that the Wingfields had hired him to transport the goods to Aylesbury and that along with them and Charlotte Butcher he had assisted in the loading. This meant that Mrs Butcher must be close at hand. She was nabbed in New Road struggling to make her way out of the city with an excessive amount of goods concealed about her person and was taken to gaol.

As for Hugh Butcher, Clarke caught up with him 6 miles from Aylesbury, equally laden down with goods. Butcher was indignant and complained bitterly that having robbed the county of £1,600 of goods he would have to dispose of the haul from gaol, presumably rather than at his leisure. Annoyed, he said that if he had had two more days and if it had not been for the 'jumping shopkeeper and Bennett' he would have got away with it. The Wingfields and the Butchers were now behind bars, but Hugh was not going down alone; he led the police to Charlotte Smith of Aylesbury. Perhaps she was their fence, for when the police turned up at her house they discovered a good deal of the purloined property.

Several shopkeepers had been duped, including the over-eager silversmith Steele, but it was Ellison who was most aggrieved, some putting his losses at nearly £500. When the five people concerned were brought before the Mayor to be questioned on 23 November, word spread rapidly and the Mayor's office was soon packed with traders baying for blood. The Mayor attempted to start proceedings, but the commotion and number of bodies were too much for the small space and he left his office and reconvened in the Town Hall. Henry Jacob, as the clerk to the guardians of the united parishes of Oxford, was responsible for collecting Mr Butcher's numerous debts. The Butchers had little cash to hand, since their children – of whom nothing previously had been mentioned – were currently lodged in the workhouse. On visiting him in gaol, Jacob asked Butcher how he would settle his accounts and likewise support his children. Butcher was again indignant and acted aggrieved, saying, 'If the furniture and goods had not been taken from the house, there would have been plenty to keep them', and that he had not a farthing in the world. It was like a line of dominoes fanning out; once a footing had been obtained with Ellison, other tradesmen rapidly furnished the Butchers with goods which led to ever increasingly expensive operations. The local paper reprimanded the traders for their promiscuity in giving credit, saying that living in the 'country' would not save them from the tricks played in London.

The Butchers faced trial on 6 January 1832 charged with multiple counts of fraud. The finger of suspicion was also waved at Esther Bennett, it being pointed out that she was very active in her constant assistance to Mrs Butcher. Mrs Butcher had even stayed at the Bennetts' house on occasions and Esther had received a scarf into the bargain. But the Bennetts said that they too had lost out, having not received any rent for their property. Steele was repeatedly asked if he had 'forced' his wares on the Butchers and whether the Bennetts would have rather not had them? It was proved by William Lyne of Stent, near Devizes, who coincidentally enough rented land from New College, that he knew of no Hugh Butcher let alone one, a farmer, living near Devizes, William having lived there all his life. However, he travelled to all the fairs and had seen the 'Butchers' two or three times before.

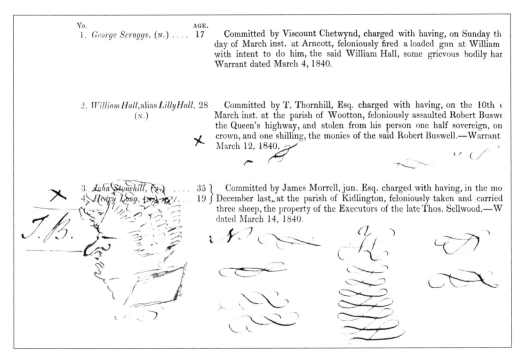

No.   AGE.
1. *George Scraggs*, (N.) 17   Committed by Viscount Chetwynd, charged with having, on Sunday th
                                     day of March inst. at Arncott, feloniously fired a loaded gun at William
                                     with intent to do him, the said William Hall, some grievous bodily har
                                     Warrant dated March 4, 1840.

2. *William Hall*, alias *Lilly Hall*, 28   Committed by T. Thornhill, Esq. charged with having, on the 10th (
   (N.)   March inst. at the parish of Wootton, feloniously assaulted Robert Buswe
                                     the Queen's highway, and stolen from his person one half sovereign, on
                                     crown, and one shilling, the monies of the said Robert Buswell.—Warrant
                                     March 12, 1840.

3. *John Stonehill*, (N.) .... 35 ⎱   Committed by James Morrell, jun. Esq. charged with having, in the mo
4. *Henry Long*, (N.) .... 19 ⎰   December last, at the parish of Kidlington, feloniously taken and carried
                                     three sheep, the property of the Executors of the late Thos. Sellwood.—W
                                     dated March 14, 1840.

Doodlings in the Calendar of Prisoners for the Summer Assize of 1840 may have been of Sir James Parke, the Justice of the Assize. (ORO)

The jury consulted for a short time and delivered their verdict of guilty against both Mr and Mrs Butcher, sentencing them to the maximum allowable by law: seven years' transportation. This being concluded, a new trial commenced at which the Butchers were charged with Charlotte Smith and the Wingfields with conspiracy to defraud and cheat. The evidence against this 'miscreant band of plunderers' was the same as before and on being found guilty Smith and the Wingfields were sentenced to two years' hard labour. The Butchers having already received sentence of transportation were merely charged the nominal fine of 1*s* each.

The jury stated pompously that it had broken the knot of an extensive game of confederate villains, disbursed in towns near Oxford, in the midst of their depredations. But the last laugh was on the greedy and unwary traders for, though some of the items were recovered, a great deal remained forever unaccounted for.

26

FRAUD, FIRE AND ODDBALLS

END OF THE MONKS

A passage running underground between what is now the Chequers pub on one side of the High Street and the Mitre Inn on the other side existed during the Middle Ages. It was at this time, acting on behalf of Henry VIII, that soldiers drove a group of monks into this passage and walled up both ends. It is said that you can still hear the screams late at night when the Mitre is quiet.

PLAYING WITH REALITY

In the seventeenth century members of Jesus College (traditionally Welshmen) attended a play in which an actor depicted the attack of fellow countrymen. One of the members stormed the stage and proceeded to kick six shades out of the offending thespian.

Turl Street in the nineteenth century with Exeter College, left, Jesus College, right, and Lincoln College and All Saints Church in the background. (OCCPA)

ODE TO JOY

Having sold a houseful of seats for a 1602 performance of *England's Joy*, Richard Vennar of Balliol did a runner. In fact, the play did not exist. Vennar was brought before the magistrate, Sir John Popham, a Balliol man who took the affair to be a joke. But Vennar was never allowed to forget what he had done and finally ended his existence in a debtors' prison.

HELP THE AGED

In the eighteenth century, Mr Scott, later Lord Chancellor, heard an invalid grumble that the view from his window down the High Street was interrupted by a tree in All Saints churchyard, and sent his servant, a Yorkshireman, to cut it down. It was too much for the servant, and the young gentlemen who were standing around watching were forced to pitch in to fell the tree. Next day the magistrates were offering a reward for the conviction of the offenders.

PROCTOR'S PUNCH

Fletcher of University College was expelled from the University for punching a Proctor in December 1711.

CASHING IN

Mr Heyman, the bursar of Merton College in 1712, ruptured a vein when lifting a £600 bag of silver. He died soon afterwards and was buried in the college chapel.

LIGHTLY TOASTED

Cuthberth Ellison died in front of his fire in November 1719. The Fellow of Corpus Christi College passed away peacefully in his chair. But before his body was discovered the heat of the fire had burnt one side of his face.

AGE BEFORE BEAUTY

At 2 p.m. on 4 September 1723 battle commenced. A scaffold had been erected next to the theatre for the purpose of holding a smoking contest. These days smokers are more likely to be found trying to give up rather than smoke until they keel over. But in 1723 the competition was very simple: anyone, man or woman, who could smoke 3oz of tobacco without drinking or getting down would win 12s.

A number of people tried and failed and then a tailor of St Peter-in-the-East looked to be romping home, being several pipefuls ahead of the others, but before finishing he was so violently sick that the spectators thought he was about to die. An old soldier, sitting and smoking gently, carried on until, at last, the 3oz was all smoked. In fact, he was said to have smoked another four or five pipes that very evening as well.

LAST MOONLIGHT WALK

John Holloway, a tailor in St Peter-in-the-East, walked out to a pub on a hill near Horspath at the end of December 1729. There he drank with two other Oxford men. Leaving the pub between 5 p.m. and 6 p.m., he wandered back to Oxford. As he rarely left Oxford, he was not familiar with the route home. Eventually Holloway wandered into Temple Cowley at 8 p.m. It was dark by this time, but he obtained directions for Oxford and set off again. Unfortunately he went the wrong way and ended up in Church Cowley. Here he woke someone up between 11 p.m. and midnight. Gaining further directions, Holloway set off, but never made it home. His body was found the next morning a little way from the house he had stopped at in Church Cowley.

STANDING ROOM ONLY

September 1733 saw the end of a horse race meeting on Port Meadow. There had been a near-death escape for one of the jockeys, but of more concern was the fact that the stand had fallen down almost killing the spectators, most of whom were battered and several had broken limbs. It had been erected by an Oxford carpenter named Prickett who had previously built two stands, both of which had collapsed.

THE TOOTH FAIRY

An eminent dentist of St Thomas's Parish, was no less a celebrity for his stature as a poet than his love of the high life, particularly his ruling passion, gambling. During the second week of December 1763, having been induced by free-flowing food and a never-empty glass to play cards, he was outsmarted by those more ingenious than himself. Day after day they wiped him out of ready cash. He wrote an IOU for 31 guineas and eventually was required to hand over the mortgage deeds to his two houses in the parish, at which point he left the card table. Just as he was returning to deliver the deeds he met a friend who recommended he obtained the opinion of a lawyer. The lawyer found a 'wholesome statute' to save one of the better classes and overturn his misfortune, restoring the dentist's peace of mind, as well as his cash.

MAD CAT DIPPING

In March 1764 a rabid cat belonging to a Merton student attacked his bedmaker's son. The cat tore the boy's leg and the bedmaker rushed to help. She became entangled and was forced to shake the cat off, but it became caught up in her clothes. The cat had previously bitten a dog and was shut up and left to die, which it did a few days later. The boy was immediately sent to the coast to be dipped, since salt water was considered helpful in the treatment of rabies.

THE NAKED TRUTH

On passing through the Parks on 10 June 1766, a labourer was stopped by a stranger who told him that he had just found a woman, stripped to her petticoat, in a nearby cornfield. They went to her and found her bound head and foot, with a bloody nose. The woman cowered from the men. The stranger was greatly perturbed and afraid to unbind her lest it was a trick. The woman had told him that the previous evening she had been stripped and robbed of 16s 9d, taken to the field, tied up and left there overnight. She then proceeded to describe the man who had robbed her.

A general alarm was raised and while she was conveyed to Holywell workhouse to be looked after, a search was made for the robber in question and her lost clothes. The 'stranger' who had first found her visited her rather too frequently and, becoming suspicious, the police arrested him. The day she was found, two men, matching the description she had given, were arrested and brought to her for identification. Meanwhile, the stranger in custody finally admitted that the woman was his wife and that he had stripped her. He led police to her clothes, which had been hidden under a heap of old thatch in a rick yard near to where she said she had been stripped and 'robbed'. The couple were detained in the Bridewell for questioning.

The husband and wife had hoped to defraud people by exciting pity owing to the woman's plight and thereby obtain money. They went under the names of Robert Seward (25) and Elizabeth Parsons (30) and came from Birmingham. On 21 June 1766, during market time, the two were brought out to the whipping post for execution of sentence for their fraud. Elizabeth was spared, as it was discovered that she was pregnant. Her husband did not escape punishment and was severely disciplined, after which they were both thrown out of town.

TWO FOR THE PRICE OF ONE

A gentleman passing through Oxford on 18 September 1769 stopped the night at one of the inns and, going to bed, found his door difficult to lock. The man checked under the bed and there, by candlelight, he saw someone who withdrew their legs as the light approached. The man ran to the door and shouted for help; the uninvited guest bolted out of the window and escaped under the cover of night.

WRONG HIDING PLACE

A 15-year-old errand boy went absent without leave on 3 January 1777 to go ice-skating with his friends. Since he was afraid that his master would throw him out, and too ashamed to go to his friends, he took shelter in a hovel near Holywell Parish cockpit (Turf Tavern), covering himself with hay. After some time a man in a smock frock accompanied by a woman entered the hovel, but they did not see the boy concealed beneath the straw. They were in conversation about a robbery they had recently committed in Oxford and another which they were about to execute.

The boy was terrified lest they discover him. He tried to make a run for it, but they seized him and cut his throat, slicing nearly the whole way through his windpipe, and left him for dead. He lay in the cold all night, which probably saved him by stemming the blood flow. He finally staggered to the Radcliffe Infirmary the next day for treatment, but no sign could be found of the robbers.

JUST NOT CRICKET

A request was printed in *Jackson's Oxford Journal* on Saturday 29 March 1783. The paper addressed those people who had been exercising their firearms against Mr Redwood's garden door adjoining Wadham College walls (just behind Holywell Street). It asked for them to desist in such practices. Several bullets had penetrated the door, causing wooden splinters to fly across the garden and making walking there very dangerous, especially for children.

WHEELY BAD BEHAVIOUR

Joshua Smith, servant to Mr Watson, was convicted on 24 January 1786 at a meeting of the Commissioners for Paving and Lighting for wheeling a hand barrow on the footpath.

EASY COME, EASY GO

One of the Trinity College bedmakers went to the bank on 14 July 1792 to get 10 guineas for one of the students. On his return he was guided, money in hand, by strangers into the Chequers Inn. They sat around gambling; he sat down and was induced to believe one of them had just inherited a fortune. The bedmaker noticed that this particular young man was reckless and decided to join in. At first the bedmaker won 4 or 5 guineas, but then lost the student's money and more of his own.

The men paused play and two of them stepped outside to 'feed their horses', leaving the bedmaker with the remaining man. This man said he had money and would help the bedmaker win back his cash. Leaving the bedmaker, he stepped outside to call the others back in. By the time the bedmaker realised what was going on, all three had disappeared with the bedmaker's cash.

DEAD BUT STILL SHOPPING

A man dressed as a servant walked into an Oxford shop during the first week of January 1798 and ordered some 3s worth of goods, saying that they were to go to Dr Neve.

Unknown to the shop, Dr Neve then lay dead. The goods were taken by the shop boy who was heading for the good doctor's house when the servant who had called at the shop overtook him just before he arrived. The man gave the shop boy an earful for being late and told him that he had already returned to the shop and left a guinea with his master; that he would take the goods and the change himself, saying that the boy should not ring the bell as it would disturb the family.

The boy did as he was told, but when he returned to the shop he found out that it was a scam. No money was left, but by now it was too late to do anything about it and the man had disappeared with the goods and cash.

THE LOYAL VOLUNTEER?

Sergeant Rae of the Oxford Loyal Volunteers was convicted at a court martial in Oxford Town Hall on 18 March 1805. Rae was up on charges of enlisting in another regiment and embezzling the money given to him to pay the soldiers of his company. For this crime he was reduced to the ranks and sentenced to receive 300 lashes, the punishment being executed two days later.

FAMILY FOR HIRE

Francis McKew, a one-armed beggar, turned up in Oxford on 4 April 1814 and applied to the Oxford magistrates for benefit for his wife and two children. McKew was required to present his family. He was taken aback, but duly returned with a woman and two children and was given the cash. It transpired that the woman, Margaret Brackenridge, was not his wife, and she had borrowed the children from another beggar that afternoon. McKew and Brackenridge were convicted and sentenced on 6 October to six months in gaol.

BIG LITTLE VOICE

A beggar was arrested in St Clement's on 8 February 1818. Pinned to his chest was a note that stated he had been liberated from Algiers by Lord Exmouth. It went on to explain that he had been beaten and had had his tongue cut out before he could be rescued. The notice requested charitable donations from all its readers. On forcing open his mouth, the police found that the beggar's tongue was intact and that he rolled it back to make it appear as though it had been cut out. After being banged up in gaol the man suddenly regained his speech and confessed, saying that the marks on his back had been inflicted by the residents of Stokenchurch who had readily donated money to him, but had stripped and flogged him severely in the streets of the town when they had discovered the deception.

CUSHIONS LEAD TO DEATH

James Bruge was charged on 3 March 1819 with entering a dwelling-house and burning six hair cushions, stealing a key and a brass cock. Bruge was duly sentenced to death.

RAILING AGAINST THE CROWD

The remains of Vincent Hudson, a corporal in the Oxford militia, were about to be interred on 24 January 1822 in Magdalen churchyard. The event was attended by a large number of his comrades and a vast crowd besides. The assembled masses stood on the coping stones and leaned on the iron railings. The stones gave way and 25yd of the railings collapsed with them, bruising and battering many people, not least young master Clarke who had one of his legs broken.

A SWIFT RECOVERY

Lying stretched out on a street in Magdalen Parish at 7 p.m. on 20 January 1824, a poorly dressed 50-year-old man writhed around in a fit, hands clenched and eyes rolled up. Passers-by rushed to attend to him, but to no avail and someone was sent to get a doctor. Suddenly the gentleman made a remarkably quick recovery and was able to walk and talk. He explained to the crowd that he was an out-of-work stonemason and people, feeling sorry for him, gave him some cash. So much was collected that he walked away with a fist full of coins. One man even took him to the pub where the old-timer related his tale of woe and was bought brandy and beer; even the landlady chipped in, feeding him bread and meat. Enjoying himself as if nothing had happened, he even had the cheek to ask for a pipe of tobacco. But when it came to an in-depth questioning by those in the bar of what he did, where he had come from and where he was going, he waffled, made his excuses and left the pub.

Half an hour later he was flat on his back again, this time in St Ebbe's, lying in a similar state as earlier that evening. This time the crowd set to with some 'scientific' experimentation: they poured a bucket of water over him but there was no response. Then they made use of a thick stick about his shoulders and back, at which point he recovered instantly, even faster than in Magdalen Parish. He put his limbs and tongue to good effect and got down on his knees and prayed for mercy, while the crowd made threats and told him exactly what they thought of him. Presumably they let him go and he, for his part, made a hasty exit from Oxford, for no more was heard of him.

BLAME THE PARENTS

On 30 September 1826 at the city court were Charles Billing and Sarah Serjeant. They were both around 12 or 13 years old and were convicted of stealing apples from a garden in St Thomas's, value 3s. They were fined treble the cost of the apples plus 1s as a penalty. The magistrate criticised the parents and told them to be more vigilant over their children in the future as it was his experience that the vices contracted by children were attributable to the neglect of their parents.

NEW FOR OLD

An advertisement in *Jackson's Oxford Journal* on Saturday 14 October 1826 cautioned people against a couple who were going from house-to-house collecting silver-plated goods under the pretence of replating them, and then disappearing with the booty.

THE UNNATURAL MOTHER

At 4 p.m. on 1 April 1828 a 6-month-old infant was found lying in the shadow of the boundary wall of Wadham College garden. The Holywell Parish officers decided that the infant should be taken to the workhouse and directed someone to do so. As the man passed through the parks with the baby, he asked everybody he met if they knew anything of the child. Near Wadham he stopped a well-attired woman and asked her the same question. She appeared very nervous and finally broke down, saying that the child was hers.

The child was returned to the woman, who hastily disappeared. It was conjectured that the infant had only been left a while and that the 'unnatural' mother was seized by a fit of guilt and was on her way back to retrieve the child. Since nothing was known of her, the affair was shrouded in mystery.

TAKEN FOR A RIDE

A young girl by the name of Marianne Sanders, aged 16, was induced to accompany a man to Beckley in December 1828. He said his mistress, a spinster, had sent him to Oxford to find a servant. On that Tuesday afternoon, 2 December, they stopped at the Cape of Good Hope and the Port Mahon pubs in St Clement's and drank beer and spirits the fellow stating that his mistress's gig would collect them. He encouraged her to walk up to Headington, saying that the gig would overtake them. Passing the Headington turnpike, they turned left into the fields where the man seized Sanders, threw her down and, not withstanding her screams, 'effected her ruin', and then left her. She staggered home to Queen Street, arriving at 8 p.m. in a state of shock, to tell her friends what had happened. The man was described as 35, tall, wide-eyed, lame in one leg, with a smock frock and patched trousers.

The police searched high and low and took several men into custody; they were presented to Sanders and subsequently eliminated from the inquiry. Having travelled 100 miles all over the county, Oxford policemen Gardner and Bossom went to Wheatley on 5 January 1829 and arrested a man by the name of James Barker. He was brought before one of the magistrates, Revd Dr Ingram at Trinity College, the next morning. The girl identified him. Barker was not unknown to the law, as some years before he had been sentenced to transportation at the Old Bailey for stealing fowls at Acton, Middlesex.

THE DEATH OF THE FLOWERS AND ERMINTRUDE

Samuel Cooper had been employed by John Smith of St Giles's Parish for some time when he was tried before the Mayor on 20 May 1829. He was charged with wilfully and maliciously destroying flowers to the value of £4. Smith said that he had always treated Cooper well and that without the least provocation Cooper had jumped over the wall into Smith's garden, throwing a pan of lead, which was in the garden, into the neighbouring field and destroying Smith's flowers. Two of Mr Preston's cows,

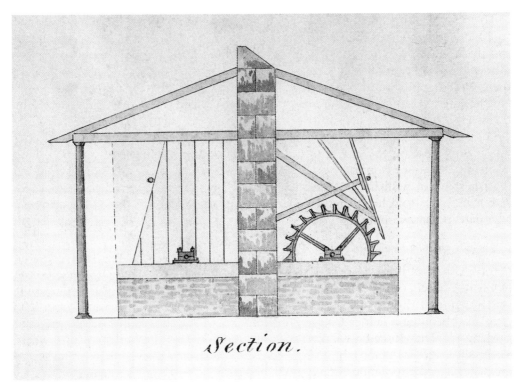

Section.

A plan for the proposed treadwheel for the Castle gaol, drawn in 1842 by architects John Richmond of Chelmsford, Essex, was submitted to the city authorities for their consideration. (ORO)

grazing in the field, partook of the lead and died, a serious loss to Mr Preston. Cooper was found guilty and fined £4 and costs, but in default of payment he was committed to walk the treadwheel for two months.

STEALING FROM THE POOR

The guardians of the poor for the city were in the habit of procuring large quantities of leather, which they had made into shoes by local shoemakers so that they could sell the shoes at a reduced rate to the impoverished. For this purpose leather had been given to James Boswell, a shoemaker. Boswell had kept the high-quality outer leather for himself and used the remainder, as well as old scraps of leather, to make poor-quality shoes. In court Boswell was sentenced on 25 September 1829 to two months inside, though the magistrates did not inflict a whipping, which the law allowed for.

TOO GOOD TO MISS

Two little girls were walking through the Parish of St Peter-le-Bailey on 9 July 1829. They found a dirty little bag containing three sovereigns, which one girl picked up. At home, the girl presented the bag to her mother, while the other little girl told her mother what the two had found. The second mother went round to the house of the first and demanded half the money. In reply, the first woman said that they should not divide it then, as somebody might come looking for it and it would be better to hold it back rather than take what was not theirs. The other woman again urged her to split the money, without success.

The second mother hit upon the following plan: she went to the town crier and told him she had lost three sovereigns and that he should cry it in one certain place and that place only. When the money was brought to him, he should give a reward of 10s. Thereafter he should take the sovereigns to another designated place and leave them for her, but he must on no account bring them directly to her at her own house. Not finding this suspicious in the least, he duly cried and the money was returned by the first mother and later handed over to the second mother.

For one reason or another these events came to light and the second girl's mother was brought before the city magistrates the next day, 10 July. She acknowledged receiving the money from the town crier, but said she had lost it subsequently, adding that she did not wish her husband to find out anything about what had happened. The magistrates told her to return the money to them and postponed the case to a later date, perhaps hoping that the real owner would turn up before it all went to trial.

DANGEROUS DAMSONS

During a spate of break-ins robbers entered the house of the Revd Dr Pusey, Canon of Christ Church, on 24 or 25 September 1830. As at the other burglaries, the family was not home, though three servants were asleep in the top of the house. The burglars, obtaining a ladder from a hovel in Christ Church meadow, scaled the high garden wall. They forced a window and picked the lock to the butler's pantry where all the silverware lay before them. But they were discerning thieves, filing the edges of the plates in order to deduce which were solid silver and which were merely plated.

The robbery was discovered when the servants came down in the morning. One of the maids entered the pantry and heard an enormous bang. Supposing she was being shot at by robbers armed with a blunderbuss, she ran out screaming into the college. Several people arrived with pokers, spits and suchlike and charged into the pantry ready to fight. What they found was not what they were expecting. The noise was caused by a bottle of damsons exploding, and wiping out another bottle and the pantry window. The burglars had left the way they came, and two sets of prints were traced across the flowerbed in the garden, one with short wide feet and the other with bare feet leaving imprints 12in long.

Thereafter, the colleges employed their own servants to patrol their properties, hoping that eventually there would be improvements in the state of the local police. Though the police may have improved over the years, college porters still patrol the grounds at night.

FIRE WATER

One of the bedrooms at the Roebuck was found ablaze at 10.45 p.m. on 5 June 1831. The alarm was raised and the fire engines arrived, along with a great crowd of people. The fire was confined to the room where it had begun, but all the furniture and clothing inside were destroyed. It was thought to have been started by an army officer who set light to the curtains while drunk. Praise was given to several members of the University and town for stopping looting during the fire.

WEE WILLIE WINKY

James Ward was convicted on 18 June 1831 for indecent exposure with 'intent to insult females' and sentenced to a month's imprisonment with hard labour, whereupon he gave notice to appeal. Perhaps he wanted a second opinion on his manly physique.

ONE MORE FOR THE ASYLUM

At the Quarter Sessions of 15 October 1832 there were the usual number of prisoners for trial: sixteen on this occasion, but only one serious offender, John Tyror aka Taylor. Tyror was charged with the murder of an 8-month-old boy, John Gibbs, two weeks previously in the Parish of St Aldate's. The jury decided that there was a case to be heard and the trial commenced, but the defence counsel immediately objected on the grounds of insanity and the jury subsequently heard evidence to this effect.

Several witnesses were brought forward, including Edward Thurland, formerly assistant surgeon at the Radcliffe Infirmary, who had known Tyror for more than fourteen years and had seen him as a patient on several occasions. He had observed Tyror a few weeks before running round and round on the Broad Walk outside Christ Church, pointing at a dog and making hideous noises. Tyror took no notice of Thurland even though he was standing next to him. The surgeon considered Tyror to be in a worse state than when he first knew him and that Tyror could not make the distinction between right and wrong. Thurland concluded that, in his opinion, the defendant did not understand the nature of the proceedings now against him.

Mr Hutchings, the Oxford surgeon, had known Tyror for thirty years and thought him to be of 'weak intellect'; likewise he thought Tyror did not understand the situation he was now in. Another surgeon, Mr Cleobury, had known Tyror for more than four years. When Tyror first came to Cleobury, he complained of spiders and insects crawling about under his skin and asked the surgeon to get rid of them. Soon after, Cleobury discovered Tyror to be insane, as he repeatedly returned and told the surgeon the same story. Cleobury had often seen him moping about Christ Church meadow, and there was no doubt in his mind that Tyror was out of his.

Finally it was down to William Court, hairdresser of St Aldate's, who had known Tyror for more than twenty years, to state that Tyror had always been known as 'silly Johnny' or 'silly Jack'. Williams said that Tyror usually talked randomly, darting from one thing to another, never finishing the stories he started. The jury concluded that

The Broadwalk running alongside Christ Church Meadow has always been a popular venue for a Sunday walk. (OCCPA)

Tyror was indeed insane, whereupon he was taken away and confined to the lunatic asylum, where he spent the remainder of his days.

AN EASY WAY OUT

Thomas Quinlan was brought before the Mayor on 9 May 1832 charged with stealing a gold watch. The previous evening, at Mr Salter's on the High Street, the shopman heard the smash of glass and ran outside to find Quinlan standing, watch in hand. Quinlan said he was so poor he wanted to be transported rather than stay.

BELATED BURIAL

During an outbreak of cholera in July 1832 a widow of St Aldates was convicted and fined £5 for not burying her husband within twenty-four hours of his demise, as it was considered to endanger public health not to do so.

DOWN AT HEAL

Harvey Robinson turned up on the doorstep of the guardians of the poor in St Giles's in May 1833 and asked for charity, but they did not think he deserved it and refused. An annoyed Robinson set to, kicking the shins of the assembled board members. The beadle came out to calm Robinson and soon fell foul of him, though the beadle did eventually manage to handcuff him after a struggle. The beadle went for a policeman, but while he was gone, Robinson ran off, still handcuffed. The police and the beadle went to Robinson's house and found him at home. They took him back into custody, but not before Robinson had given the police a few kicks as well as a blow with a poker. Robinson was sentenced in October 1833 to six months' hard labour.

CRIMINAL ANATOMY

The remains of a child were found in Preacher's Pond in St Ebbe's one Wednesday morning. The following day, 3 April 1834, an inquest was held at the Bull in the same parish. Mr Webb, the surgeon, stated that a fisherman by the name of Beesley had found an arm, a leg and a thigh, as well as part of the spine belonging to a 4-year-old child. The arteries were filled with wax and it was the surgeon's opinion that the body had been used for anatomy. An Act of Parliament ruled that bodies used for dissection were to be buried in consecrated ground following their use under a penalty of three months' imprisonment or a fine of £50. At the inquest the jury's verdict was that the body parts had been thrown into the pool after dissection by an unknown person.

SLEIGHT OF HAND

Mr Pike, an elderly farmer of Cowley, had attended a fair in Oxford on 21 December 1835 and had gone into the bank to cash a cheque. He was followed by a powerfully built man who watched him cash the cheque for £14 and some shillings. As Pike left the bank this man struck up a conversation, saying he was about to go into the Mitre Inn to conclude a deal to buy a farm, and asked Pike to join him for a glass of gin and water. Pike agreed and, sitting down in the bar, they were joined by another man who was equally chatty, telling Pike he was a landowner with farms to let. The conversation turned to Pike's bag of money, which sat on the table. The men told Pike he could not be too careful with it and that it would be safer if Pike put it in his pocket, which the stranger kindly assisted him with, and soon after the two left. But Pike was shocked to find that all that was in his pocket was a fistful of coppers wrapped up in brown paper. Police were alerted and two men were arrested, but Pike could not recognise them and they were set free, Pike having to bear the loss of his cash.

MOTHER DEAR MOTHER

In St Thomas's Parish on 1 November 1835 William Brooks (aged 6) was at home with his mother. She was washing up with a kettle of boiling water on the table. Endeavouring to grab hold of him, in a hurry to beat him, her dress caught the kettle and the boiling water dropped all over William, who had fallen in his attempt to get away from her. His burns were considerable, but he survived until the 4th when he finally died. At an inquest held on Friday 6 November the jury returned a verdict of accidental death, since there were no bruises or marks of violence on the body. It was hardly justice for a child whose mother was not the most kind-hearted.

BALLS TO IT

William Gale was fined 5s and costs on 8 February 1836 for throwing snowballs, much to the annoyance of the local inhabitants of Oxford.

IN SEARCH OF GAS

In digging outside Mr Chaundy's tobacconist shop on Cornmarket, on 19 March 1838, the gas main was cracked and the gas was left to escape. The leak continued for most of that day, becoming increasingly intolerable towards the evening.

Chaundy was so concerned he decided to sit up all night. At 1 a.m. it became too much for him and he wandered around the house trying to trace the leak, carrying a lighted candle. He found gas in a corner of his sitting room, causing the first explosion. The whole neighbourhood bore witness to the explosions that followed at intervals thereafter.

Miraculously the flame was extinguished before the fire engine arrived and the gas flow was then turned off at the gas works. It does not say how extensive the damage was, but *Jackson's Oxford Journal* commented that 'The prompt adoption of these measures [calling the fire brigade and switching off the gas] put a stop to what might have been a serious accident.' Surely multiple explosions of gas in a residential street should count as a serious accident?

The journalist also noted that it was an uncommon event to be wondered at, considering the prevalence in the use of gas in the city, and added, 'The above occurrence is one that arose from peculiar circumstances, over which neither the company nor the consumer had any control.' Surely if the gas company could switch off the gas after the explosions it could have contemplated doing so beforehand? Likewise, surely Mr Chaundy wandering around his house with a lit candle had some control over the resulting explosions? It can only be wondered at that Chaundy had miraculously escaped unhurt.

THE KINDLY INSURERS

On 16 May 1838 at Messrs Drewitt and Towle's paper mill at South Hinksey an employee went to clean the brasswork. In cleaning the brasses, he chose not to unclog them with a knife, but to wrap brown paper around them and set alight. The oily paper burnt well – all too well. It set alight the large quantity of paper above that was hanging to dry. The thatched roof rapidly caught alight as well. Several fire engines were called and arrived soon, but it was too late. Two hours later the mill and neighbouring house were razed to the ground and their entire contents reduced to ash.

The cost of the fire was expected to be huge. The insurance premium was high and had not been renewed because Mr Towle had made recent alterations in order to bring down the cost. *Jackson's Oxford Journal* stated: 'We hope, however, as the premises have been insured for so many years that the Office [insurance] will take the matter into consideration, and allow the insurance to be valid.' And that was the last that was reported on the matter.

UNGRATEFUL BEGGAR

At the beginning of March 1839 Mary Ann Holbird, a tramp, was passing Mr Souter's, the watchmaker, on the High Street. She saw a gentleman in the shop and went to solicit charity. She told them she had not eaten for two days; the gentleman remarked that if she had not eaten she had certainly not been without alcohol. On being asked to leave the shop, Holbird pulled off her shoe and smashed three panes of glass and several pieces of jewellery. The men grabbed hold of her and handed her over to the police. At her trial on 15 March Holbird was convicted as being a vagrant and sent to gaol for fourteen days.

FIRE LOOTERS

A fire broke out on Cornmarket on the night of 23 April 1840 in the house next door to Mr Laney. As the fire took hold it burnt into Mr Laney's and much of the property in his shop was in danger of being reduced to ash. There was only one thing for it; the goods would have to be removed. But where there was fire and confusion there was an opportunity to loot.

Thomas Bustin with William Forster, Laney's brother-in-law, were in the shop that night between 11 p.m. and 1 a.m. making their best efforts to protect the contents. Through the shadows cast by the fire came Henry Cox, who was rummaging around the shop for a quick steal. He was not the only one. Bustin yelled out that the first person to take anything away would be arrested. It did not quite have the desired effect. Cox told Bustin where to go and asked what it had to do with him as he lifted a handful of cigars. As Cox walked out of the shop door Bustin called for him to stop, but he was knocked down by somebody else.

The man whom Bustin had failed to notice had a fair swing, and knocked out two of the poor man's teeth. Bustin managed to stay until 2.30 a.m., but by then the heat was too intense and he was forced to leave before he too went up in smoke.

In the aftermath of the fire a search was conducted which yielded several pieces of Laney's property: Thomas Bennett had a pair of brass scales, ten boxes of matches and a pipe; Stephen Howse was caught with a snuff box. Cox, Bennett and Howse pleaded not guilty to theft at their trial on 29 June 1840. When Cox was also charged with threatening behaviour he was found guilty only of the lesser charge.

Cox was sentenced to twelve months' hard labour with the first and last months in solitary confinement. Bennett had been caught trying to sell the scales on 16 June, but claimed he had bought them from somebody else, but he could not remember the man's name. Even more cunningly, Bennett claimed he had found the matchboxes lying on the ground outside Laney's shop. It was all very suspicious, but he was given good character references and, as a result, found not guilty. Howse was likewise given a good write-up, Laney did not press charges and Howse was eventually acquitted.

AND SO BACK TO BED

Two young men were walking home one evening in December 1841 at 11 p.m. in the Parish of St Clement, whereupon they were passed, at a rapid pace, by a man dressed only in his nightshirt, muttering as he went and heading down Bath Street towards the river.

The gentlemen, supposing the walker deranged, set off in hot pursuit. When they eventually grabbed hold of him the man came to and complained that the stones hurt his feet. His name was Wharton and it turned out that he had been asleep until awoken by the men. Returning the man to his house, as they approached the front door his brother came charging out in pursuit of Wharton, having missed him from bed. Surprisingly, Wharton had not left by the front door, but by the back and over a wall into the street beyond.

DEFENDING A BAD CHARACTER

Thomas Hazel took Richard Price to court for slander in January 1842. Price had entered the Lamb and Flag on 8 October 1841 and when he saw Hazel in a group said, 'You are one of the Hazels of Summer Town; you stole some wood from old mother Harris's cow-house, and I caught you at it!' Hazel asked if he could prove it and Price said he could. The Hazels were notorious, but at the trial the jury retired and consulted together for seven hours before finding a verdict in favour of Hazel. The judge awarded him 40s damages, but recommended to Hazel that he should not accept it because his name had been cleared.

MAGIC RECIPE

George Sparrow, a shoemaker in St Peter-in-the-East, told Ann Pauling he could cure her epilepsy with a special potion. In December 1842 Sparrow slipped her a piece of paper with the miracle cure on it, begging her not to share it with anyone. For this Sparrow charged Pauling 3s 6d.

The note read: 'A pigeon is to be kept alive for thirteen days, the heart to be then removed, mixed with two drops of antimony wine and a small quantity of gin; taking two drops every morning for thirteen days.' Sparrow said he would call again in a few days with a pigeon. This he did, telling Pauling that she, and only she, could feed it for the thirteen days, and demanding 18d for the bird. Pauling had not got the money so he took the pigeon back. When Pauling demanded the rest of her money back Sparrow told her he could not give it or even let her see it as it would break the charm.

Sparrow was convicted at trial as a vagabond, rogue and con man, and sentenced to five weeks' hard labour.

FREE FUEL

On the evening of 22 November 1842, in Summertown, Miss Abbott heard the sound of breaking wood. The noise came from the garden of the Norreys Arms, owned by Mr Simpson. Abbott soon saw Joseph Dawson walk past with wooden rails wrapped up in his apron just yards from what was left of the fence. Abbott told Simpson, who went to Dawson's house and found him stoking the fire with some of the wooden rails.

Dawson, needing an alibi, put forward John Hazel, one of the notorious Hazel family to swear in court that Dawson was at work in Hazel's house at the time of the robbery. The magistrates would have none of it and fined Dawson £2 1s 6d plus costs.

UNSUNG HERO

In October 1843 James Turner of Binsey fell into the canal near Medley Lock and was rescued by Mrs Bossom, her daughter and Mr Bleay. William Hedges came up to Turner on 1 November and told Turner that he should be grateful as he, William Hedges, had rescued Turner from the canal. Hedges then demanded something for his services even taking Turner to the Hollybush pub in order that Turner could change a sovereign and Hedges could get 5s out of him.

In court it was proved that Hedges had no part in the rescue, but Hedges' defence was that he had only borrowed the money from Turner and the sum was 3s not 5s. This excuse was thrown out of court, and Hedges was found guilty of fraud and imprisoned for two months' hard labour.

AN EXPENSIVE DUCK

James Davenport and Robert Godfrey were out with others in the first week of October 1844 at Binsey. Some of the group doubted the power of Davenport's 'big single' and he presently whipped it out and, letting rip at three nearby ducks, blew them all away. Godfrey picked up one of the ducks and walked off.

Mr Simmons, to whom the ducks belonged, was none too pleased, but a compromise was reached and Davenport agreed to pay £5 on behalf of himself and his 'sporting' companion. Mr Simmons stated generously that the money should be used to send coals to the poor of Binsey.

THE GIFTED SALESMAN

Mr Kensell's storeman was in his master's shop on Holywell Street on 3 January 1846. The storeman felt that the gas tap did not work to his satisfaction. So with a lit candle in one hand he removed the tap with his other. The gas immediately ignited and the University fire engine was called for – but before the it arrived the flames had been extinguished. The salesman, like the shop, survived.

COW ARRESTED

George Howse, George Carr and George Mills were charged with releasing a cow impounded by Mr Cripps in Summertown. It was May 1849. Mr Howse's cow had taken a liking to Mr Cripps's field next door, and frequently visited. Cripps had eventually impounded the cow and, demanded 5s from Howse for its keep and damages. Howse refused, and with Carr and Mills liberated the cow. Mills's role is a little uncertain, as he was a policeman and was there in his capacity to 'keep the peace', which appeared to extend to liberating cows. The case against Mills was thrown out by the magistrates at trial and Carr and Howse were fined 1s each.

LOVE THY NEIGHBOUR

In June 1849 Thomas Clark gave notice to his tenant and next-door neighbour George Carr on Plantation Road. This angered Carr and he proceeded to draw coffins, gallows complete with a figure of his landlord and a few other things agreeable to his feelings, on Clark's front door. Clark, a nervous man, was freaked out by this.

Carr's defence was that he was 'at liberty to indulge his taste for drawing'. The magistrates disagreed, hearing that Carr had used abusive language towards his landlord. Rather than fining him 40s, they suggested that Carr apologise, promise never to do it again and leave the house within a fortnight, which he agreed to do.

A SMASHING TIME

In August 1849 Mr Hales, the baker of Clarendon Street, was in for a surprise. John Johnson, being drunk at the time, came up to Mr Hales's shop and repeatedly ran his head through the glass panes in the shop window. Johnson smashed five panes before he was stopped. He was found guilty as charged and fined in court, but as he was unable to pay the fine the magistrates committed him to gaol for a month, where 'a little helpful recreation on the tread wheel it is hoped will have the effect of checking his propensity of popping his head through shop windows'.

FOR WANT OF LOVE

An inquest was held into the death of 8-year-old George Bench on 17 March 1845. The jury was horror-stricken at the emaciated and almost skeletal appearance of the corpse. Witnesses were called who proved that the father, Henry Bench, earned a good wage and had done so for a considerable time, but that he provided nothing for his family.

   The conclusion of the post-mortem was that the poor boy had wasted away as a result of starvation. It was then that George's younger brother was brought into court and the assembled body was equally stunned to see that he was just as emaciated as his deceased older brother. The final verdict was that George died of natural means, but that this was accelerated by starvation. Henry Bench was sent for and on arriving was given an earful by the disgusted jury for his appalling conduct. The younger brother was taken into care in the hope that he would be better looked after.

YOUTH CLUB

Complaints were made in court on 30 April 1847 by the residents of Paradise Square owing to the damage caused by young boys who tied large stones to the end of string and catapulted these through windows and roofs. The police were directed to look out for any offenders and to arrest anybody they found destroying property in such a manner.

CONVICTION OVER DEATH

Henry Best, aged 19, was found guilty on 6 April 1858 of stealing a carved ivory article representing a death's head and crossbones and a shirt link, the property of Anthony Reilly. He was sentenced to twelve months' hard labour.

TEACHING THE TEACHERS

A Balliol student purporting to be Emil Busch from Frankfurt, exponent of the Freudian System, gave a lecture in Oxford in 1918. He even answered questions as he was accompanied from the college to the station to catch the London train, and was given full press coverage following the lecture.

CUCUMBERS UNDER FIRE

In 1919 Balliol accepted a German artillery gun from the War Office, much to the displeasure of the returning veterans. Despite weighing half a ton, it was manhandled over a wall into Trinity College, destroying a cucumber frame – complete with cucumbers in the process.

FOOLPROOF PLAN

In 1938 there was a plan to kidnap Lord Nuffield. It was proposed to bundle him onto a yacht lying off the Essex coast complete with torture instruments, to twist his thumbs or elongate his spine until he signed a bank draft for £100,000. The plan failed.

HOUSE PET

In 1970 the Dean of Somerville (a women's college for many years) impounded a student's pet, in accordance with the college statutes which disallowed animals 'of any description' in student rooms. The pet in question was a python.

27

To Outsmart a Quack

Richard Matthew Goldberg and David Romaine were summoned before the Abingdon magistrates on 31 August 1846. At their trial the next day they denied having made a disturbance or using vulgar language towards Ralph Martin. They said the whole case was a diversionary tactic to prevent them proceeding against Martin himself, Goldberg claiming he had been fleeced of 20 sovereigns by Ralph Martin, Edward Wyatt and John Hale. This particular affair occurred at the White Horse on the Abingdon Road on 22 August and had arisen out of a gambling transaction. This is why Goldberg and Romaine had visited Martin and why subsequently they were charged with a breach of the peace.

Goldberg, having suffered his loss, had gone with Romaine to Martin's on 23 August. Martin had introduced Goldberg to a group of gamblers and Goldberg said he wanted his money back. Goldberg and Romaine had rolled up that morning in a coach and hammered on Martin's front door in Market Lane – Martin worked for Mr Wheeler, a fruit seller. Martin was accosted with foul language, punctuated by Romaine's accusations. Goldberg chipped in, saying Martin was a thief and a

The view into Oxford from Abingdon Road in the eighteenth century shows the familiar skyline of the city's spires. (OCCPA)

vagabond. Romaine said, 'I can fight and play cards, and if you want to rob a man, why don't you come out on the highway and do it.' Martin would have none of it and went back inside; Goldberg ran off for a policeman, leaving Romaine on his own.

John Day, returning down Market Lane from church, made the mistake of getting involved. He had seen the confrontation at the front door and Romaine told him how Goldberg had been cheated out of his money. Day, finding out that it was from gambling in a pub, which was illegal, said the magistrates would not investigate a crime which had arisen out of a criminal activity. Romaine asked him if Day was therefore one of the gang that had robbed his friend.

At the trial, Romaine and Goldberg were found guilty of disturbing the peace and using improper language and were fined 10s each.

The whole affair had started on 20 August when Goldberg, who was staying at the Blücher, had been visited in the evening by John Burton, who said he knew someone with tapeworm. Goldberg was a self-proclaimed travelling medical botanist, and Burton said that if Goldberg removed the worm he would more than likely get £1 for his trouble. Goldberg was not able to go immediately, as he was about to leave town and would not be returning until Saturday, but he would go and see the afflicted person on his return.

Soon afterwards, Ralph Martin arrived and badgered the 'eminent' man: 'I suppose my friend has told you of the case; when will you attend?' Goldberg said, 'Saturday', and Martin replied, 'Very well, then I will meet you here and go with you, but do not say anything to your partner about it.'

Saturday 22 August came and between 5 p.m. and 6 p.m. Martin came up to Goldberg, who was standing at the door of the Blücher, and asked if he was ready to attend the patient. Goldberg said he was and went upstairs to fetch his coat. Romaine went over to talk to Martin. The two men knew each other well and Romaine told Martin that he hoped he was not planning to trick Goldberg, since Romaine would take it personally; Martin said he was not. Goldberg returned and, with Martin, the two walked down the Abingdon Road to the White Horse.

The pub was 50yd from the railway station. Mr Wyatt, the landlord, was at home and Goldberg enquired after his patient. Martin told him that the man would not be there until after nightfall. They settled in the garden – Martin calling for two glasses of brandy and water – and there they met John Hale. After a short while Goldberg complained of the cold and they moved inside.

Goldberg was invited to play whist but, never having played, refused. Nevertheless, Wyatt stood up from the table, went to the bar and returned with a pack of cards. Martin, Wyatt and Hale began to play, stopping only for bread and cheese. Play continued and Goldberg was egged to bet, even though he said he did not have the cash, let alone the bottle, to join in.

Finally, after nearly three hours, Goldberg took twenty sovereigns out of his pocket and held the money in his hand. Hemmings, the coachman, had arrived and Martin said he would bet with Goldberg. Now it became exciting. The cards were dealt and Goldberg, seeing some winking and nudging going on, was amazed to see Hale slip a card up his sleeve and said he wanted out, telling them they were a bunch of swindlers. Wyatt grabbed the money from Goldberg's hand and, with Martin, threw him down, kicking him while Hale did a runner with the cash. Goldberg was down, but heard what he thought was a coachman say, 'That's right, knock the bastard's brains out; it serves him right, he lost it fair.'

Goldberg struggled to his feet and escaped, returning to the Blücher and his friend Romaine, to whom he spoke of the night's events. Goldberg did not know at the time, but there were policemen at the railway station just round the corner from the pub. Goldberg and Romaine returned to the White Horse and Romaine went inside, eventually being served after first being refused. He asked for a private word with Wyatt, who agreed and took him into the parlour. Romaine told him that he was surprised Wyatt would allow gambling, let alone someone to be robbed. Relating all he knew, Romaine said that if the money was not forthcoming there would be trouble. Outside and out of earshot, Goldberg waited. Wyatt denied everything and Goldberg was eventually brought in, but Wyatt refuted ever having seen Goldberg before. Goldberg and Romaine went to the Oxford police station – it was by now 10.15 p.m. The Oxford police refused to help as the pub was officially in Berkshire and out of their jurisdiction, so the men went to the University police who, taking names, told them to get an arrest warrant.

In fact, Romaine's assistance was not all it seemed; Romaine had initially refused to go with Goldberg, but Goldberg had said that if he did not he would implicate Romaine, since it was Romaine who had first brought Goldberg to the Blücher.

Goldberg roamed the streets the whole night, stopping off at a few public houses. The next day he obtained a warrant from an Oxford magistrate for Wyatt, Hale and Martin, and then made for Martin's house, which is what led to the initial court case. On the day he visited Martin, when Goldberg failed to find a policeman he went to threaten Hale 'with the consequences'. Romaine, believing Goldberg had likewise gone after Hemmings the coachman, with a mind to apprehending him, slept the night at a friend's house.

Despite having an arrest warrant from Oxford, Goldberg went to Abingdon to get one valid in Berkshire. He returned to the White Horse with Romaine on their way back to Oxford, not to have Wyatt arrested, but to sit outside and have a beer. Wyatt himself served them and they happily told him they had a warrant out for him. That night Goldberg slept at the Air Balloon, the next night telling the landlord and landlady that he had been outwitted and had lost his money. He told others at different times the same story.

The case finally came to trial on 20 October in the Shire Hall in Abingdon. Goldberg's credentials were brought into question and he being evasive at every turn, often giving contradictory answers. He was a medical botanist, but not a herbal physician. He had had business cards printed, but not flyers, advertising one Professor Goldberg and enumerating numerous cases of curing blindness, cataracts and deafness. But he denied that this was him. He had not distributed flyers, but Romaine's son had done this for him. Goldberg made further confusing statements, saying that he had not played cards; had not intended to withdraw his bet; had not intended to bet and was likewise positive he never did bet. Goldberg refused to answer any more questions, though the court did establish he was an Englishman born at Upton Pyne near Exeter, but Goldberg could not swear that his name was entered in the register there.

Romaine's story was different. He was a licensed hawker travelling with, but not in partnership with, Goldberg, stating Goldberg might as well have been a Turk for all Romaine knew. Several witnesses stated that on many occasions Romaine had openly said he wished he had nothing to do with the affair and that he had only done so as Goldberg had frightened him into it, having told him that Goldberg would have him implicated and transported because of it. He added that Goldberg was an awful man whom he regretted having anything to do with. Despite Goldberg being present during many of these conversations, he never said anything or disagreed with what Romaine had said.

The trial lasted several hours and caused a lot of excitement – the case being viewed by a packed court – when the jury found all three men not guilty. However, the judge rebuked Wyatt, cautioning him against allowing gambling, saying that if it ever happened again Wyatt would lose his licence. He promised it would never happen again, and all three men were discharged.

The parts played by Goldberg and Romaine in the whole affair remain unclear, muddied as they were by the refusals to confirm or deny many of the statements put to them. As for Goldberg's role, whether induced or otherwise to gamble, he seems to have sought to hedge his bets: he would hold his money in his hand, and if the result fell in his favour he would bet, but should it go against him, he would say that he was merely holding it in his hand. Romaine seems to have opted for the line of least resistance and just shrugged his shoulders. Possibly he neither confirmed nor denied anything in the hope that he would upset the least number of people and, in particular, that he would not upset Goldberg himself.

28

DEATH THROUGH INSECURITY

On 14 February 1887 Charles Smith, along with his wife Lucy and their children, Oceana (aged 16) and Prince Albert (aged 11), arrived at Open Brasenose, near Cowley, having previously been at Cumnor and Bampton. They had swapped their house at Bampton for a tent and all four slept on the ground, which they had lined with straw. Charles made his living by making skewers, pegs, baskets, toasting forks and washboards, which Lucy sold. Smith daily beat his wife with his fists as well as a thick stick, often for no more reason than she dared to speak. As a result, Lucy's body was black and blue. He regularly beat his two children until they were unable to stand.

When Lucy returned from selling pegs in Oxford on 17 February Charles yelled at her because she had earned only 4s 6d that day, and then he beat her. After tea Charles beat Lucy again and eventually they went to bed. Charles had earlier blurted out to his children one of the reasons for his anger: he was jealous of James Dean. James was Lucy's cousin and Charles complained that years ago, when the couple lived at Hunger Hill near Aldershot, James had 'messed and mauled' Lucy. For this jealousy Charles beat Lucy likewise, because five years previously she had gone to church with James. Though Lucy had not seen James since, Charles continued to beat her. Later on the night of the 17th he threw her out of the tent at 2 a.m. It was winter and she was outside in the rain wearing only her chemise and her son's coat, which she had managed to claw from the tent after her ejection.

At 1 p.m. on the 18th Kate and George Smith (no relations) found Lucy still half-naked and about 20yd from the tent. She was in a dishevelled state, arms folded, wet and shivering violently. She could hardly see through the swelling of the black eyes Charles had given her. Charles was building a fire and George went to talk to him while Kate consoled Lucy. The woman was petrified and would not return to the tent, but Kate coaxed her into sitting by the fire to warm herself and drink a cup of tea. Meanwhile, Charles explained to George that he was angry with Lucy for what she had done thirty years previously. George told him to forgive Lucy. Despite the obvious terror that Lucy had for her husband, Kate said they would have to leave her. Lucy pointed to the stick and said she would be beaten with it again when Kate left. Sadly Kate said to Lucy, 'I do not think he will.'

After the Smiths had gone, Charles grabbed his stick and beat Lucy, telling her it was because she had been to church with James. He continued to beat her throughout the day, threatening to throw her into the ditch and stamp on her. During that week Charles repeatedly thrashed Lucy, even throwing water on her. At the end of the week she told her children that if she received one more beating Charles would kill her. How close to the truth she was would soon become clear. For more than five years Charles had beaten his wife and Lucy had complained to the police on many occasions, but to no avail.

Oceana slept between her mother and father and was awoken at 2 a.m. on the morning of the 19th by her mother's screams. In the half-light she could see her father leaning over Lucy and hitting her repeatedly with a hammer. Charles swung the hammer back and forth, striking Lucy a dozen times on the legs and back. Lucy screamed that he was going to kill her, to which he repeatedly said he was and that he did not care. He yelled at her, saying how dare she scream out, and smashed her head three or four times before she collapsed. Lucy, covered in blood and severely beaten, was able to crawl out of the tent, with the children calling after their mother.

Oceana was sent out by her father two minutes later. She found her mother's body just yards from the tent. Lucy was lying flat out with her mouth wide open, her feet in the ditch and her head on the bank. Prince Albert followed his sister out of the tent and his sister told him that their mother was dead. The children returned to the tent and informed their father that Lucy was dead. Charles said he did not care, but when his children cried for their mother he threatened to kill them as well. Then, followed by the children, Charles went to the body, calling Lucy's name and splashing water on her face, even blowing on her. He seemed to cling to the hope that she would bounce back as she always had, but this time she did not. Charles told Oceana to grab hold of her mother's legs while he took Lucy's shoulders, and together they moved her body inside the tent. In a matter-of-fact way Charles told his children to go to the Smiths' house and say their mother was dead.

Oceana and Prince Albert ran to the house, crying. Oceana frantically called, 'Mistress, my mammy is dead, he killed her with a hammer', waking Kate first, then George. It was 4 a.m. on the morning of 19 February. George, half clothed, jumped straight out of bed and went outside to bring the children indoors. He dressed, went to Thomas Jarman's and woke him up and both men went to the tent at Open Brasenose. When they arrived George called out, 'Smith, what's up?' From inside

The Original Swan in Temple Cowley, built in 1854 and rebuilt in 1930, was, like other pubs, often the location for coroner's inquisitions. (Giles Brindley)

21st April	Baron Huddleston	Guilty of unlaw-fully wounding.	... ...	6 calendar months hard labour.
Ditto	Baron Huddleston	Not guilty of arson	... ...	To be discharged.
22nd April	Baron Huddleston	Guilty of wilful murder.	... .	To be hanged by the neck until he be dead, and his body to be afterwards buried within the precincts of the prison.
Ditto	Baron Huddleston	Ditto.		

An extract from the Calendar of Prisoners shows the death sentence passed by Baron Huddleston on Charles Smith for murder in April 1887. (ORO)

Charles replied that his old woman was dead. The men joined him in the tent. Crawling across the straw George stopped, lit a candle and saw the battered and bloody corpse of Lucy. Things did not look good and George said so. Charles said, 'Yes what are we to do now?' George said he would return with a doctor and Charles asked that he send one of the children back to keep him company. George agreed, but had no intention of sending either of the children back for fear of the treatment they would receive.

    Instead of finding a doctor, at 5.30 a.m. George woke William Sly, the policeman, and Sergeant Quarterman and they all returned to the tent. By the time they arrived at 6 a.m., Charles was outside gathering firewood. Quarterman stepped forward and said, 'Good morning.' Charles replied, 'Good morning, we've got a dead 'un in here – my old woman died this morning.' Maybe Charles thought the police would be deceived and come to the conclusion that Lucy had died in some freak accident or that the police would not notice the injuries. In the tent the sergeant took one look at the body, turning Lucy's head aside, and immediately told Charles he was being arrested for murder.

    The sergeant asked Charles to produce the hammer that had been used to bludgeon Lucy. But Charles denied all knowledge of a hammer, though in searching the tent the police found Lucy's blood-soaked bonnet and the hammer, which was concealed, but not very well, under the straw near her body. Charles said the bloodstained hammer was his and put his hand out to receive it back. Instead, Quarterman put the hammer in his pocket and told Charles that he was going to keep it. Pointing into the ditch, Charles said that was where Lucy had fallen. Quarterman looked across at Smith and the blood-splattered coat he was wearing. He formally charged Smith with murder and had him marched off to the police station. The sergeant then arranged for Lucy's body to be taken by carriage to the Original Swan at Temple Cowley, but not before the children had returned at 8 a.m. to see their mother's body still in the tent where they had left her.

A post-mortem was conducted and on 21 February an inquest was held, both at the Original Swan. It was revealed that Lucy had several cracks in her skull; some were 3in long. These were the result of hammer blows delivered as her stone-cold-sober husband, in a frenzied attack, had killed her. When Charles was formally charged with Lucy's murder on 26 February, Oceana poignantly said her mother was kind to them all and never hit Charles back despite all the abuse.

A letter was written on behalf of Charles, on which he placed his mark, in which he asked the judge if a defence counsel could be found for him as he was a 'poor and ignorant' man. That was almost certainly true, but when the trial came, on 9 April 1887, Charles was reduced to representing himself. His attempts at cross-examination were farcical. Aged 63, Charles Smith waited in court for the jury to return a verdict. It finally came: guilty of murder and sentenced to be 'hanged by the neck until he be dead, and his body to be afterwards buried within the precincts of the prison'.

CONCLUSION

The history of Oxford is long and diverse, both as a city and seat of learning. Outwardly, beneath the majestic towers and spires, the people of town and gown appear to mingle happily. But a deeper investigation into the city's criminal past reveals that this was not always the case.

Life in all its routine was peppered with individuals who had strange notions. Often their crimes never quite delivered on their promise to pay. For some of the victims and accused alike they were in the wrong place at the wrong time – for them there was no justice, save that their story was recorded and has been reported.

Many landmarks are no longer: the Norman tower of St Michael at the North Gate remains, but not the gate itself or the Bocardo prison that flanked it; the Castle gaol has succumbed to redevelopment. Likewise, the city's residents, students and workers come and go, but what remains are their stories; stories of love, life, suffering and death which give a window to the past.

BIBLIOGRAPHY

Primary Sources

Bodleian Library
Oxford University, Chancellors Court: Act Books, 1732–1834
—— Court Registers, 1835–1905
—— Solicitors Accounts, 1822–25

Oxfordshire Record Office
Oxfordshire Quarter Sessions Minute Books, QS/C/A1/1–13: 1687–1839
Oxfordshire Quarter Sessions and Assize Calendars, QSP I/1–11: 1778–1913
Plans and Specification for County Gaol, QSE/19, 20: 1819–1852

Oxfordshire Studies
Jackson's Oxford Journal, 1753–1849

The National Archives (TNA)
TNA: PRO, Oxford Assize Circuit: Crown Minute Books, 1734–1906
TNA: PRO, Indictment files, 1753–1848
TNA: PRO, Criminal Depositions and Case Papers, 1719–1889

Secondary Sources

Adams, P. *Somerville for Women: An Oxford College, 1879–1993*, Oxford, Oxford University Press, 1996
Buxton, J. and Williams, P. *New College, Oxford, 1379–1979*, Oxford, The Warden and Fellows of New College, Oxford, 1979
Cooper, J. (ed.). *The Oxfordshire Eyre, 1241*, Oxford, The Oxfordshire Record Society, vol. 56, 1989
Fasnacht, R. *A History of the City of Oxford*, Oxford, Basil Blackwell, 1954
Green, J.R. and Robertson, G. *Studies in Oxford History Chiefly in the Eighteenth Century*, Oxford, Oxford Historical Society, 1901
Green, V.H.H. *A History of Oxford University*, London, B.T. Batsford, 1974
Headlam, C. *Oxford and Neighbouring Churches*, London, J.M. Dent and Sons, 1925
Hearne, T. *Remarks and Collections of Thomas Hearne*, vol. I, ed. C.E. Doble, Oxford, Oxford Historical Society, vol. 2, 1885
—— *Remarks and Collections of Thomas Hearne*, vol. II, ed. C.E. Doble, Oxford, Oxford Historical Society, vol. 7, 1886
—— *Remarks and Collections of Thomas Hearne*, vol. III, ed. C.E. Doble, Oxford, Oxford Historical Society, vol. 13, 1889
—— *Remarks and Collections of Thomas Hearne*, vol. IV, ed. D.W. Rannie, Oxford, Oxford Historical Society, vol. 34, 1898

—— *Remarks and Collections of Thomas Hearne*, vol. V, ed. D.W. Rannie, Oxford, Oxford Historical Society, vol. 42, 1901

—— *Remarks and Collections of Thomas Hearne*, vol. VI, eds Committee of the Oxford Historical Society, Oxford, Oxford Historical Society, vol. 43, 1902

—— *Remarks and Collections of Thomas Hearne*, vol. VII, eds Committee of the Oxford Historical Society, Oxford, Oxford Historical Society, vol. 48, 1906

—— *Remarks and Collections of Thomas Hearne*, vol. VIII, eds Committee of the Oxford Historical Society, Oxford, Oxford Historical Society, vol. 50, 1907

—— *Remarks and Collections of Thomas Hearne*, vol. IX, ed. H.E. Salter, Oxford, Oxford Historical Society, vol. 65, 1914

—— *Remarks and Collections of Thomas Hearne*, vol. X, ed. H.E. Salter, Oxford, Oxford Historical Society, vol. 67, 1915

—— *Remarks and Collections of Thomas Hearne*, vol. XI, ed. H.E. Salter, Oxford, Oxford Historical Society, vol. 72, 1921

Horan, D. *Oxford: A Cultural and Literary Companion*, Oxford, Signal Books, 1999

Irving, J. *Stories from the History of Oxfordshire*, Oxford, Clarendon Press, 1908

Jebb, M. *The Colleges of Oxford*, London, Constable, 1992

Jones, J. *Balliol College: A History*, 2nd edn, Oxford, Oxford University Press, 1997

Martin, G. H. and Highfield, J.R.L. *A History of Merton College, Oxford*, Oxford, Oxford University Press, 1997

Overnell, R. F. *The Ashmolean Museum*, Oxford, Clarendon Press, 1986

Thompson, J.M. 'The Robbery from the Ashmolean Museum, 1776', *English Historical Review*, vol. 46, no. 181 (1931), 96

Wood A. *The Life and Times of Anthony Wood, Antiquary, of Oxford, 1632–1695, Described by Himself*, vol. I, ed. A. Clark, Oxford, Oxford Historical Society, vol. 19, 1891

—— *The Life and Times of Anthony Wood, Antiquary, of Oxford, 1632–1695, Described by Himself*, vol. II, ed. A. Clark, Oxford, Oxford Historical Society, vol. 21, 1892

—— *The Life and Times of Anthony Wood, Antiquary, of Oxford, 1632–1695, Described by Himself*, vol. III, ed. A. Clark, Oxford, Oxford Historical Society, vol. 26, 1894

MAIN INDEX

INDEX OF NAMES